MANAGERIAL ECONOMICS

MANAGERIAL ECONOMICS

KULWANT SINGH PATHANIA
SABINA BATRA
RAJIV SALWAN

REGAL

REGAL PUBLICATIONS
New Delhi - 110 027

ISBN 978-81-8484-141-1

Printed in India at
DEEPAK PUSTAK BANDHNALAYA
468, Bhola Nath Nagar, Lane No. 7, Shahdara, Delhi - 110 032

Published by
REGAL PUBLICATIONS
F-159, Rajouri Garden, New Delhi - 110 027 • Phone : 45546396
E-mail : regalbookspub@yahoo.com

Contents

Preface

Economics of Business or Business Economics or Managerial Economics all are inter-changeable terms. Managerial Economics assimilates concepts and methods from all disciplines viz. micro economic theory, macro-economic theory, the theory of decision-making, operations research and statistics and thus trains managerial economist to integrate all these concepts and methods to enable him to tackle managerial problems in the business organisation. This relationship of managerial economics with other disciplines and areas forms its subject matter. Managerial Economics shows, how to apply economic concepts and theories to business decision-making and planning.

Managerial Economics is a part of Economic Theory which deals with business activities in general and in particular suggests solutions to business problems, arising in the process of decision making in a business organisation. Thus, Managerial Economics implies restricted connotation. It is the study of the application of economic theory and methodology to decision making problems faced by business organisations. It trains a business manager and equips him with managerial skills to make decisions in diverse business situations involving intricate problems of resource allocation, choice of inputs and product mix, the quantification for a product, the scope for marketing the product in relation to demand by measurement and forecasting of demand, pricing of the product in different market situations etc. The word "managerial" conjures up notions of control, direction, decision making. "Economics", to most people, means money. Managerial Economics can be applied to number of decisions in which money enters directly.

This book is of great significance for the students, scholars and teachers.

KULWANT SINGH PATHANIA
SABINA BATRA
RAJIV SALWAN

CHAPTER

1

An Introduction to Managerial Economics

MEANING

Managerial Economics shows how to apply economic concepts and quantitative methods to business decision-making and planning.

Managerial Economics is a part of economic theory which deals with business activities in general and in particular, suggests solutions to business problems arising in the process of decision making in a business organisation. Thus, Managerial Economics implies restricted connotation. It is the study of the application of economic theory and methodology to decision making problems faced by business organisations. It trains a business manager and equips him with managerial skills, to make decisions in diverse business situations involving intricate problems of resource allocation, choice of inputs and product mix, the quantification for a product, the scope for marketing the product in relation to demand by measurement and forecasting of demand, pricing of the product in different market situations, etc.

The word "managerial" conjures up notions of control, direction and decision making. The main functions of management are decision making and forward planning. Decision making means the process of choosing from among available alternatives to achieve the desired objectives of the organization and forward planning refers to planning for the future. "Economics", to most people, means money. It is the study of the optimum utilization of limited resources to satisfy human needs and desires. A broad classification of economics into Micro Economics and Macro Economics has been done by the famous economist Norway Ragnar Frisch. Microeconomics deals with the behavior of individual economic units like a consumer, a producer and a market, whereas Macroeconomics incorporates the study of the economic problems of the economy as a whole like national income, total employment, general price level etc. Managerial economics applies economic theory, particularly microeconomics to business and administrative decision making. Managerial Economics can be applied to a number of decisions in which money enters directly. Economics of business or Business Economics or Managerial Economics all are inter-changeable terms.

DEFINITION

In the words of *Mansfield*, "Managerial economics provides a link between economic theory and decision sciences in the analysis of managerial decision making."

According to *Samuelson and Marks*, "Managerial economics is the analysis of major management decisions using tools of economics."

Spencer and Seligman are of the opinion, "Managerial economics is the integration of economic theory with business practice for the purpose of facilitating decision making and forward planning by management."

RELATION OF MANAGERIAL ECONOMICS WITH OTHER DISCIPLINES

Managerial Economics assimilates concepts and methods from all disciplines viz. micro economic theory, macro-economic theory, the theory of decision making, operations research and statistics and thus trains managerial economist to integrate all these concepts and methods to enable him to tackle managerial problems in the business organisation. This relationship of managerial economics with other disciplines and areas forms its subject matter.

(I) Managerial Economics and Micro Economic Theory

Managerial Economics makes use of different micro-economic concepts and tools, viz. price theory (known as Marshallian Economics), kinked demand theory, model of price discrimination and elasticity of demand, marginal costs, the short and long run market structures and resource allocations. Estimating demand and cost relationship in short-run for fixing price of products and quantity of production is made by using micro economic analytical concepts. However, certain concepts of micro economics have not been familiar with Managerial Economists, like the use of qualitative measures of demand, because, improbability of practical application of indifference analysis in measurement of variables has kept it away from immediate applicability to business problems.

(II) Managerial Economics and Macro Economic Theory

In long-run managerial decision-making, different concepts of Macro Economics are often made use of. For instance, forecasting of future demand is based on forces influencing overall economy like Gross National Product, Theory of Income and Employment of post Keynesian period, etc. Macro Economic literature is repeadedly made use of; for example, consumption and saving pattern of the general population and specific groups of the population are some of the macro parameters which are taken into account in deciding the product price and for making long run business decisions for expanding or contracting production and distribution facilities for developing and marketing new products. Even, significant issues of acquisition and mergers involving decisions about economies of scale, capital expenditure etc. warrant frequent use of macro economic theory. Particularly, different macro economic concepts of capital, cost of capital and methods of capital budgeting are reduced to micro applications for facilitating decisions determining capital structure of a business organisation.

(III) Managerial Economics and Decision-making Theory

Decision Theory has been developed to deal with problems of choice or decision-making under uncertainty, where the applicability of figures needed for the utility calculus are not available. The theory of decision-making is in contrast to much of economic theory based on assumptions of a single goal, whereas decision theory breaks new ground by recognising multiplicity of goals and pervasiveness of uncertainty in the real world of management. Thus, decision theory is made use of in managerial decision making under odd situations and complexities involving future uncertainty.

(IV) Managerial Economics and Operation Research

There is a close affinity between managerial economics and Operations Research. Where managerial economics focuses on maximization of profits or minimization of costs, Operations Research too emphasizes on concept of *optimization*. While managerial economics is an academic subject aiming at understanding of business problems and then taking decisions, operations research is a functional activity pursued by specialists within the firm, helping them to improve the quality of their decisions. Thus, both the subjects contribute towards taking effective decisions. Use of Operations Research is made in managerial decision making for finding out best of all feasible decisions. It suggests to the business economist to discard rules of thumb by systematically seeking to determine the very best of available possibilities. Use of linear programming is a great aid in decision making in business and industry. Determination of facilities or machine scheduling, distribution of commodities, determination of optimum product mix and allocation of labour and other resources are but a few examples of the type of problem which can be solved by linear programming. In deciding inventory level or pricing a product or fixing up advertisement budgets, use of Operations Research is frequently made. Although Operations Research techniques are mathematical in character as opposed to the more subjective and qualitative techniques usually used by management, yet Managerial Economics makes use of these techniques to pursue accurate business decision-making.

(V) Managerial Economics and Statistics

Statistical methods provide most important and reliable data for business decision making. Statistics helps in empirical testing of theory. On the basis of empirical testing of data better decisions are made relating to demand and cost functions, production, sales or distribution. Better decisions are made through theory of probability in circumstances of risk and uncertainty of future events. Use of statistical methods is frequently made in reading business situations and environment and making decisions to solve many business problems like demand forecasting and pricing of products, and other such decisions in fluctuating business situations through time series. Thus, Managerial Economics is heavily dependent on statistical methods.

(VI) Managerial Economics and Mathematics

According to Savage and Small, "Recent advances suggest that managerial economics should be both conceptual and metrical, for while measurement without theory can only lead to false precision, theory without measurement can rarely be operationally useful." Mathematics helps in estimating various economic relationships and predicting economic quantities for decision making and planning. Managerial economics uses various mathematical techniques like geometry, algebra, calculus etc. in arriving at reliable and accurate solutions.

(VII) Managerial Economics and Psychology and Sociology

In the words of Simon, Cyert and March, "The study of what motivates an individual to work and the study of group behavior is essential for any decision making." Therefore both psychology and sociology provide the basis of behavioural theory of the firm. For introducing any change or installing any new equipment in a firm, the study of the reaction of employees is must, thus emphasizing the use of psychology in managerial economics.

(VIII) Managerial Economics and Accounting

Accounting means recording, classifying and summarizing data for its analysis and interpretation. A business manager needs a lot of accounting data for appropriate analysis for decision making and policy formulation. Management Accounting, a new branch of accounting was developed to help managers take accurate decisions by presenting the data and information in a methodological manner, as required by the managers.

Thus, it is clear that managerial economics is closely related to certain subjects and an experienced managerial economist integrates concepts and techniques of all these subjects to improve the quality of his decisions.

MANAGERIAL ECONOMICS : NATURE AND METHODOLOGY

In the words of Spencer and Selligam, "Managerial economics is the integration of economic theory with managerial practice for the purpose of facilitating decision making and forward planning by management." It is the application of economic theory, particularly of microeconomics to managerial decision making. Managerial economics is pragmatic as it guides the managers as to how to achieve the goals of the organisation. In the words of Haynes, "Managerial Economics is pragmatic, it is concerned with the analytical tools that are useful, that have proven themselves in practice or that promise to improve decision making in the future."

Managerial economics is regarded as multi-disciplinary, as it is concerned with using the tools and techniques of different disciplines like statistics, management, mathematics, economics and psychology to improve the quality of managerial decisions. According to Haynes,"Managerial Economics is concerned with using the logic of economics, mathematics and statistics to provide effective ways of thinking about managerial decision making." Managerial economics is also regarded as an applied social science as it formulates theories in a systematic manner about possible cause and effect relationships. It is applied by the managers in determining whether the resources are effectively utilized or not and further the principles of managerial economics can help the managers respond to various economic indicators like price or demand fluctuations.

Managerial Economics is both normative (prescriptive) as well as positive (descriptive) science. It combines methodologies of both normative and descriptive economics. As a normative science, it specifies what action should be taken in order to achieve a given goal or objective like profit maximization, sales maximization etc and also predict the outcomes of specific managerial decisions. For instance, managerial economics helps a manager in setting price or output at the point where marginal revenue equals marginal cost for maximising profits of the organisation. As positive science, it deals with accurate description of phenomenon. It explains what is, what was and what will be. That is, managerial economics focuses on description of the manner in which economic forces operate without explaining how they should operate. The descriptive model of managerial economics helps to explain and predict economic behavior. According to Prof. K.K. Sen,"Since most business decisions are related to optimization of some function, prescriptive models are the principal tools of managerial economics. However, descriptive models are often helpful in the development of such optimization models."

Thus, managerial economics becomes deductive in nature when, in certain business situations, it prescribes a set of initial assumptions, specifies an objective function and a set of constraints in terms of relevant variables as it is done by following linear programming techniques in which final solution is reached by solving for values which optimise the value of objective function. Use of Calculus and Lagrangian multipliers is often made in finding solutions to the models which are formulated as an optimization technique. Managerial Economics also makes use of the main body of Economic Theory which consists of descriptive hypotheses where an attempt is made to generalise relations among variables without judgement about what is desirable or undesirable. Law of Diminishing Returns is an example of such generalisation which clearly depicts the net result of adding more inputs to fixed requirements of inputs without hinting towards remedial solutions about decisions that ought to be made. Likewise, quantitative measures used in finding out actual relationship existing among variables are useful in business decision-making in situations entailing determination of level of demand for a product by finding out actual relationships existing among different variables like price, income, price of substitutes, and tastes of consumers through price elasticity or income, elasticity.

Managerial Economics thus uses economic tools for empirical study of economic variables and testing hypotheses. Econometric techniques of regression and correlation are other examples of inductive reasoning used in Managerial Economics for decision making purposes. To sum up, managerial economics has both normative orientation as well as descriptive orientation. Better use of Managerial Economics shall depend upon the skills of the business manager in making appropriate decisions in different problematic business situations. William J. Baumol is of the view that "a Managerial Economist can become a far more helpful member of a management group, by virtue of his study of economic analysis, primarily because there he learns to become an effective model builder and because there he acquires a very rich body of tools and techniques which can help him to deal with the problems of the firm in a far more rigorous, a far more probing and a far deeper manner."

ROLE OF MANAGERIAL ECONOMIST

A Managerial Economist shares heavy accountability in the decision making process in the business organisation. His correct and accurate predictions may bring prosperity to the business and his slight lack in understanding any business problem may bring doom to the entire set-up of the enterprise. In view of this, a managerial economist exercises leadership in the whole group of management personnel. He is responsible for optimum utilisation of the scarce resources of the organization. His prescriptions for business performance in uncertainties of future are significant for forward planning. Thus a managerial economist is a person who specializes in basic economic theory and applies this knowledge to ensure prosperity for the business organization.

His suggestions for minimising cost by adopting different measures are crucial to the growth and survival of the enterprise in conditions of perfect or imperfect competitions. His analysis of hidden costs like opportunity cost of alternate use of the resources are significant for assessing true worth of the efforts of the enterprise. Besides his duties and responsibilities towards the business enterprise, a Managerial Economist has a formidable task to perform towards social responsibilities of the business enterprise. He has to take into consideration different sociological reasons and circumstances while making decisions towards fixing up profitability ratios of the business performance or recommending a price structure for the products of the enterprise and likewise, so that the decisions of the enterprise do not result into exploitation of the common people by monopolistic price situations or restrictive trade practices.

The two primary tasks of a managerial economist are: making decisions and processing information. That is, a managerial economist must be able to obtain process and use information so as to make intelligent decisions. The decisions taken on the basis of information collected by a managerial economist can take two forms:

(i) Specific Decisions

Professor K.J.W. Alexander and Alexander G. Kemp have outlined the following specific functions of the managerial economist in an industrial organization:

1. Market Research
2. Production Scheduling
3. Demand Forecasting
4. Economic Analysis of the Industry
5. Investment Appraisal
6. Security Management Analysis
7. Advice on Foreign Exchange Management
8. Advice on Trade and Public Relations
9. Capital Projects
10. Pricing and Related Decisions
11. Analysing and Forecasting Environmental Factors
12. Advice on the Purchase of Raw Materials and Inventory Building

13. Economic Analysis of Competing Companies
14. Market Survey to determine the Nature and Extent of Competition.

(ii) General Assignments

In trying to find correct solutions for various business problems, a managerial economist is guided by the economic theory and he must analyse the information and use it in accordance with the available theoretical and statistical tools to make best possible decisions.

To be more practical in decision making, a Managerial Economist is supposed to have knowledge of other disciplines too, so that the extraneous and internal factors affecting the existence and the performance of the business organisation in the prevailing environment should not prejudice the interest of the business enterprise and restrict its growth. Extraneous factors which may influence business decisions may include governmental policies, international trade situations, trade or business cycles, labour situation in the country, firm's share in the market, input costs, different economic legislations like foreign exchange regulations, taxation policies, knowledge about foreign collaboration and institutional finance etc. The role of managerial economist in internal management is as important as his contribution to the management of external factors. The internal factors which need managerial economist's attention are pricing and profit policies, investment decisions, technological developments, business plans, statistical records, supply of economic information, etc.

Thus a managerial economist has an indispensable role to play in an organization as he not only manages the internal factors but also analyses the external factors renders useful advice to the firm on the likely impact of the these factors.

MANAGERIAL ECONOMICS : ITS NATURE AND SCOPE

Managerial Economics is related to solving all problems concerned with business affairs. It implies policies of planning and development of business. The subject matter of Managerial Economics is divided as under:

(i) Consumption Analysis,
(ii) Production and Cost Analysis,
(iii) Product's Pricing Decisions, Policies and Practices,
(iv) Profit Management,
(v) Capital Management, and
(vi) Decision-making.

CONSUMPTION ANALYSIS

For Spencer and Siegelman a business firm is an economic organism which transforms productive resources into consumable goods which are meant for sale in the market. As such, a firm before producing any consumable commodity must assess the nature of demand for the product. It has to search out and measure the forces that determine sales. With a view to estimate the future demand, the manager has to take into consideration the Income Elasticity, Price Elasticity and Substitution Elasticity of Demand. Demand analysis covers Demand Determinants, Demand Distinctions and Demand Forecasting. Demand analysis is significant benchmark for appraising salesman's performance and for setting up sales quotas.

PRODUCTION AND COST ANALYSIS

It is another sphere of study of managerial economics. It helps the manager to attain efficient allocation of productive resources which are scarce. The production and cost analysis is inevitable for effective project planning.

The costs of production of a firm are estimated from the accounting records. From these records, the business manager will be in a position to compare costs of production of different periods and thereby evolves suitable policies in controlling costs and deriving suitable profits. The production analysis is related to proper product mix and what factors are to be combined in what manner to produce a given product. It is done in physical terms while cost analysis is done in financial terms. The significant topics discussed in this field are cost concepts, classifications, cost input relationships, economies and diseconomies of scarce, production function and cost control.

PRODUCT PRICING DECISIONS, POLICIES AND PRACTICE

Pricing of the product or products produced by the firm is a very significant field of managerial economics. The chief function of the firm is pricing. This depends upon the cost of production and at the same time, the price of substitutes and the nature of competition. Price affects profits which in turn determine the existence and growth of the firm. The Manager is needed to have a thorough knowledge of the theories of production and the pricing in order to make sure that the firm gets profit continuously. The Manager has to determine suitable price policies applicable to short and long-term production.

CAPITAL MANAGEMENT

A business firm is organised in view of making profits. In order to organise a business firm, the most important requirement is capital. Capital management is' efficient use of scarce capital. Capital management is done by means of preparing a capital budget. It comprises both investment capital and working capital. It also involves short term and long term requirement of capital. Briefly, capital management implies planning and control of capital expenditure. Further it deals with three things-cost of capital, rate of return and selection of project.

PROFIT MANAGEMENT

It is central matter in managerial economics. A business firm is an organisation designed to make profit and profits are the primary measure of success. Social criteria of business relate to the quality of the product, rate of progress and the behaviour of prices. But these are tests of the desirability of the entire profit system. Within this system, profits are acid test of the individual firm's performance. The business firm's objective is to make profit but it has to make profit under the situation of uncertainty. This is because of different factors like the prices of resources, the cost of production etc. Since the firms have to work in a world of uncertainty, profit planning becomes very difficult. Yet, it is essential to plan the future profits in a realistic manner, taking into consideration the element of uncertainty. Profit planning, profit measurement and profit management are the significant areas of managerial economics.

Decision-making

It is the most significant function of a business manager. Faced with scarce resources, uncertainity and competing ends, the choice of a final end is to pass value judgment. Because of uncertainties like demand uncertainty, cost uncertainty, price fluctuations, sales uncertainty, interest uncertainty, profit and capital uncertainty, decision making for the managerial economist becomes very difficult and complex. To try to achieve optimum satisfaction is to realise the objective which may be considered good and proper. The economic agent has to act on the principle that scarce resources are put into optimum utilization and should not be wasted. This is obviously a 'universal human value' affecting all economic behaviour. It is in this context that decision making occupies a central place in management.

Inventory Management

Inventory comprises of stock of raw materials, work in progress and finished goods. A very important issue for the manager is to decide an ideal inventory level as overstocking leads to wasteful investment of capital and under stocking entails risk of shortages and consequently disruption in production. Thus managerial economics uses various techniques of inventory control like ABC Analysis, simple simulation exercise and also mathematical models so as to minimize inventory cost.

Advertising

Another area which the managerial economist embraces is the decision about advertising. It includes matters relating to determination of the cost and budget of advertising, measuring the economic effects of advertising, etc. Thus, advertising forms an integral part of decision making and forward planning.

Resource Allocation

The optimum utilization of scarce resources to meet competing ends is a very important matter to be decided by the managerial economist. It incorporates two types of problems. First, what should be the appropriate combination of inputs to arrive at maximum output? Second, if the prices of any input increase, what substitute should be used to ensure least cost combination?

Thus, from the above discussion it is evident that two important areas covered by managerial economics are decision making and forward planning. Since forward planning and decision making pervade all important areas like production, marketing, distribution etc., therefore managerial economics plays a vital role in the successful operations of an enterprise.

MANAGERIAL ECONOMIST : HIS RESPONSIBILITY

Managerial economics is a composite discipline. It comprises quantitative statements as well as statements touching ethical aspects. Managerial economics is more practical than theoretical and as such the managerial economist has to study practical economic implications of any decision taking. The chief responsibilities of the managerial economist are as under:

BETTER RESOURCE MANAGEMENT

Though managerial economics is normative, it cannot ignore the positive aspect. Positive economics is a scientific discipline while normative economics is a branch of ethics. If the firm is to attain success in business, it has to produce products of exceptionally high quality and sell it at reasonable prices. This needs better management of men and resources. The optimum utilisation of production capacity, exploitation of hidden talents in the manpower and better financial management are sine qua non for success of a business organisation. It is said that the opinion of the managerial economist on a normative question is of no more value than guessing the outcome of a football match. This field rests with management itself. But the role of the managerial economist in the organisation is that of a pure scientist leaving the normative aspect to the management.

Forecasting

The firms function in certain social, economic and political systems. For instance, we assume the existence of a mixed economy in which individuals enjoy right to property. We also assume that law and order prevails in the country and everyone is subordinate to rule of law and there exists stable political system. The existence of free markets is assumed. The markets keep buyers and sellers of a commodity in touch with one another. That is how prices are determined and a uniform price prevails for a product in the market. The managerial economist works in such a social and political environment and thus manages the affairs in perfect coordination and understanding. He cannot work in an ivory tower. He functions in realities. Therefore, economists have to function in an environment where resources are scarce and technical factors put a limitation on industrial output, etc. Though the managerial economist works in an uncertain environment, he is needed to forecast the demand for the product, the sales turnover, the net profits etc in realistic terms. His analysis should indicate the risks that the company may experience in varied situations.

The economic forecast is like weather forecast, as such, in the midst of uncertainties, the forecast should suggest how the management can adjust the production and marketing of the product and withstand the economic fluctuations. The managerial economist is needed to watch carefully the outcomes of his forecast and keep the management alert. The managerial economist is a thinker. He is a friend and philosopher of the industrialists. He should, therefore, be both conceptual as well as practical. He must have a good knowledge of working of the individual units as well as the industry as a whole and the behaviour of the market and business conditions and likely changes that take place in the economy. Then only he can successfully function as an economic adviser. Apart from being an adviser of the organisation, he is also a researcher. Economic research is an effective tool for any realistic forecasting. Therefore, he is needed to come in contact with data sources and collect the inevitable data related to his field, to use it whenever essential.

To Maximise Profits

The most important function of the managerial economist is to help the firm achieve its goal of profit maximization i.e., there should be harmony in his objectives and the desired objectives of the organization.

Researcher

In addition to the advisory function, a managerial economist is also a researcher. Therefore, he is required to collect the required information from different data sources for effective decision making.

Conceptual as well as Practical

A managerial economist is expected to be a friend and philosopher for the industrialist, so he should be both conceptual and practical. He must have adequate knowledge about the individual units as well as the industry as a whole, the market environment and the changes taking place in the economy.

Thinking, Discussing and Criticising

A managerial economist should devote sufficient time to thinking, discussing and criticizing various economic problems without involving himself in controversial matters.

Taking Challenging Tasks

A managerial economist should always be ready to take up challenging tasks and make his services indispensable and most sought after in the organization. Whenever given any assignment, he should be ready to accept it with full seriousness and devotion.

To conclude, the managerial economist has a significant role to play in any organization by helping the management in decision making and forward planning. He has to recognise his responsibilities and obligations in the firm, if he has to perform an effective role.

Objectives of the Firm

A firm is an organisation carrying on economic activities like production, distribution and marketing of goods and services with a view to earn profits. Traditionally, a firm is defined as an organisation of an individual or a group of individuals formed to achieve economic objectives. A firm in modern period is defined as a joint stock company in which decisions are taken by the shareholders and they are executed by the company officers. Whether the firm is owned by an individual or by group of persons, the goal is to make profits. Once this goal is ensured, the next goal, namely the expansion of the firm comes into existence.

The traditional economists, keeping profit maximisation as the objective of the firm, formulated a theory which is known as equilibrium of a firm. They said that when a firm is in equilibrium position, it is earning maximum money profits. With regard to objectives of a firm, Prof. Galbraith in his book 'The Goals of Industrial System' says, 'Any organisation, as for any organism, the goal has a natural assumption of pre-eminence', it is the survival of the organisation". Survival here means to obtain normal earnings. Once a firm accomplishes this objective, it plans to expand the activities of the firm, which means assuming more resposibilities in the organisation. The objectives of expansion are followed by growth and then by technological development. This means taking up of innovation. In course of time, a business firm with a simple objective grows to a goal institution with multiple objectives. The goals of a business firm are divided under five heads i.e., production goal, inventory goal, the sales goal, the market share goal and the profit goal.

OBJECTIVE OF PROFIT-MAKING

In a modern business firm the producer is interested in maximising profits. The term profit maximisation implies generation of largest absolute amount of profits over a period of time. Here the term 'period of time' refers to both short period and long period. The term profit maximisation refers not only to normal profits but also to super-normal profits. The normal profits are minimum income which an entrepreneur must get if he wants to stay in business. The normal profit is a fixed amount which a firm earns independent of the level of the output. Since the normal profit is included in average cost, it does not come under the principle of profit maximisation. It is the super-normal profits which are the residual income of the entrepreneur which he aims at maximising. There has been a controversy regarding this objective.

Some economists stick to this assumption while some others oppose it tooth and nail. Some economists hold the view that businessmen are interested in maximising the profit for each accounting period. For them, immediate profit is more significant than future profit. But there are some economists who object to this view saying that businessmen emphasize on the future in the concept of profits. According to them, profit is defined as the maximum dividend that a company can pay without impairing its ability to pay the same dividend in the subsequent years.

REALITY OF THE CONCEPT

A doubt has been expressed by many regarding the reality of the concept of maximising profit. In fact, profit maximisation theory justifies its stand on the ground that it is essential for a business to meet the social welfare obligation. Secondly, the goal of profit maximisation is forced on him by the impact of competing firms, namely, if he can make profit, he survives, otherwise, he will have to disappear from business. These justifications of profit maximisation have been criticised on the following grounds.

As criticism it can be said that enlightened businessmen vehemently oppose the concept of profit maximisation as their business objective. They say that service to society rather than personal profit is their aim. In a modern industrial organisation, decisions are taken by salaried executives rather than by the owners of the firm. They aim at sales maximisation. As long as competition is keen, the demand for the product is high and any firm, however inefficient, can make profits. Profit maximisation in such circumstances will not be the objective. Then, the goal of profit maximisation is difficult to realise. If a businessman wants to maximise his profits, he has to fix a price, so as to equalise marginal cost and marginal revenue. This means that he must be able to estimate the demand at all prices and marginal cost at all outputs. This is a very difficult task and it is not practiced anywhere. Further, some have considered profit maximisation as immoral. Thorns J. Hailstones in his book 'Readings in Economics' observes, "Profit maximisation requires the businessmen to use every trick he can think of to keep wages and fringe benefits down to extract the last feasible dollar from the consumer to sell low quality merchandise as he can legally hoodwink the customer into buying, to use income solely for the benefits of the stock holder, to disclaim any accountability to the community, to wrangle the lowest feasible price from his vendors regardless of its effect on them" and so on. It is also a fact that business practices followed by the businessmen are not consistent with the profit maximisation principle. Businessmen are also guided by a sense of fairness, adequacy etc. in fixing the prices for their products. If they get a certain percentage of profit, they are highly satisfied. Thus, profit maximisation is far from the realistic objective of business firms. We can conclude by quoting Dorfman, "on balance, the maximisation hypothesis is not as firmly grounded in the facts of life as a fundamental scientific hypothesis should be. But substantial and prolonged divergences from the behaviour, it implies, are rare especially in industries with several participants. It therefore can still be entertained as a sound working hypothesis"

THEORY OF LONG TERM SURVIVAL

The theory of long term survival as an objective of business was developed by Prof. Rothschild. It is said that when a businessman fixes the price for his product, his aim is not to get maximum profit but to satisfy his sense of security. It means that he aims at getting good income for several years to come, so that he does not suffer from insecurity. In other words, the objective of the entrepreneur is to get a steady flow of profit for a long time to come.

According to Prof. Rothschild "profit maximisation has until now served as the wonderful master-key that opened all the doors leading to an understanding of the entrepreneur's behaviour. But there is another motive which cannot be so lightly dismissed and which is perhaps of a similar order of magnitude as the desire for maximum profit, the desire to secure profits". In a market structure like imperfect competition and monopolistic competition, where there are big number of firms operating, profit maximisation may become valid objective. But under perfect competition, where the price is fixed by the industry and the individual firm has to accept the prevailing price, but has no option, the question of profit maximisation does not arise. In the case of monopolistic competition and absolute monopoly, the entrepreneurs are in a position to fix the price. The oligopolist has both desire and the power to achieve a secure position. In such a market situation, the need for security is more desirable than profit maximisation.

MAXIMISATION OF SALES

Prof. Baumol has developed a model in which he says maximisation of sales revenue is an alternative goal of maximisation. He says that maximisation of sale rather than maximisation of profit is the eventual objective of the entrepreneur. He added that sales have become an end and not only a means of improving operational efficiency and profits. Baumol regards sales maximisation as the most valid assumption governing the behaviour of the firm. Sales maximisation means maximum revenue from sales. The goal of the firm is to sell as high as possible, so that the firm gets more revenue. Prof. Baumol also calls his model 'Revenue Maximisation Hypothesis'.

In his book 'Business Behaviour Value and Growth', Prof. Baumol expounds his approach. According to him, when the sales of the firm increase, the profits of the firm will also increase.

Therefore, by increasing the sales, the firm is fulfilling the objective of profit maximisation. He makes his position very clear by analysing this concept that the entrepeneurs promote sales without incurring extra costs so that his determined rate of return of investment is not affected. He maintains that the firm is not going to sacrifice its assumed profit if sales were to increase. So he observed, "As long as profits are high enough to keep stockholders satisfied and contribute adequately to the financing of company's growth, management will bend its efforts to the augmentation of sales revenue rather than to further increase its profits". The sales maximisation hypothesis is explained with the help of the following diagram:

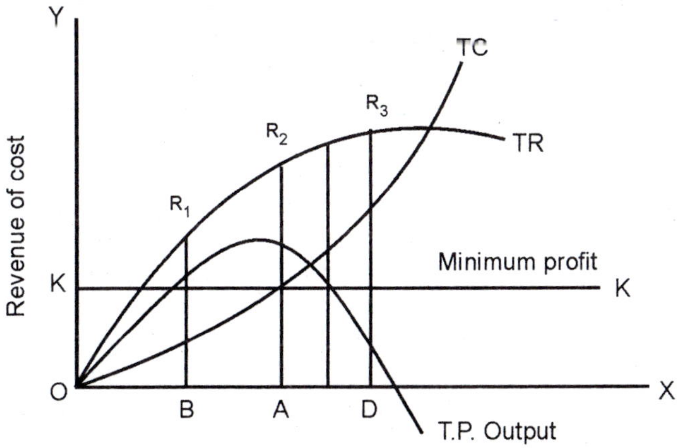

FIG. 1

In this diagram, the firm aims at selling a maximum output, earning minimum profit. TR is the total revenue from the sales of the product. TC is the total cost incurred for producing the output. TP curve represents the total cost incurred for producing the output. TP curve represents the total profit. At the output OA, the profits are maximum. If the firm aims at producing the output OD, the sales revenue is DR_3. At this level, total profit is less. Then, the firm sells OB output and at this output, the total sales revenue is BR_1 and the firm is earning minimum profits. Thus, Prof. Baumol concludes that the firm maximises total revenue without incurring any loss but his minimum profit is maintained.

BALANCED RATE OF GROWTH : ITS MAXIMISATION

The balanced rate growth model is propounded by Prof Morris. He suggested a variation to Baumol's model of sales maximisation and called it maximisation of growth. For

Prof. Morris, the objective of the firm is to achieve a balanced rate of growth. The executives of the firm are interested in salary, status, power, prestige and security, while the owners (shareholders) are concerned with profit, market share and output, etc. Thus, the objectives of the shareholders differ from that of the manager. Prof. Morris, correlating the goals of the owners and the managers, reduced the variables to a single variable, like the size of the firm. Thus, he concluded that the managers are related to the rate of growth of the size of the firm. Morris defined the size of the firm in terms of corporate capital which is equivalent to sum of the value of the assets, the inventories and the cash at the office. Prof. Morris added that the balance of growth model is not without constraints. He says that the firm has to face two limitations. Firstly, the constraint comes from the limit of the expansion of managerial skill. Secondly, it comes from finances. Keeping the above constraints in mind, Prof. Morris has said that the managers aim to have a balanced growth of demand for the product and supply of capital. If the managers decide to expand the firm too rapidly by establishing risky projects, then the balanced rate of growth concept will be defeated. The balanced rate of growth involves not only bringing adequate profits to the shareholders, but also safeguarding the interests of managers. Thus, the rationale for this objective is that by combining the objective of shareholders and the managers in a proper manner, the balanced rate of growth of the firm can be achieved

BEHAVIOURAL THEORY

Prof. Simon put forth the behavioural theory of the firm in 1955. Behaviour theory is purely psychological in character but it combines with industrial economics. This approach centers on the decision making process of the big multi-product firm under uncertainty in an imperfect market. Prof. Simon calls his model satisfying behaviour of the managers. The managers in each firm take decisions for the future on the basis and of the information they get. This information might not be accurate. As an outcome of this, any decision taken might not be practicable. Management under such uncertainty and incomplete information takes decisions which satisfy their calculations. In fact, the management determines a 'satisfactory aspiration level' on the basis of past experience and judgement about uncertainty of the future. If the aspiration is fulfilled easily, the future operations are revised upwards and if the expectation is not fulfilled, then the future operations are revised downwards. In these calculations, the management is satisfied with the decision taken. The management tries to satisfy, but not to maximise either profits or sales. In other words, the firm wants to see that the overall performance is executed in accordance with the desired goals. The satisfying behaviour concept also suffers from certain flaws.

Prof. Simon talks about the nature of information and says that it is usually incomplete and imperfect. It is not clear, how information supplied by the organisation is imperfect. The significant fact in Simon's approach is that the management is needed to adjust to the changing conditions. Prof. Simon makes an ambitious aim, namely coordinating the objectives of both the owners and the managers. The behaviour model of Prof. Simon was later modified by Cyert and March. According to them, assuming that the world is uncertain and market conditions are changing is imperfect. Under these conditions, the firms expect for a reasonable profit and a reasonable sales of the product or products. Before any firm can arrive at a decision, it has to keep in mind the restrictions under which it has to operate. These restrictions can arise in two ways.

Sometimes, they may come from within the organisation i.e. they are internal to the firm. For instance, a firm, which has capital at its disposal, need not explore all alternative possibilities of goods and services that it can produce. Knowing that it has limited capital, it may explore only a few feasibilities and decide to produce one of the goods. Here, capital is the constraint which has to be kept in mind before arriving at the decision of what to produce. Conversely, sometimes there are restrictions imposed by external factors like limited quantity to be produced, non-availability of sufficient quantity of raw materials or restrictions imposed by laws and regulations etc. Some of the significant external restrictions are discussed below:

Output Related Restrictions: In case of most of the commodities, the quantity that has to be produced by the firms is determined by an external authority. This authority has the liberty to specify how much can be produced which can act as a restriction to the producing firm. Again, the licensing authority can specify the rules relating to the quantity of the commodity and the firm is expected to abide by these rules. This can also act as a constraint to the producing firm. For instance, the firm producing baby foods may be expected to meet certain nutritional requirements specified by the competent authority.

Resources Related Restrictions. Quantity of resources available to a firm may be fixed or limited, keeping in view the availability of resources, on the basis of which the firm has to take an appropriate decision. Especially in a developing country like India, scarcity of resources acts as a major obstruction to the firm's production levels.

Governmental Restrictions: The government may impose certain restrictions on the firm's activities. It may define particularly the level of wages and bonus, or the measures to be taken to maintain the health and safety of employees. Restrictions may also take the form of taxes, subsidies, quotas, differential rates of interest on loans etc. Before the firm can arrive at any decision, it has to consider all these legally imposed restrictions.

Restrictions by Environmental Factors: All firms have to operate within the framework of a given economic, social and political environment. These environments may vary from country to country. The decision making firm, therefore, requires to have a clear knowledge of these environments both within the domestic economy and also outside it, because today no economy is a closed economy. The decision maker must have a thorough knowledge about all aspects pertaining to objectives and policies of the government like plan objectives, industrial policies, fiscal and monetary policies, foreign trade policy etc. He is also required to have a fair idea about the relevant macroeconomic trends like national income, money supply, levels of poverty and unemployment etc. It is essential for him to keep track of the changing social and political environment in the country. It is in these matters that the service of economists and analysts can be of great use to the producers. They and specialists who are in regular touch with the changes that are occuring in the economy have a responsibility to keep the top level management well informed about the forthcoming changes.

MAKING OF DECISION

The objective of managerial economics is to solve practical problems of business. This requires decision making at the level of the firm. Decision making is the process of selecting the appropriate action from among different alternative actions. Decisions have far reaching effects on the firm and are generally easy to make. The following steps should be followed to arrive at right decisions:

(i) To establish objectives,
(ii) To express the decision-problems,
(iii) To identify alternatives,
(iv) To assess alternatives,
(v) To select the best feasible alternative,
(vi) To implement the decision,
(vii) To monitor the performance.

At the outset, it is essential to be clear about the objectives of a firm. In today's complex world, there are many alternatives available to a firm and also many constraints under which they are to operate. With a view to have a clear understanding of these, a through examination of the environment opportunities and constraints is essential. An evaluation of alternatives involves collection of all relevant data and their analysis through appropriate techniques. Once the above four steps are completed, it is simple to choose an alternative on the basis of the chosen objective. However implementation of the decision taken requires resources, an explanation to those who are affected by it and an ability to face the results. After implementing the decision, its performance must be monitored in comparison with expectations, so that errors are minimised in the future. Ours is a dynamic economy and decisions have to be made within the time constraint. Things change over time and an undue delay in decision making may turn opportunities into risks.

ESSENCE

The business firms have some goals to be fulfilled. The chief goal is to produce and market the goods and services which satisfy the buyers and thereby earn a-profit sufficient for the survival and growth of business. While discussing about the business objective, Peter Drucker says that the goals of the firm are market standing, innovation, productivity, economical use of productive resources including finance, improved performance of men and machinery, co-operation and public accountability. He says that a firm has to earn profits and also meet the social objectives. Profit making is no doubt an inevitable function of a business firm. Adam Smith considered that profit is a device which transforms the selfishness of mankind into channels of useful service. Prof. Drucker also holds the same view. According to him, profit serves three chief objectives:

(i) It measures the effectiveness and soundness of the business enterprise.
(ii) It helps to cover the risk in business.
(iii) It makes sure supply of future capital for investment, expansion and thus enhance the wealth of the society.

Profit as such is not at all a defective objective. The future growth of the economy depends upon generation and reinvestment of profit. Profit serves as a motivation for expansion, diversification and lastly innovation.

QUESTIONS

1. What do you know about Managerial Economics? Define it.
2. Describe in brief the nature and scope of Managerial Economics.
3. Mention the importance of Managerial Decision Making.
4. Briefly discuss the objectives of a firm ?
5. Describe the Economic Theory in detail.

CHAPTER

2

Theory of Demand

DEMAND ANALYSIS

Demand Analysis in Decision-making: The concept of demand is the fundamental concept in managerial economics which acquaints a manager with the relationship between the price of a commodity and its quantity which could be purchased at a given price by consumers. The study of such a relationship provides the business manager with essential facts which could be analysed for measuring the forces that influence sales volume. This study is called 'Demand Analysis' which serves the following important managerial objectives in the process of decision-making :

(i) It aids in forecasting sales and revenues;
(ii) It provides guidance for manipulation of demand;
(iii) It provides basis for analysing market influences on different products manufactured by a business organisation and helps in adjusting and adapting such influences;
(iv) It provides basis for appraising salesman's performance and for setting his sales quota;

(v) It is also used to match the competitive strength of the organisation;

(vi) Guidance is sought through demand analysis in formulating production schedules. It also helps in planning for inventory control and assessing working capital requirements.

Thus demand analysis occupies a central place in the process of decision making in the business organisation. According to Savage and Small, "through demand analysis, it is feasible to identify and understand the nature of variables influencing demand for firms' products and those variables could be used in planning and budgeting". Demand Analysis provides the technique with which these variables could be manipulated in planning for profit. Demand Analysis assumes the forms of demand schedule, demand curve, demand function, shift in demand curve and factors affecting demand curve, elasticity of demand and its different forms and relationship with marginal revenue and incremental revenue. All these forms are discussed below:

DEMAND SCHEDULE

Demand Schedule is the simplest quantitative expression of demand analysis that studies demand relationship. In the words of Leibhafsky, "Market Demand Schedule is defined as the quantities of a given commodity which all the consumers will buy at a given moment of time." Demand Schedule is a list of prices and corresponding quantities of a commodity that would be demanded by some individual or individuals at those prices. For instance, following is the demand schedule for commodity 'X' which displays prices of the 'X' and the quantity which could be purchased at such prices:

It may be observed from the Table 1 demand schedule that at a higher price of Rs. 10, the quantity of 'X' demanded is very less, i.e. 100 units only clearly indicating that as the price declines the quantity of 'X' demanded by consumers increases. As a result, at Rs. 6,260 units are demanded. So, with lower price, a greater quantity of the commodity is demanded. This is the law of demand which indicates an inverse or negative

TABLE I

Price (in Rs.)	*Quantity Demanded (Per time period)*
10	100
9	120
8	150
7	200
6	260

relationship between price and the quantity of demand. There are two reasons for the above phenomenon. Firstly, decline in the price increases disposable income in the hands of consumers so that with the same amount of money they can obtain larger quantities. This is called 'Income Effect' of price change. Secondly, a decline in the price of a commodity attracts the consumers in comparision to other commodities which are relatively high priced. This is called 'Substitution Effect'. These two effects are dependent on the utility function of a commodity for the consumers. i.e. greater the utility for the commodity, the greater the effectiveness of these effects. This subject will be referred to in the study of elasticity of demand at the end of this section.

DEMAND CURVE

The "law of demand," as referred to above, indicating negative relationship between price and quantity demanded, can be explained through geometrical expression in the shape of demand curve. In the words of Leftwitch, "The demand curve represents the maximum quantities per unit of time that consumers will take at various prices."

The demand schedule as discussed above can be explained in terms of demand curve as displayed in Figures 1 and 2.

Demand Curve in Figure 1 is a straight line whereas in Fig. 2 it is a nonlinear curve. The slope of straight line is uniform along the length of the line and measures the steepness of the line d-d′. This slope has been defined as change in price divided

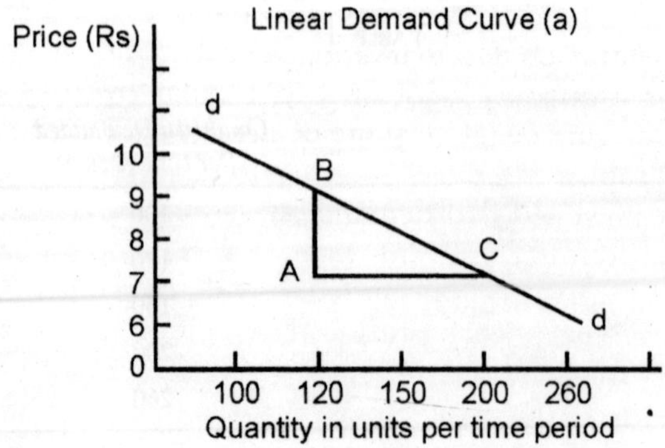

FIG. I

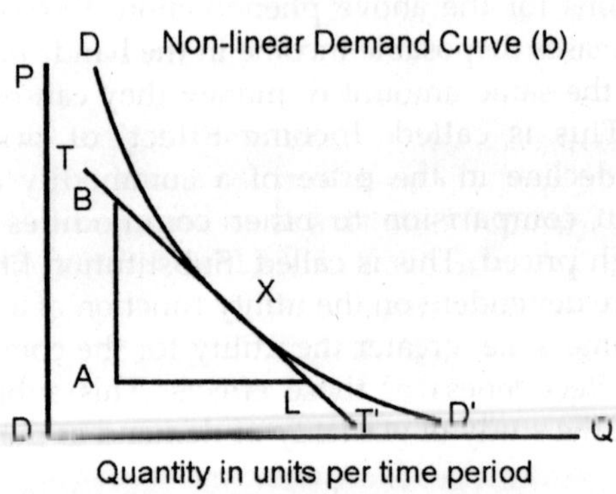

FIG. 2

by corresponding change in quantity. Let us refer to triangle ABC in Fig. I wherein AB=2 and AC=80. The slope is equal to AB/AC, i.e. 1/40. The slope is negative because as price declines there is increase in demand for the commodity. However, in case of non-linear demand curve, slope of curve D-D′ at point X may be found by calculating slope of tangent T-T′ i.e. AB ÷ AC as in previous example. The demand curve is based on the assumption that there are no changes in other variables which may affect price and quantity relationship. This has been done for simplification of the study of price-quantity relationship. In practical situations other variables affect the price besides quantity, which are taken into consideration by business managers while using 'demand analysis' for a particular commodity for making effective decisions with regard to production and marketing. The demand curve depicts demand for a quantity of X on a particular price as may be observed from the negative slope of the demand curve D-D′ in the above graph.

It may be stated that demand curve may be plotted for an industry, individual and the firm viz. (a) For an industry, showing the quantity purchased by all consumers of that industry's product at each price (b) For an individual consumer, showing the quantity one purchases at different prices as may be observed from the above demand curve (c) it may be plotted for a particular product of a firm showing how much it would be sold out at each price. The following characteristics of 'demand curve' are worth noting:

(i) Contrary to usual mathematical practice, it is customary for economists to represent price level on the vertical axis and quantity demanded on the horizontal axis. This is so because demand is treated as a function of price being the independent variable based on assumptions.

(ii) The curve implies a single point of time say at particular hour on a particular date. So that all but one of the prices and quantities must be hypothetical and the curve answers the question of how much quantity could be demanded on a particular price.

(iii) The demand curve has a negative slope indicating that other things being equal, more quantity will be demanded on lower prices. There are two feasible exceptions to this general phenomenon (a) cases of snob appeal like demand for jewellery and (2) cases where consumer should judge quality by price like a costly fountain pen and so on.

DEMAND FUNCTION AND SHIFT IN DEMAND CURVE

The basic assumption in 'Demand Schedule' and 'Demand Curve' has been the relationship between price and quantity of a commodity, signifying a change in price to bring a change in quantity demanded with all other variables assumed constant and the same. In "demand function', this assumption is relaxed and it is held emphatically that besides change in price there are other variables which influence demand for a particular commodity. So, demand is a function of a number of variables besides the price as listed below. Algebraically demand function is represented as under :

$$Q_D = f(X_1, X_2, X_3 \dots X_n)$$

Where,

Q_D is quantity demanded and

$X_1, X_2, X_3 \dots X_n$ refer to number of variables, some of which are listed in Table 2.

TABLE 2

Change in Variables	*Effect on Demand*
1. Increase in Consumer's income level	Increase in quantity demanded QD
2. Decrease in Consumer's income level	Decrease in QD
3. Increase in price of substitute goods	Increase in QD
4. Decrease in price of substitute goods	Decrease in QD
5. Increase in price of complementary goods	Decrease in QD
6. Decrease in price of complementary goods	Increase in QD
7. Increase in the amount of advertisement and promotional expenditure	Increase in QD
8. Decrease in the amount of advertisement and promotional expenditure	Decrease in QD
9. Expected price increase for	Increase in QD
10. Expected price decrease for QD goods	Decrease in QD
11. Increase in Consumers' desire for QD goods	Increase in QD
12. Decrease in Consumers' desire for QD goods	Decrease in QD

The above variables exercise a crucial impact on the demand function. The difference can be noted in comparison with the demand schedule or the demand curve where changes in price of a commodity result in movement along the demand curve. But in the case of demand function changes in other independent variables cause a shift in demand curve. This shift may be illustrated graphically as under :

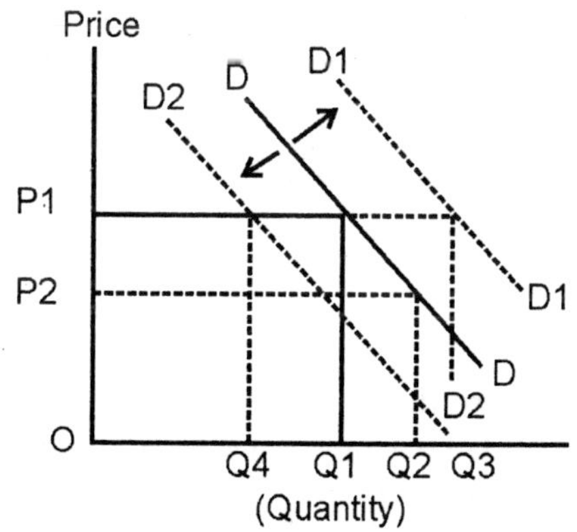

FIG. 3

In the above figure D-D is the initial demand relationship. At price P1, quantity Q1 is demanded and with reduction in price to P_2 increased quantity Q_2 is demanded. With change in other variables the position of D-D changes either upward or downward depending upon the nature of variables and magnitude of the change. For instance, increase in dearness allowance enhances the feasible income of consumers. As a result deman curve will shift to D^1-D^1 and at P_1 increased quantity Q_3 will be demanded. However, if the government raises taxation rate on the increased income to the extent that existing disposable income is also reduced then at the given price P1 the consumer would demand a lesser quantity Q_4 and the demand curve would shift downward to the position D_2-D_2.

Shifting of demand curve renders the demand analysis difficult. Therefore, demand function makes use of mathematical formulations to arrive at correct results. Recently, more sophisticated methods have been developed for the study like simultaneous equation estimation and mathematical programming which help in arriving at accurate results.

THE LAW OF DEMAND

In economics, the relation of price to sales is known as the 'Law of Demand'. It implies "higher the price, lower the demand and vice versa, other things remaining the same." Producers make goods to satisfy the wants of people. If no one consumes, there will be no production at all. Consumption is thus, the end of productive activity. What goods are to be produced and in what quantities depend on what is demanded by the people. Thus, the knowledge of demand is indispensable for managers to determine what to be produced and how much to be produced. Here also lies the significant thing, namely the price of the product.

Demand analysis is related to the size of the demand for the product. There are three managerial aspects of demand-one is the Analysis and Forecasting of Demand, second is the Effect of Demand on the activities of the firm and the third is the Positive Approach of meeting the demand. Demand Analysis has two chief managerial purposes: (1) forecasting sales, (2) manipulating demand. The first is passive managerial aspect of demand because it represents factors which influence the firm, the second is active which represents what the firm can influence. Forecasting means knowledge of the factors likely to affect demand in a given situation. Sales forecasting is passive because it estimates external economic factors and predicts the amount of sales that the firm can make. But in a free economy, since consumers enjoy absolute freedom to consume, the producers have to take up production of those commodities which people hope to buy. The demand analysis unearths the main issue of what people want and how much do they want.

DETERMINANTS OF DEMAND

Product's demand is inevitably the attitude of consumers towards the product. The consumer's attitude gives rise to actions in buying so many units of a product at different prices. Briefly stated, the demand for a commodity is the amount of it that a consumer will purchase or will be ready to take from the market at different prices at a given time. Thus, demand in economics implies both the desire to buy and ability to pay for a product. It is to be noted that only desire does not constitute demand, if it is not supported by the ability to pay for it. For instance, a poor man wants to have a car, but this does not constitute demand, because he does not have the money required to buy it.

Again, a miser has plenty of money but he has not got the essential desire to have a car. These do not constitute demand. Thus, demand in economics means desire backed up by adequate purchasing power to pay for the product when demanded. Demand for a product is determined by many factors such as price of the product, taste and desires of the consumers for commodity, income of the consumer, the prices of related goods like substitutes and complements, advertising and sales promotion. These factors have the greatest influence on sales of the products. Let us discuss fully these variables which influence demand.

Commodity's Price: This is the basic factor in determining demand. There is a definite relationship between the quantity demanded and the price of the product. If a person wants to pay a certain price to the commodity, he must get satisfaction which is equivalent to the price paid for the product. No rational human being will pay for a product more than what it is worth to him in terms of utility. If the price is high, the individual has to sacrifice much, therefore he purchases less. If the price falls, his sacrifice is less, he purchases more. This inverse relationship between the price and the quantity demanded is known as the Law of Demand.

Income of Consumer: Consumer's income is another significant variable which influences demand. The ability to buy a commodity depends upon the income of the consumer. The higher the income, larger is the quantity of a product that the consumer will buy. For instance, a rich man can afford to buy more because his purchasing power is high. When the income of consumers increases, they buy more at a given price or at a higher price. When the income falls, the consumers are forced to buy less.

Consumer's Tastes and Preferences: Commodity's demand depends upon tastes and preferences of consumers. These depend upon the cultural and social standard of consumers. If the consumers develop taste for a commodity, they buy whatever may be the price. The particular life style influences the consumers to buy luxury goods and quality products. For instance, a few years back, the demand for soft drinks was very low. But now the demand for soft drinks has increased very significantly, which is because of change in taste. Advertisement and sales campaign and improved knowledge are some of the factors which cause changes in consumers' tastes and preferences.

Price of Substitutes: Product's demand is also affected by the prices of substitutes and complements. Generally, commodities have alternatives and also they are used as complements. For instance, coffee and tea are substitutes. Ink and pen are compliments. When coffee becomes cheaper, the consumers's substitute coffee for tea and as a result the demand for coffee increases and that of tea decreases. If the price of ink rises, the demand for pen falls. Likewise, when the price of cars falls, the demand for them would increase which in turn will increase the demand for petrol.

Advertisement and Sales Campaign: In modern civilization era, advertisements and sales campaign in newspapers and television influence the demand for products very significantly. They can change the demand pattern of the upper class people. Thus, all these factors contribute to the demand for a commodity. We can analyse the concept of demand in the form of a formula as q = f(pyprw), where q stands for quantity demanded, p stands for the price of the commodity, y stands for income of the consumers, pr stands for price of the concerned goods and w stands for tastes and preferences.

If income, price of concerned goods, tastes and preferences are assumed to be constant, the quantity demand for a commodity depends upon the price. Then, the formula for demand is q = f (p).

Demand Schedule: It is a statement displaying the relationship between the price and the quantity demanded. The following table displays price-quantity relation.

The demand schedule displayed above reveals the relationship between the price and the quantity of the commodity bought. If the price is Rs. 2, 16 units of the commodity are demanded. If the price rises to Rs. 10, then only 1unit is demanded. It displays that lower the price, higher the

TABLE 3

Price	*Quantity Demanded*
10	1 Units
8	2 Units
6	4 Units
4	8 Units
2	14 Units

TABLE 4

Price	*Market demand schedule assuming there are several buyers with different income and tastes*
10	10,000 Units
8	20,000 Units
6	40,000 Units
4	80,000 Units
2	14,00,000 Units

quantity of the commodity demanded and higher the price, lower the quantity of the commodity demanded. Assuming there are many consumers with different incomes and tastes, by adding up all the individual demand schedules, a market demand schedule is obtained. The demand schedule when plotted on a graph gives the following demand curve:

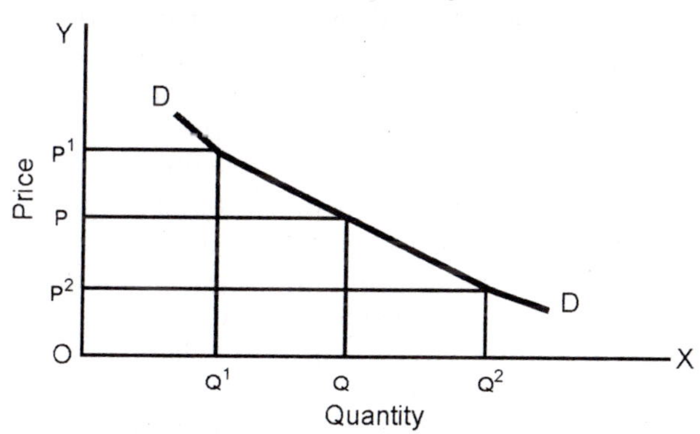

FIG. 4

The demand curve (DD) simply displays the relationship between the price and the quantity of the commodity demanded. The demand curve slopes left to right downwards, indicating that when prices rise, lesser amount of the commodity is purchased and when price falls, more is demanded. The slope of the demand curve is negative because as price declines, more units of the commodity are bought. It is conventional to show the quantity demanded on the X-axis and the price on the Y axis. The demand curve is also known as Average Revenue Curve (AR) because the price paid by the consumer is revenue per unit for the seller.

Law of Demand: Chief Features

(i) The law states that demand varies inversely with price, not necessarily proportionately. If the price falls by 10 percent, it does not follow that demand will rise exactly by 10 per cent. It may be more than 10 per cent or less than 10 percent.

(ii) Price is an independent variable while the quantity demanded is a dependent variable. It means that demand is entirely dependent on the price.

(iii) The law of demand depends upon certain conditions like constancy of tastes and preferences, incomes of the individuals, prices of substitutes, etc. If these change, demand also changes.

Law of Demand: Income and Substitution Effects

According to law of demand, if the price of a commodity falls, the demand for the commodity rises and vice-versa. It implies that demand responds to the price in the reverse direction. This aspect can be explained with reference to the behavior of buyers. The buyers are divided into marginal buyers and intra-marginal buyers. Intra-marginal buyers are those who increase or decrease their consumption of goods but do not start or stop their consumption when faced with price variations. The behaviour of marginal buyers can be explained in terms of income and substitution effects.

Effect of Income: The fall in the price of a commodity is equivalent to an increase in income of the consumer because he spends less while buying the same quantity of the commodity as before. A part of the money so gained can be used to buy more of the same commodity. When the price rises, the consumer's income is reduced since he has to spend more money to buy the same units of the commodity by curtailing the consumption of other commodities. If the consumer does not want to buy more units of the same commodity when price falls, he may use the surplus money to buy some units of a superior commodity. The reverse takes place when price rises. Thus, income effect of a change in price is negative for superior goods and Positive for inferior goods.

Substitution Effect: The substitution effect is the effect that a change in relative prices of substitute goods has on the quantity demanded. Substitutes are goods that can be used in place of each other. In order to get maximum satisfaction with a fixed income, a consumer will substitute a low priced good for a high priced one. When the price of a commodity falls, the consumers can buy more units of the same commodity or they can substitute that commodity for some other commodity or commodities which have now become comparatively dear. For example, tea and coffee are substitutes. If the price of tea falls, the consumers may substitute tea for coffee, although the price of coffee remains the same. Thus, the demand for tea extends due to its becoming less expensive. Contrary to it, if the price of tea goes up, the consumer will substitute relatively less expensive coffee for tea. Consequently, the demand for tea contracts. To get maximum satisfaction, a consumer will buy more units of that commodity whose price in relation to its substitute, has gone down.

A change in price leads to the rise to both substitution effect and income effect. Income effect is positive and substitution effect is negative—The sum of income and substitution effects measure the price effect. For superior goods, both the income and substitution effects work in the same direction, while for inferior goods they work in opposite directions.

Law of Demand: Exceptions

The demand curve often slopes left to right downwards. But seldom, it may rise from left to right upwards. This is known as exceptions to the law of demand. It means, when prices rise, more units of a commodity may be demanded. If price falls, less units of the commodity may be demanded. This is displayed in the form of a rising demand curve. Such cases are very rare. However, there are some cases in our every day life. They are often referred to Giffen goods. Giffen goods are those inferior goods on which consumers spend a large part of their incomes. Giffen paradox states that the demand is strengthened with a rise or weakened with a fall in price.

(i) People belonging to a poor community spend a major portion of their income on staple foods such as wheat, jowar, etc. If the price of wheat or jowar falls, the people are compelled to give up buying of these goods and buy more of rice and other superior goods. When the price of wheat or jowar rises, the consumers buy more of wheat or jowar and forego the buying of other goods. Sir Robert Giffen found that in the 19th century in Ireland, the people were so poor that they spent a major portion of their income on bread and a small amount on meat. Bread was so cheap while meat was very costly then. When the price of bread rose, they spent their entire income on bread and abandoned meat. Thus, a rise in the price of bread resulted in increased sales of bread. This phenomenon happens in all communities when they spend a major portion of their income on staple commodities.

(ii) When a shortage is feared as in days of war or emergency, people become panicky and buy more even though the price is rising.

(iii) There are some commodities named Veblen Goods which are purchased by the upper sections of the society for their 'snob appeal' or ostentation. If price of goods of ostentation rise, some people purchase more units of these goods, Veblen calls this clear consumption. For instance, diamonds. When the price of diamond rises, rich people buy more in order to exhibit their superiority in society. When the price of diamond falls, its demand will also fall for it loses its prestige.

(iv) Sometimes, people buy at a higher price in sheer ignorance.

(v) In the speculative market, a rise in price of shares and stocks is followed by big purchases, while a fall in their prices is followed by less purchase. When the prices of shares rise, people expect that their prices would rise further and rush to buy. When the price falls, they anticipate further fall in the prices and stop buying the same.

(vi) The commodity on which a very small part of the total expenditure is incurred, e.g. post card, salt, etc, the law will not operate because of the change in price of such items.

Law of Demand—Its Basis—Diminishing Marginal Utility

The basic question in the demand analysis is, why do consumers buy more when the price falls and vice versa. The answer is that the consumer acting rationally, calculates intentionally the satisfaction he gets from the consumption of different units of a commodity at a given time. The goal of a consumer is to derive maximum satisfaction or utility from the purchase of different units of a commodity. In order to maximise satisfaction or utility, the consumer allocates his expenditure on a commodity in such a way that he receives the same marginal utility for the last unit of money spent on that commodity. The peculiar characteristic of the law of utility is its diminishing character. The law of diminishing marginal utility states that as a consumer goes on purchasing more and more units of a commodity, the utility from every additional unit keeps on decreasing. The purchases of most of the people are governed by this law. For instance, the utility of a text book on Managerial Economics will be higher to a student who does not possess the book. After having bought the book, he does not need the second book of the same title. If he purchases the second book, the utility from that book will be less than the first book. This means that utility of several units of a commodity to an individual diminishes with every increase in his stock of that commodity. This is known as the law of diminishing marginal utility. When he is forced to buy the second, the third and the fourth unit of the same commodity, he is not prepared to pay the same price for the succeeding units.

Since he derives diminishing marginal utility from every succeeding unit, he offers lower prices for those units. Otherwise, he will not derive maximum satisfaction from every unit of money spent on the commodity. It implies, the consumer will not pay for a commodity more than the money value of its marginal utility to him. Larger the units of the commodity purchased, lower the marginal utility. Therefore, the consumer will not buy more units of a commodity unless its price is low. This behaviour of the consumer will make him attain equilibrium. Consumer's equilibrium will be at a point where the utility from a unit of a commodity is equal to money value spent on that commodity. A formula is worked out as under:

$$\frac{\text{Mu of a}}{\text{Price of a}} = \frac{\text{Mu of b}}{\text{Price of b}} = \frac{\text{Mu of c}}{\text{Price of c}} \text{ etc.}$$

If this condition is not satisfied, then he will not attain equilibrium. If Price of a > Price of b, then the consumer will transfer money from b to a, which will result in an increase in total utility, since utility received from a exceeds the utility from b.

Thus, the basis of law of demand is operation of the law of diminishing marginal utility. The consumer will buy more only if the price falls, because the more he buys, the lower is the marginal utility.

Research of Market and Law of Demand

It is said that a consumer behaves in a rational manner and implicitly follows the law of demand in most cases. Marketing executives have generally found that the law of demand is not relevant to them in organising the sales of the commodities. Therefore, market research is now needed to propound a viable theory of consumer behaviour relevant to marketing executives. Market research comprises consumer surveys, i.e., studies of buyers' motives, attitudes, preferences and purchasing habits. Information is gathered from personal interviews and mailed questionnaires and the same is supplemented by indirect study like interviews with market observers who study the behaviour of the buyers through observation.

When such surveys are conducted, they throw light on the characteristics of demand for different products. It can bring about the sharpening of marketing targets, improvement of distribution methods and adoption of sales improvement techniques. In a free economy with exposed competition, the consumer is a king. Neither the price nor the quality can influence him in buying the product. The demand analysis is used to determine exactly what kind of product he wants. Whenever a new product is introduced, it should be made acceptable to people. The product has to be improved on the basis of market research. Economic analysis takes little interest in classification and summarization of past sales. But producers may formulate their production and pricing policies on the basis of past sales. Some of the researchers have found that sales of the commodity are related to single price. They found that some commodities, though best, could not be sold as forecasted due to their lesser price.

Since the prices were low, the consumers considered the quality of these products as low. When the producers increased their prices, they found that sales increased very significantly. One researcher found that several consumers feel that it is risky and uncertain to go in for a low priced product. The customer who purchased high priced products was cautious. Thus, it can be concluded that the consumer behaviour is not so simple as buyers do not behave according to the law of demand.

Individual Demand and Market Demand Function

The quantity demanded by an individual purchaser at a given price is known as individual demand whereas the total quantity demanded by all the purchasers together is known as market demand.

The market demand, that is, the total demand for a commodity, can be calculated by adding the quantities demanded by all the purchasers. Suppose five persons, viz., A. B, C, D and E purchase eggs in the market. The market demand will be calculated as follows:

The last column of table gives the total demand for eggs at different prices, that is, the 'Market Demand'. The market

TABLE 5
Market Demand for Eggs

Price per dozen Rs.	*Quantity Demanded in Dozens by*					*Total*
	A	*B*	*C*	*D*	*E*	
10	1	3	0	0	0	4
9	2	4	1	0	0	7
8	3	5	3	1	0	12
7	4	6	5	2	1	18
6	5	7	6	3	2	23
5	6	8	7	4	3	28
4	7	9	8	5	4	33

demand curve will as such be a lateral summation of individual demand curves.

Elasticity of Demand

Law of demand is a mere qualitative statement about the direction of change in demand for a good as a result of change in its price, i.e. it does not explain as to how much the demand will change. The concept which elaborates the proportionate change in quantity demanded of a good as a result of change in its price, is called the concept of elasticity of demand.

Meaning, Types and Importance: Elasticity of demand forms part of demand analysis and offers solution to various business problems. Its usefulness is noted in those cases where demand curve analysis becomes unreliable because in many cases demand curve does not slope downward at a uniform rate for the simple reason that change in price does not stimulate the demand in the same proportion.

Demand curve provides a measure of responsiveness to price change and deals with absolute change in quantity and price which makes it difficult to compare the responsiveness of different commodities which might be measured in different units say labour in hours, land in acres and beer in quarts. These commodities with different measures can't be compared with similar units or magnitude. In such cases the concept of elasticity of demand provides us with an accurate way of measuring the responsiveness of demand for a product to a fall in its price. In view of this, elasticity of demand can be defined as a "measure of the responsiveness of the quantity sold to price change, assuming all other variables constant." According to Dr. Alfred Marshall, the first economist to clearly explain the concept of elasticity of demand, "Elasticity is a measure of the responsiveness of one variable to change in another."

In other words, elasticity is a ratio of the relative change in two variables. Elasticity could be measured for marginal effect of price change as or to use the derivatives. But this measure would give large values of elasticity while dQ will differ according to the degree of flattening of the demand curve. For absolute change, the formula is correct but it is not useful to divide tones or bushels by rupees and get meaningful results. Therefore, it is suggested to employ a measure of elasticity which deals with proportionate or percentage change in price and quantity.

Price Elasticity of Demand

Price elasticity of demand is the ratio of the percentage change in the quantity demanded of a commodity to the percentage change in its price. Keeping in view the explanation contained in the above paragraphs, price elasticity of demand Ep can be defined as the ratio of percentage change in quantity demanded to percentage change in price i.e.

With other things being equal,

$$Ep = \frac{\%DQ}{\%DP}$$

Where, DQ = change in quantity demanded
Where, DP = change in price.

Where, minus sign is inserted to make the elasticity number non-negative, because demand curve is negatively inclined presenting inverse relationship between price and quantity demanded. A rise in price (DP positive) will lead to a fall in quantity (DQ negative) so that numerator and denominator in elasticity fraction will be of opposite sign i. e. one in minus and another is plus. With the result, the fraction will be a negative number and 'minus' is needed to make it a 'positive' number. There are a number of formula for computing elasticity of demand varying in accuracy and sophisilication. For specific measure of clasticity, W.J. Boumol has suggested the following formula:

$$Ep = -\frac{\Delta Q}{Q} \cdot \frac{P}{\Delta P} = -\frac{\Delta Q}{\Delta P} \cdot \frac{P}{Q}$$

The above formula is the same as under

$$Ep = -\frac{100\Delta Q/Q}{100\Delta P/P}$$

If we cancel out the numerator 100 by denominator 100 then we have

$$Ep = -\frac{\Delta Q/Q}{\Delta P/P} \text{ or } -\frac{\Delta Q}{\Delta P} \cdot \frac{P}{Q}$$

Since division by fraction $\Delta P/P$ is the same as multiplication by its reciprocal $P/\Delta P$.

The above formula is based on percentages on the basis of original prices and quantities and does give only rough estimates. For reliable estimates it is needed to depend upon another measure known as Arc elasticity.

Arc Elasticity: Arc elasticity is a measure of average responsiveness to price change exhibited by a demand curve D–D′ in Figure 5 over some finite stretch of the curve D_0–D_1. The logic advanced in this regard stresses that range of value of Q along arc DQ–D_1. Therefore,

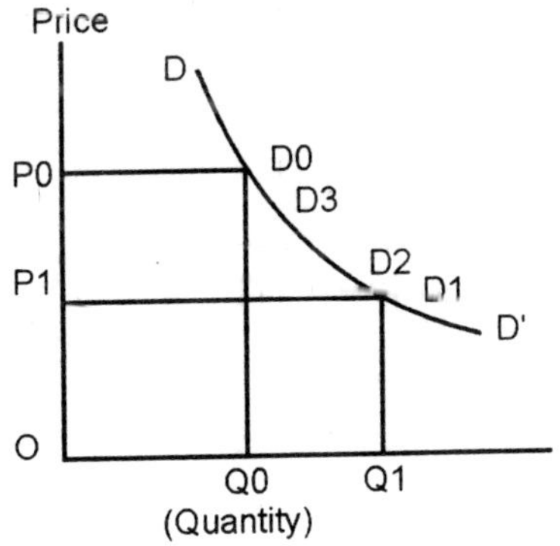

FIG. 5

Use of average of the two end values of Q are taken with consideration viz. Q = $Q_1 + Q_0 \div 2$ similarly, we take average of price change as P = $P_1 + P_0 \div 2$. This gives us the measure of arc elasticity of demand with :

$$\text{Arc Ep} = \frac{Q_1 - Q_0}{P_1 - P_0} \cdot \frac{(P_1 + P_0)/2}{(Q_1 + Q_0/2)}$$

Since numerator and denominator have common which cancels out by multiplication to give :

$$\text{Arc Ep} = \frac{Q_1 - Q_0}{P_1 + P_0} \cdot \frac{P_1 - P_0}{Q_1 + Q_0}$$

The following example will clarify the above concept : Given the following demand schedule:

TABLE 6

Price (P) Rs.	*Quantity Q (Units)*
10	2
9	4
8	6
7	8
6	10
2	18
1	20

Based on the above schedule, if it is assumed that the original price was Rs. 10 at which 2 units are demanded then Ep between the price of Rs. 10 and new price Rs. 9 will be :

$$\text{Arc EP} = -\frac{Q_1 - Q_0}{P_1 - P_0} \cdot \frac{P_1 + P_0}{Q_1 + Q_0}$$

$$= -\frac{4-2}{9-10} \cdot \frac{9+10}{4+2} = -\frac{2}{-1} \cdot \frac{19}{6}$$

$$= -6.3$$

Suppose, if original price P_0, was Rs. 2 with quantity demanded Q_0, 18 units and new price P_1. is I with Q_1, 20, then price elasticity of demand is as under :

$$= -\frac{20-18}{1-2} \cdot \frac{1+2}{20+18} = +\frac{2}{-1} \cdot \frac{3}{38}$$

$$= -.16$$

The above measure is for the arc elasticity which bears further modification in the shape of point elasticity.

Point Elasticity : The price elasticity shall differ from demand curve from point to point as the arc becomes smaller and smaller between two points as may be observed from the Figure 4 where arc D_0-D_1 becomes smaller between D_0-D_2 and D_0-D_3. This gives the following formula for measuring point elasticity :

$$\text{Point Ep} = \frac{dQ}{dP} \cdot \frac{p}{Q} \text{ Ceteris Paribus,}$$

When : $\frac{dQ}{dP}$ are the partial derivatives of quantity with respect to price (that is the inverse of the slope of the demand curve). It is analogous to $\frac{Q_1 - Q_0}{P_1 - P_0}$ in Arc elasticity measure.

Q = Quantity demanded at price P
P = Price at-some specific point on demand curve.

The following example may help to clarify the concept of point

Suppose, demand function is defined as Q = 150-10 P then what is the point elasticity P and Q.

Taking the partial derivatives and substituting the relevant quantities in the above formula, we have

$$\frac{dQ}{dP} = -10, \frac{P}{Q} = \frac{5}{100}$$

$$\text{Then Ep} = \frac{+dQ}{dP} \cdot \frac{P}{Q} = (-10)\left(\frac{5}{100}\right) = .5$$

Readers may note the above difference between the Arc and Point Elasticity.

Income Elasticity of demand: Elasticity concept can be adapted to measure responsiveness in variables other than quantity and price. For instance, we may measure the income elasticity of demand.

In income elasticity of demand, responsiveness of change in quantity demanded to a change in the consumers' disposable income is measured. It may be expressed as under :

$$\text{Ey} = \frac{\text{\% change in Qunatity Demanded}}{\text{\% change in income}} \quad \textit{Ceteris Peribus,}$$

Point income elasticity of demand is calculated from the following :

$$\text{Ey} = \frac{dQ_D}{dY} \cdot \frac{Y}{D}$$

When Y = disposable personal income

Q_D = quantity demanded of some commodity

$\frac{dQ_D}{dY}$ = Partial derivative of quantity with respect to disposable personal income.

Cross Elasticity of Demand : Cross elasticity of demand is a measure of the responsiveness of changes in the quantity demanded of product A to price change for product B. It is measured by the following formula :

$$\text{EX} = \frac{\%\Delta QDA}{\%\Delta PB} \quad \textit{ceteris peribus,}$$

When EX = Cross Elasticity of demand

Q_{DA} = Change in quantity demanded of product A

P_B = Price change for product B

Finally, the formula is

$$= \frac{\%\Delta QDA}{\%\Delta PB}, \text{ or} = \frac{\frac{\Delta QDA}{QDA}}{\frac{\Delta PB}{PB}} \text{ or } \frac{\Delta QDA}{\Delta PB} \cdot \frac{PB}{Q_{DB}}$$

Interest Elasticity of demand: Change in interest rate of money can affect the supply of a particular commodity and the responsiveness of this change can be measured with the following formula:

$$\text{Interest Elasticity of Supply or ES} = \frac{\%\Delta S}{\%\Delta I} \text{ or} - \frac{\Delta S}{\Delta I} \cdot \frac{i}{S}$$

Where, S is change in supply of some Commodity to a change in interest rate

Di = change in interest rate,

To conclude, it may be said that in the above manner, the concept of elasticity can be extended to cover other aspects of business enterprise like income elasticity of imports and interest elasticity of investment, etc.

Elasticity of Demand: Its Interpretation

Interpretation of Elasticity of Demand shall depend upon the degree of elasticity of demand which is divided in to five categories as given below:

Perfectly Elastic Demand: Perfectly elastic demand is defined as e = (i.e. elasticity is equal to infinity). In the presence of

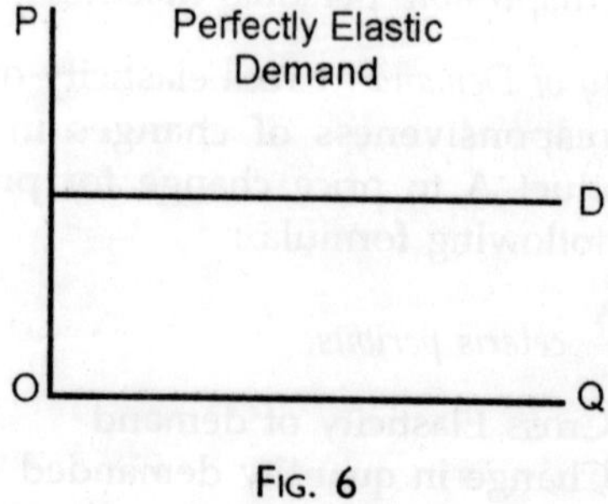

FIG. 6

perfectly elastic demand, no reduction in price is needed to increase demand for the quantity of a commodity. Perfectly elastic Demand Curve is a horizontal line parallel to the horizontal vertix as displayed in Figure 6.

Perfectly Inelastic Demand : Perfectly inelastic demand is defined as e=o. In this case, a change in price does not cause any change in the quantity demanded. It is reflected through a vertical line parallel to price line as displayed in Figure 7.

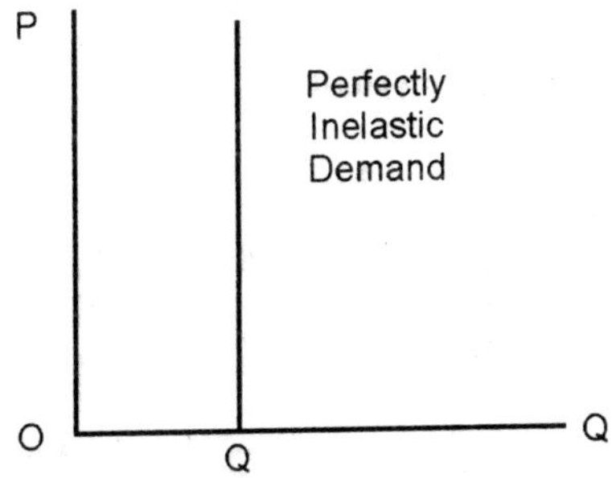

FIG. 7

Unit Elastic Demand: Unit elasticity of demand. is defined as e = 1. In this case, a proportionate change in price causes an equal proportionate change in quantity demanded. The demand curve takes the form of a rectangular hyperbola as displayed in Figure 8.

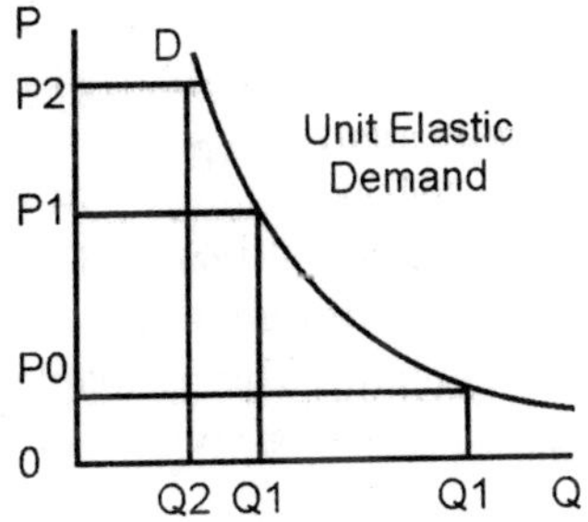

FIG. 8

Relatively Elastic Demand: Relatively elastic demand is defined as e> 1. In the case, a change in price causes greater than proportionate change in quantity demanded. This is displayed in Figure 9.

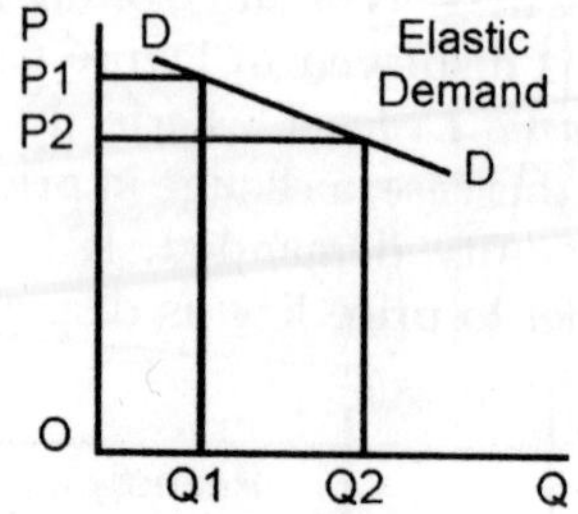

FIG. 9

Relatively Inelastic Demand: Relatively inelastic demand is defined as e< 1. A change in price causes less than a proportionate change in quantity demanded. This is displayed in Fig. below :

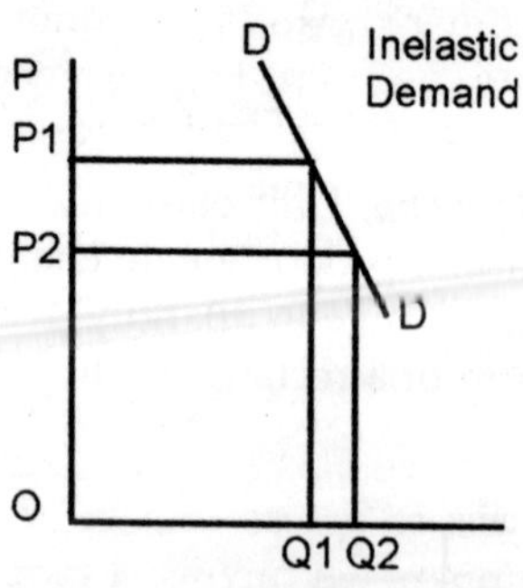

FIG. 10

Income Elasticity of Demand: Another Important interpretation of elasticity of demand is done with reference to income elasticity of demand. This is displayed in Figure 11.

From the Figure following conclusions are worth noting:

(i) Income elasticity of demand is high where it is greater than one, i.e. (e>1). Those commodities which are luxury items generally have high income elasticity.

(ii) Income elasticity of demand is less than one, i.e. (e< 1)

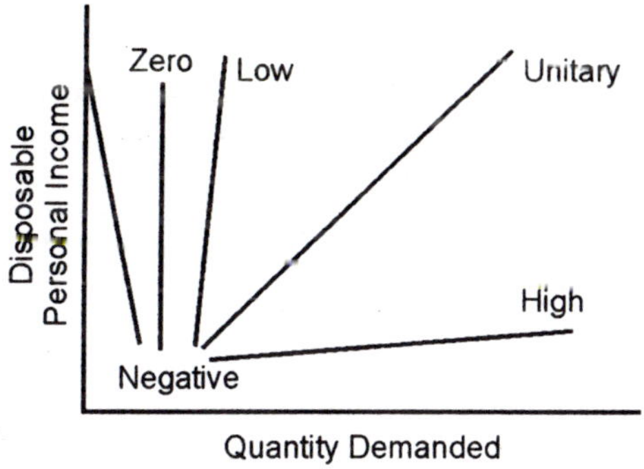

FIG. 11

and this happens in respect of goods which are necessities.

(iii) For most of the goods, income elasticity in expected to be positive i.e. e >o and/or e= 1.

(iv) For inferior goods, income elasticity is always negative, i.e. e<o. For instance, such goods include low-income diet which loses demand as soon as income level increases.

(v) Zero income elasticity is observed in certain goods whose demand is not affected by increase or decrease in income.

Study of Income Elasticity of Demand is significant in forecasting analysis to assess impact of increase in disposable incomes of consumers for buying a particular product.

In the case of Cross Elasticity of Demand between two products A and B, higher cross elasticity would mean that A and B are equal substitutes of each other. Where as, a negative cross elasticity indicates that two product are complementary. For the study of market structure, cross elasticity of demand provides requisite insight and guidance.

RELATIONSHIP BETWEEN TOTAL REVENUE, MARGINAL REVENUE, AND INCREMENTAL REVENUE

Total Revenue (TR): There exist a formal relationship between Elasticity of Demand and the Total Revenue of a business organisation. This relationship is summarised below:

(i) With rise in price of a commodity having elasticity less than unity ($e < 1$) *total revenue rises* because this is a case of inelastic demand and change in price causes a less than proportionate change in quantity demanded and consumers' expenditure is not curtailed.

(ii) With rise in price of a commodity having unit elasticity ($e = 1$) *total revenue remain the same* because a percentage change in price is exactly offset by same percentage change in quantity demanded with the net results being a constant total consumers expenditure.

(iii) With rise in price of commodity having elasticity greater than unity (i e. $e > 1$) *total revenue falls* because change in price causes more than proportionate change in quantity demanded reducing the proportion of consumers' expenditure on such a commodity.

(iv) On the other hand, with fall in price with e <I for a commodity, *total revenue falls* on the same logic as given in sub-para (1) above.

(v) With fall in price with $e = 1$, *total revenue remains the same* for the reasons given in sub-para (ii) above.

(vi) With fall in price with $e > 1$ *total revenue rises* for the

The above relationship, between elasticity of demand and total revenue of a firm can be summarised as displayed in Table 7.

Marginal Revenue (MR) : Elasticity of demand has also formal relationship with MR in the same way as with TR. Marginal revenue is the addition to total revenue resulting from additional sale of commodity to the organisation, i.e. MR is equal to addition to total revenue (R_1-R or DR) divided by addition to output (Q_1-Q or DQ) viz. $\frac{\Delta R}{\Delta Q}$. In terms of calculus, the formula for MR becomes :

$$MR = \frac{dR}{dQ}$$

TABLE 7

	$e < 1$	$e = 1$	$e > 1$
Rise in Price	TR rises	TR the same	TR falls (More than proportionate change)
	MR rises	= MR remains 0 neither positive nor negative	MR have negative change
Fall in price	TR Falls	TR the same	TR rises
	MR Falls	MR as above	MR will be caused positive

TR = Total = Revenue MR = Marginal Revenue AR = Average Revenue which is equal to price.

Which is a derivative of total revenue curve with respect to quantity. MR can be calculated if price and elasticity of demand are known with the help of following formula :

$$MR = P\left(1 - \frac{1}{n}\right)$$

Thus, relationship between MR and demand elasticity is quite close to each other. For instance, when e = I marginal revenue is Zero because price change brings no change in total revenue, as the TR function is already at maximum. Beyond the point where total revenue is maximised, MR become negative and TR declines because at such point e < 1. However, if demand is perfectly elastic (e > 1) the MR becomes equal to price and can be calculated from the above formula. The demand curve slopes downward to right then MR is less than price.

This can be proved by an example using formula MR = $\frac{\Delta R}{\Delta Q}$ noted above. Suppose the original price for commodity X is Rs. 10 when 1000 units of X are sold. Now, price is reduced to Rs. 9 so that 1500 units would be sold. Here DR = 3500 (i.e. 13,500 minus 1000) and DQ is (1500-1000) = 500 and $\frac{\Delta R}{\Delta Q}$ is equal to Rs. 7 which is less than Rs. 9 being the price for the commodity.

Incremental Revenue (IR): Incremental Revenue changes with total Revenue and so it has relationship with elasticity of demand through TR. It also differs from marginal revenue. It measures only the difference between the old or new total revenue unlike MR and is not necessarily converted into change in revenue per unit of output change. Further, it is a measure of the effect of any kind of managerial decision on total revenue and as such is not limited to the effect of change in price and is more flexible than MR concept. Its utility is felt when the decision taken is on the whole profitable. It ignores full record of changes in output. The formula for calculating IR is as given under:

$$IR = R_1 - R = DR$$

Thus, it become clear that incremental revenue implies the change in Total Revenue and its relationship in demand analysis comes into existence through the relationship which exists between TR and elasticity of demand.

COMPANY'S PRODUCT AND MARKET COMPETITION : THE NATURE OF DEMAND

Assessment of nature of demand for a company's product is a complex problem in the theory of demand analysis because demand for company's product cannot be studied separately from the demand of the industry for the same product. All the decisions regarding pricing of the product and sale are made in relation to the demand of the product for the whole industry which includes competing firms manufacturing the same type of product.

However, the nature of demand function for the industrial firm is largely dependent on the some conditions viz. number and relative size of firm in the industry homogeneity of the products sold by firm in the industry, product differentiation amongst the firms in the industry and degree to which decision-making by an individual firm is independent. In the light of above conditions, assessment of nature of company's demand can be made in relation to the study of market structure in which the company as well as the industry, to which it belongs, operate. In the following paragraphs, this is discussed.

Demand in Various Market Situations: For the purposes of studying firm's demand the market structure is divided into four main types: viz. Monopoly or pure monopoly, Pure competition, Monopolistic competition and Oligopoly

Monopoly Market: In monopoly market structure, a single firm, producing one specific commodity or selling a specific service, controls the entire market. This monopolist firm is industry for that product or service. The demand curve for such firm and industry is one and the same.

The significant characteristic of demand lies in non-existence of close substitutes for the product and the absence of cross elasticity of demand between the monopolist's product and any other product. Monopoly market is guarded for entry of competitors through four types of barriers: (a) the firm has mastered production techniques with full cost advantage of economies of inputs and production processes; (b) Product is differentiated to monopolise customers, loyalty for it; (c) advantages of scale of economies which are not available to a new firm; and (d) non-availability of large capital needed by a new firm for making investment in plant, buildings, etc. However, case of single monopoly firm is rare with possibilities in public utilities where State controls the firm and industry with existing firm price-quantity relationship.

Pure Competition: Pure competition is characterised by presence of five conditions viz. (a) large number of firms as buyers and sellers present in the market. Each buyer and seller purchases and sells such a small portion of total output that none of them has perceptible influence on total market. (b) each firm produces a homogeneous product with product differentiation. (c) There are no barriers to entry and exit from market, (d) action of all firms are independent to each other; (e) buyer and seller firms have perfect knowledge of prevailing prices in the market, these conditions render the product of each firm indistinguishable from another. Under the above conditions demand for individual firm's products approaches perfect elasticity which implies that the firm can sell all, it wishes, at the market price and any increase above market price would cause fall in its sale because buyers will move to other sellers for purchasing the commodity at market price.

The following graphs would clearly depict the distinction between a demand curve of industry or a firm in pure competition showing that industry's curve is completely different to individual seller's demand curve which is a horizontal straight line at the level of the market price.

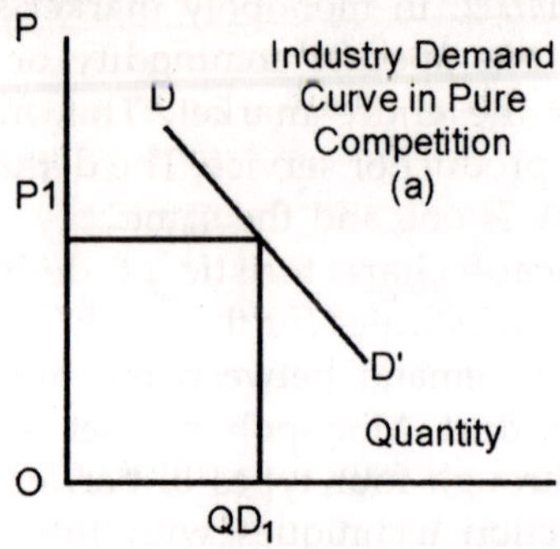

FIG. 12

In Figure 12, D.D. represents demand curve for industry including all firms in industry. Figure 13, displays individual firms demand curve d-d". Individual firm sells entire quantity at P1 which is the prevalent market price for the industry. It may be added that pure competition is other extreme from pure monopoly in the market structure and rarely exist in the real world situations.

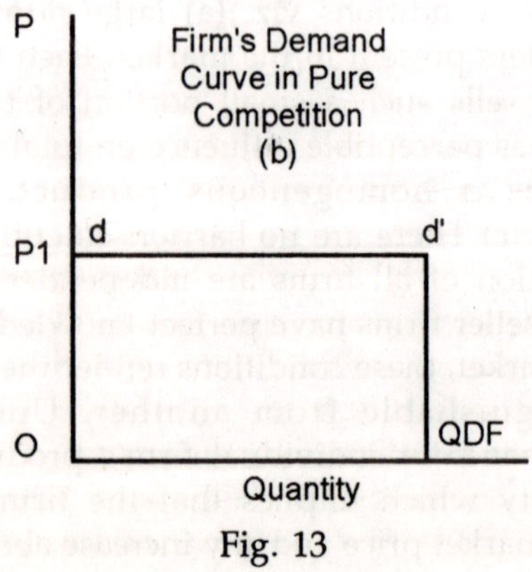

Fig. 13

Monopolistic Competition: The market structure of monopolistic competition is characterised with two main conditions, viz. (1) the sellers are numerous; and (2) product of each firm is differentiated from that of competitors. In the monopolistic competition each firm is an independent decision-maker but there is no barrier for entry or exit of a new firm in the market. The nature of the demand of the firm for the product can be distinguished with following characteristics, viz. Firm's demand curve slopes downward to the right (i.e. having negative slope) with elasticity greater than that of industry demand because of the presence of large number of close but not perfect substitutes of products available in the market. Cross elasticity of demand between the products of individual firms is high but not perfect as is in the case of pure competition. Figure 14 displays the demand curve of the price under monopolistic competition.

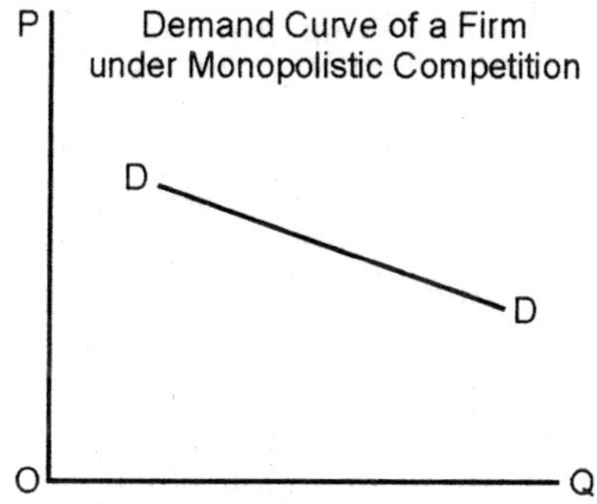

FIG. 14

Oligopoly: In oligopoly the market structure is characterised by three main conditions: viz. (1) There exist few firms selling standard products or homogeneous goods or differentiated goods. (2) Each seller firm has a perceptible impact on sales of other firms ill industry, making change in respect of price, output, product quantity and terms of sale, etc; and (3) There is a noticeable degree of interdependence between firms in the industry. This factor renders the shaping of a firm's demand curve different. In oligopoly situation, price change is dependent on competitors' responses which ultimately determine the price and output relationship. It is still controversial as to what is the shape of firms' demand curve. Under oligopoly, although some writers have proposed that Demand Curve of a firm in oligopoly is kinked as may be observed from Figure 15. It may be observed that in demand curve kink appears at existing prices while above that price demand is highly elastic and below it less elastic. The Kink brings a sharp break in the marginal revenue curve. The kinked demand is an individual firm's perception of probable reaction of competitors to this price change.

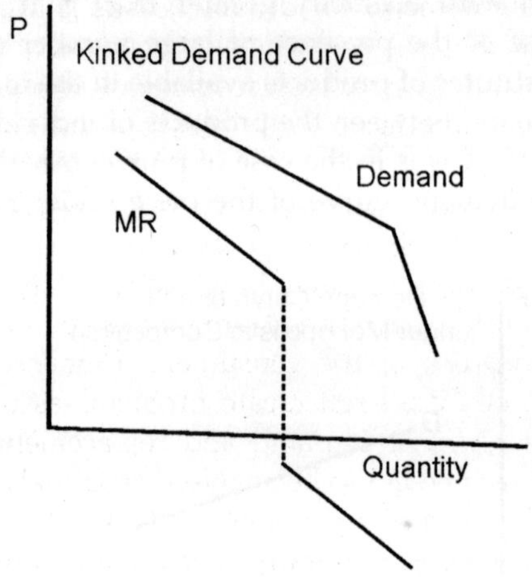

Fig. 15

In oligopolistic market situations, a firm does not face quick decisions for price change because of the dominant thinking that a raise in price will move customers to low price sellers and a reduction in price will invite retaliation from other firms who will take away market share and gains arising out of lower prices.

SOURCES OF DEMAND

Durable and Non-Durable Goods: Demand for durable goods is, in most cases, a derived demand and has a volatile relation with business conditions. Storability of durable goods and possibility of postponing their replacement both affect the nature of demand of a firm for durable goods. Estimation of demand for durable goods is made on the assessment of current inventory-sales ratio and of buyers' attitude towards increased inventories. For instance, a reduction in price will motivate buyers for increased inventories. In case of rise of prices, an opposite effect will be created on demand. However, if expectation of shortages is high, then the impact of price rise will not depress the buyers to build inventories for future consumption, hence the demand will be affected.

Further, the demand for durable goods is also affected by buyers attitude towards replacement. Higher replacement will cause the demand to rise. Replacement rate is dependent on obsolescence rate, the latter will accelerate the former. Income also plays a dominant role in demand for producers' goods. Present high income and expectation of increase in future income do affect the demand for durable goods. Non-durable goods represent current demands which are dependent on the prevailing conditions of market and the income disposability and need framework of the consumers. Demand analysis for non-durable goods does not create problems as in the case of durable goods. Current Demand and replacement demand of durable goods are needed to be analysed separately which is not needed in the case of non-durable goods. Further, demand for non-durable goods is generally a direct-demand not being derived demand like durable goods.

Producers' goods and consumers' goods: Another form of description of the nature of demand of a company's product could be made on the basis of sources of demand. Amongst direct sources of demand are the consumers who require goods for meeting their wants. There is an indirect source of creation of demand and the demand so derived from this source is known as "derived demand." Goods produced for ultimate use of consumers take different forms in the process. For instance, manufacture of products which are input in the final product meant for consumers ultimate use.

The demand for such input-goods is derived from the demand of ultimate consumers, goods and is called derived demand. For instance, demand for labour services is usually derived from the demand for the products in which labour services are consumed as input. As regards producers' goods, demand is always derived from the demand which is assessed for final product of the firm using producers' goods. If the demand for final product increases then derived demand for producers' goods will rise more rapidly. However, derived demand is generally less elastic than demand for final products. This will depend more on the cost of production and the sensitivity of demand for particular goods. In case of consumers' goods, demand may or may not be derived as in the case of producers' goods. It may be autonomous demand. The chief difference between the two is only of degree. Derived demand is less price elastic than autonomous demand.

Long-run and Short-run Demand : Differentiation of demand on the basis of amount of time in which its reaction to a price change is noticed is inevitable for making accurate forecast of sales and business performance by a firm. Because, in short-run, existing demand reacts sharply to price change, income fluctuations, etc. The long-run demand exists despite of these short-run changes. Short-run elasticity of demand is less than long run elasticity unless the fall in price is considered to be temporary. W.W. Haynes gives two reasons for this phenomenon namely:

(i) Buyers do not adjust to the new price very quickly and so they do not change their consumption habits easily because of cultural lags in information and experience.

(ii) Financial requirements for financing a shift in a consumption pattern by acquiring new equipment to use the commodity whose price has decreased may not be met so promptly as it takes time to exploit the sources. Therefore, decrease in the rate of elasticity would change habit pattern of consumers if they could finance the purchase of refrigerators, televisions, etc.

In case the fall in price is temporary then short run elasticity will be high and this will result in postponement of purchases if price increases or vice-versa. Expectation, in short-run, influences buyers motivation for purchases only when further expectation does not lead to further increase in prices. Speculation markets make use of these expectations.

Demand and Technological Innovations: Technological innovations cause sudden shift in demand pattern by causing obsolescence in both producers' goods as well as consumers' goods by creating new substitutes for old ones. According to W.W. Haynes, technological substituably of commodities contributes to substitutability in market place and to higher demand elasticities. For demand forecasting, study of probable technological changes is indispensable for planning, creation of new markets and capacities.

Determining Demand for an Established Product: For determining demand for an established product, two significant questions will have to be decided; firstly, the nature of the established product i.e. whether it is a consumers' good or producers' goods; if a consumers' product, whether it is durable or perishable, whether the demand is replacement or autonomous or derived demand; whether goods are complementary or substitutes. Secondly, whatever may be the case, demand is affected by a number of factors which should be analysed in relation to the nature of the goods. These, factors can be generalised as : (1) price and quantity of substitute items; impact of seasonal variations on the price and quantity; (2) consumers' taste, income, expectation, preferences and any change in these pattern expected in shortrun for any extra-ordinary development in social and cultural life of people viz. availability of credit facility, etc; impact of advertising upon the consumers and so on; (3) price of own goods and identical goods; (4) consumers' snobbish appeal which influence their demand pattern for durable and sophisticated goods like TVs., refrigerators or cosmetics etc. which have prestige value for consumers. For each and every type of goods, different considerations will have to be applied depending upon the circumstances and the degree of accuracy required. Demand of particular goods will be determined as a function of all these factors influencing it.

DEMAND ANALYSIS AND MULTIPLE PRODUCTS

Problems of Multiple Products Regarding Demand: Demand

analysis, so far discussed, is based on traditional logic that each firm produces or sells a single product. This simplification of demand analysis holds good in certain cases where a firm actually produces a single commodity and deals in it. In many cases a firm produces more than one product and sells more than one product. In such cases, a firm has to deal with the problems relating to these multiple products. These problems may range from product planning, deciding upon additions to product line or dropping out a product, the costing of multi products, the pricing for multi products and so on. However, in this section, it is proposed to deal with problems of multi products in relation to demand analysis of such products which ultimately leads to the inclusion of such products in the production process or selling list of the firm. According to W.W. Haynes, two situations are worth noting while considering multiple products for demand analysis, viz. multiple products which compete with each other and are substitutes and multiple products which are non-competitive but are complement in demand. There is another category of multiple products which are independent to each other in demand. A firm may produce and sell either all the above specified products or any combination of the two or more depending upon the idle capacity it has to accommodate the new product. Market conditions which a firm faces for its product may range from pure competition to a near monopoly for its different products. A firm may have monopoly in one product, pure competition in second product, monopolistic competition in third, oligopoly in the fourth product and so on. Addition of any product to product line shall depend upon the existence of demand for it, besides the idle capacity of plant, excess personnel and organisational resources which a firm may have to devote to the production, cost and pricing decisions upon which profitability of production depends.

In complementary goods, multiple product decisions are easier to take because the existence of demand or any increase in demand of one product will prove the demand for other complementary goods. Any reduction in price will increase the demand of both products which are complementary to each other. However, in respect of substitutes, opposite results might be observed. Reduction in demand for one product may cause appreciation in the demand of the substitutes and the firm might devote its full capacity to its production depending upon the cross elasticity of demand and the nature of market structure available for the disposal of this product. A business manager has to take decisions for introducing production or sale of conditional products to the existing line production processes or sale on the basis of two prime considerations, viz. (1) Technical feasibility and (2) Economic opportunity for the product. Existing technical feasibility is one ground that prompts a manager to take up production of an additional product. Technical feasibility implies the existence of idle capacity of plant, excess of personnel and organisational resources viz, management team, idle labour capacity, sales distribution facilities etc., utilisation of which may help in production of the additional product at small additional cost instead of setting up a new organisational exclusively for it. Thus, technical feasibility with all its components provides cost-wise advantage to the multiple products firm. Non utilisation of these facilities renders a firm in idle capacity which sometimes endangers continued existence of a firm. Besides technical feasibility, a firm sometimes wants to avail of the existing economic opportunities for taking advantage of a particular situation. For instance, a product may have to face the impact of a substitute's competition owing to technological developments. With the existing technical set up the firm has to take up production of the substitute product along with the continuing production of old products even at the cost of additional investment. India has switched over to the Nylon fibre spinning by putting additional plants to avail of the economic opportunities created by secular shift in demand for substitute products. In many cases, non-profitability of cotton yarn is substantiated with excessive profitable production of nylon fibre yarn.

To utilise from manufacture of the parent product new products are added as bye-products to production line without any additional investments. Another way in which economic opportunity would be availed of for production of additional products is by way of vertical integration which shall make use of idle capacity for production and distribution. Economic opportunity, some times, is created by research or innovations within the company which may inspire for taking up new product without adding any material cost to the existing investment in plant and machinery and organisational set-up. Research increases turnover, improves obsolete products, and thus offers added economic opportunity for the profitable working of the business enterprise.

PROBLEMS OF CHOICE FOR A NEW PRODUCT

Despite the fact that the business organisation has favourable conditions inspiring it to add new products in the production process, the decision for adding a new product is dependent on several other considerations. Firstly, choice of a product out of a number of alternative proposals based on recommendations of Research and Development experts, is a big problem for the management. Need of customers, value of the product, favourable acceptance by customers depending on the needs and value of the product are needed to be analysed for making a better selection of the new product. Secondly, the choice of product shall also depend upon whether the management has to incur any additional capital expenditure, marketing efforts or miscellaneous over-heads for the production and marketing of the new product. Pricing decisions and margin of profitability over additional cost are also some basic considerations which create decisional problems to the management to assess the nature and degree of return over the investment.

Thirdly, laying down market target for the new product and planning a distribution system for its marketing is another problem for management. In case, the product can be marketed in the existing market of the firm without additional efforts, choice of product becomes easier, especially in case of those products which are referred for designs of the product within the existing brand name.

VARIOUS STEPS FOR THE EVALUATION OF NEW PRODUCT FOR A RATIONAL CHOICE

To select one product out of a number of candidate products the following steps would suggest a substantive approach to a rational decision by evaluating the points of strength and weaknesses of different alternatives available for making a choice.

(i) Incremental reasoning should be applied for evaluating the cost and revenue which might affect the profitability of the whole production process by adding products. Incremental revenue should exceed incremental costs resulting from a decision. A decision is profitable if according to W.W. Haynes, it clears four tests viz. (a) increase in revenue is more than in creases in cost from the addition of new product, (b) some costs are decreased more than any increase in other costs, (c) some revenue is increased more than any decrease in other revenues and (d) the decision for adding a new product reduces costs more than the resultant revenue.

An example will make the above analysis clear. Suppose a firm decides to add a new product for utilising existing idle capacity. The incremental costs on different heads are as under for producing equal quantity of their product.

Labour	Rs. 2,000
Material	Rs. 4,000
Overheads	Rs. 2,000
Total Incremental cost.	Rs. 8,000

If the total production fetches Rs. 10,000 the firm makes a profit of Rs. 2,000. However, if full costs are estimated for addition of new products then the total cost would be on the basis of unit cost as under :

Labour	Rs. 3.000
Material	Rs. 4.000
Overheads 12% of labour cost.	Rs. 3,600
Selling Expense 20% of labour and Material cost.	Rs. 1,400
Full cost.	Rs. 12,000

On the basis of above analysis, the addition of new product seems to be unprofitable with a loss of Rs. 2,000.

So, incremental reasoning provides the best method to evaluate the decision as a whole for adding new products in the production process. If the idle capacity is not used in the above example then the firm loses rather than earning a profit of Rs. 2,000.

(ii) Time perspective is another test that should be evaluated in a decision to add a new product. In the long run the new product might require feasible variations in all inputs and production processes, but in the short run it may require only variation in one or two inputs without change in production process. Therefore, estimation of cost which will be affected by the decision should be considered alongwith the changes in revenue both in short-run and long-run perspectives. Product strategy for long-run would be the real measure to weigh a product in time perspective with reference to its costs and revenue and objectives of the firm for survival and growth in the long-run.

(iii) Opportunity cost is another reasoning that would be applied to decision making process for the choice of adding a new product. The opportunity cost for using a plant or machinery which is only party used by the firm for adding new products could be assessed in terms of its fitness for any other use. If the use of plant for a particular proposed product requires no sacrifice of other opportunities, it is cost-free. So, in many cases opportunity cost analysis helps in making decision for adding new products.

(iv) Discounting principle is another method that should be applied for making decision of adding new product in many cases. For instance, where immediate gains would be made from using idle capacity by making a new product, long-run objective may be given up. In future, risk and uncertainity is also involved besides other considerations. Cost of risk and uncertainty is more than anticipated. Although this discounting reasoning is used in selecting alternative capital projects but it can be extended to the evaluation of decision for adding new product or on the basis of gains in time perspective.

(v) The equi-marginal principle is the widely known principle of economic theory which could be applied in decision making for adding new products on the basis that new product should be so allocated that the value added by it is the same as by all other products considering new product as a marginal product in the production process. If the value of marginal product is more than the existing product, then the firm should undertake production of new product for reason of increased profitability. The optimum will be reached when the value of marginal product is equal to that of the other products.

Either one or more of the above principles should be applied for making a decision for adding new products in the production process. Joel Dean has discussed acceptance criteria for new products making a comparison of it with the existing product line in terms of inter-relation of demand characteristics with the existing product line, use of the company's distinctive know-how, utilization of common production facilities, use of common distribution channels, use of common raw material and by-products and benefits to existing products.

Dropping an Old Product Problem : Some times addition of new product compels the firm to drop out one or more of the existing old products for several reasons: viz (1) change in consumers taste because of fast change in the social environment or improvement in rival products (2) when it becomes impossible to keep the present product by improving the present operation in short-run for reason of heavy cost or less profitability and (3) when inadvertent product line additions were rendered unprofitable. A well-known Soap Factory had to give up their toilet soap brand for reasons of weaker competitive strength in the market and customers' response.

Retailers in different shopping areas drop those products which are not generally demanded by the people living in the local areas. Many textile mills had to drop the cotton textiles in preference to synthetic material to meet the increasing demand for these. Cane strips are rarely used for netting chairs because of higher cost in comparision to synthetic strips. So, whether it is a small scale production process or a large scale one, problems of dropping the unwanted products or inputs for any product is a common phenomenon. The managerial economist will have to take into consideration the opportunity cost analysis in preference to accounting costs of obsolescence of plant or machinery or any other asset rendered useless for productive purposes on account of dropping a product.

QUESTIONS

1. What do you know about Demand Analysis?
2. What is Law of Demand ? Describe it.
3. Explain Elasticity of Demand with its types and importance.
4. What do you know about Individual and Market Demand Functions?

CHAPTER

3

Theory of Supply

SUPPLY ANALYSIS

The supply of a commodity implies the amount of that commodity which producers are able and willing to offer for sale at a given price. One significant point worth noting is that supply is concerned with scarcity. This implies that it is only the scarce goods which have a supply price, goods which are freely available have no supply price. Thomas viewed that, "The supply of goods is the quantity offered for sale in a given market at a given time at various price". According to Anatol Murad,

> "The quantity supplied refers to the quantity of a commodity offered for sale at a given price in a given market at a time."

SUPPLY FUNCTION

An industry's or a firm's supply function is an algebraic expression relating the quantity of a commodity which a seller is willing and able to supply. The supply function can be written as:

$S = f(P_x, F_E, F_p, P_R, W, E, N)$

Where some significant determinants of supply are:

(i) Product price (Px)
(ii) Factor Productivities or State of Technology (F_E)
(iii) Factor Prices (Fp)
(iv) Prices of other products related to production (P_R)
(v) Weather, strikes and other short-run forces (W)
(vi) Expectation about future prospects of prices, costs, sales and the state of economy in general (E)
(vii) Number (x)

LAW OF SUPPLY

Law of supply expresses the relation between the price of a commodity and its supply. "Other things remaining the same, as the price of a commodity rises, its supply increases and as the price falls, its supply declines".

Assumptions

The following are the main assumptions of the law of supply:

1. There is no change in the prices of the factors of production.
2. There is no change in the technique of production.
3. There is no change in the goal of the firm.
4. There is no change in the prices of the related goods.
5. Producers do not expect change in the price of the commodity in the near future.

Definition

"The law of supply states that the higher the price, the greater the quantity supplied or the lower the price, the smaller the quantity supplied"

Dooley

Thus, the quantity offered for sale varies directly with price i.e., the higher the price, the larger is the supply and *vice-versa*. This can be explained by two causes: (i) An increase in price generally implies higher profits leading producers to offer increased quantities, and (ii) in the long run because of higher profitability, new producers may enter the field of production leading to an increase in output.

EXPLANATION OF THE LAW OF SUPPLY

The law of supply can be explained with the help of supply schedule and supply curve.

Supply Schedule

It is a tabular representation of data on the quantity supplied and the price of the good. Table 1 provides the supply schedules of firms A, B and C. It can be seen that as the price increases, each firm supplies greater quantity of output and vice-versa. In other words, the price of a commodity and the quantity supplied move in the same direction.

TABLE I

Supply Schedules of Firms A, B and C

Price	*Output*	*Output*	*Output*	*Aggregate Output*
	A	*B*	*C*	*A+B+C*
2	Zero	Zero	Zero	Zero
4	300	100	Zero	400
6	400	150	75	625
8	500	200	100	800
10	700	250	200	1,150
12	900	400	250	1,550
14	1,200	700	400	2,300

Supply Curve

When portrayed diagrammatically it is called the supply

curve (see Figure 1). Thus, each point on the supply curve displays the price-quantity combinations of a firm. The supply curve displays the minimum price which the firm would be prepared to receive for varied quantities of the commodity.

We can also say that the supply curve displays the maximum quantity of a commodity which a firm would be interested to sell at each feasible price, under given conditions of supply. A few points may be noted about the supply curve. First, it has a positive slope i.e., as the price of the commodity increases, its quantity supplied also increases. Secondly, the supply curve slopes downwards from right to left in contrast to the demand curve which slopes from left to right.

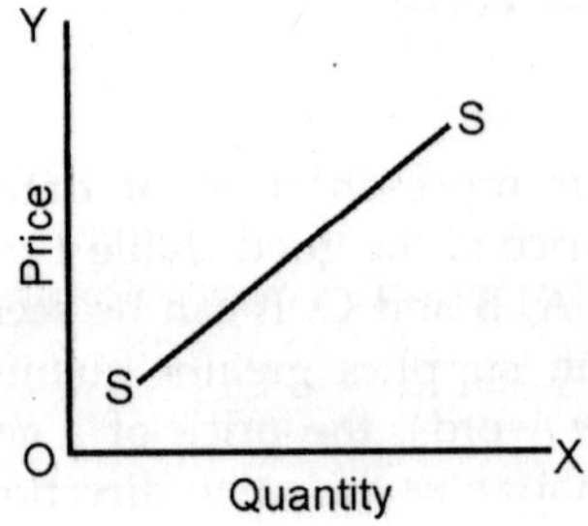

FIG. I

Reserve Price

If the price falls too much, supply may dry up completely. The price below which the seller will refuse to sell is known as reserve price. At this price, the seller is said to buy his own stock.

SUPPLY CURVE OF FIRM AND INDUSTRY

One can draw the industry supply curve from the supply curves of individual firms. For this objection, the amount supplied by each seller at different prices will have to be added so that the industry supply at different prices is arrived as illustrated in Table 1.

LIMITATIONS OF LAW OF SUPPLY

The law of supply has various limitations:

1. *Prices of Future* : When the price rises and the seller aspires for a further rise in future prices, supply will decline as the seller will be induced to withhold supplies so as to sell later and earn larger profits then. Similarly, when the price falls and the seller fears that the price is going to fall further, the supply will rise as he will be ready to sell more of the commodity in anticipation of future price fall.
2. *Output Related to Agriculture:* In case of agricultural commodities, law of supply may not apply as their production cannot be increased at once following price increase.
3. *Subsistence Farmers:* In underdeveloped countries where agriculture is characterised with subsistence farmers, law of supply may not apply. Here, as prices of foodgrains rise, marketable surplus of foodgrains falls rather than increasing as with the rise in the prices of foodgrains, farmers can get the needed amount of income by selling less and keep the remaining output for their own consumption.
4. *Factors other than Price not Remaining Constant:* The law of supply is stated on the assumption that factors other than the price of the commodity remain constant. Hence in the following cases the law of supply will not apply :
   (i) If prices of other commodities display a rising trend, the quantity supplied of a commodity may fall at a given price.
   (ii) The change in the state of technology can bring about a change in the quantity supplied even if the price of that commodity does not undergo a change.

Elasticity of Supply

Elasticity of Supply can be defined as the "degree of

responsiveness of supply to a given change in price". The formula to find out the elasticity of supply is as under:

$$e.s = \frac{\frac{\Delta Q}{Q}}{\frac{\Delta Q}{p}} \text{ or } \frac{\text{Proportionate change in quantity supplied}}{\text{Proportionate change in price}}$$

Illustration

Firm A supplied 200 units of its output at a price of Rs. 5. When price increases to Rs. 10, the quantity supplied increases to 400 units. Find the elasticity of supply.

$$\text{Elasticity of Supply Es} = \frac{\Delta Q}{\Delta P} \cdot \frac{P_1}{Q_1}$$

$$= \frac{200}{4} \times \frac{4}{300}$$

$$= \frac{200}{300} = 0.67$$

Figure 2 illustrates five types of supply elasticity. The case of zero elasticity is one in which the quantity supplied does not change as price changes. This would be the case, for instance, if suppliers persisted in producing a provided quantity Oa in Figure 2(i) and dumping it on the market for whatever it would fetch. Infinite elasticity is illustrated in Figure 2(ii). The supply elasticity is infinite at the price Ob as nothing at all is supplied at lower prices but a small increase in price to Ob causes supply to rise from zero to an indefinitely large amount, connoting that producers will supply any quantity demanded at that price. The case of unit elasticity of supply is illustrated in Figure 2(iii). Any straight line supply curve drawn through the origin has unit elasticity.

When the supply curve cuts the vertical axis, it is comparatively elastic supply [Figure 2 (iv)]. When the supply curve cuts the horizontal axis, it is comparatively inelastic supply [Figure 2(v)].

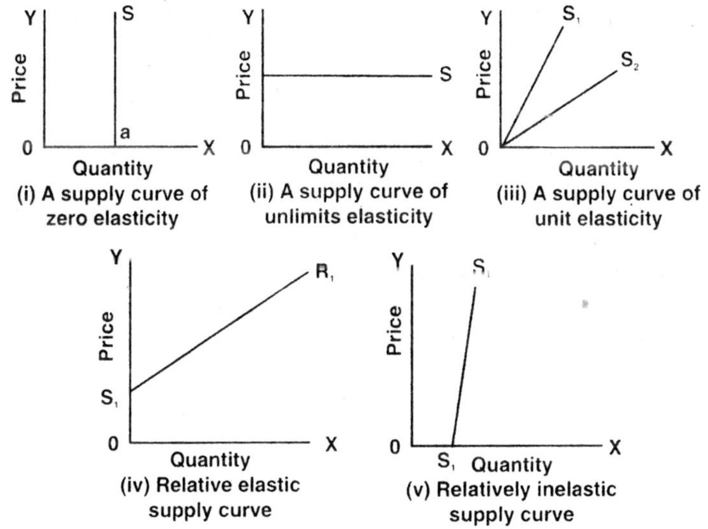

FIG. 2

Various Kinds of Supply Elasticities : The various kinds of supply elasticities are summarized in Table 2.

TABLE 2
Kinds of Elasticity of Supply

When Elasticity of Supply is		*It is known as*
(i)	Equal to zero	Perfectly inelastic supply
(ii)	Equal to infinity	Perfectly elastic supply
(iii)	Equal to one	Unit elastic supply
(iv)	More than one but not infinity	Relatively elastic supply
(v)	Less than one but not zero	Relatively inelastic supply

Supply elasticity is an important concept but not quite useful as demand elasticity for the reason that elasticity of demand has the greater additional function of telling us what is happening to entire revenue. There is, however, a significant fact that supply elasticity can describe. A given change in price will tend to have greater and greater effects on the amount supplied as one moves from momentary situation to a short-run period and on to the long-run period. Elasticity of supply tends to be greater in the long run when adjustments to the higher price have been made than in the shorter periods of time.

Cross (Price) Elasticity of Supply: Famous economists like F. Gruen, L. Ward and A. Powell introduced this new concept of elasticity of supply while estimating elasticities of supply for Australian agricultural products. The cross (price) elasticity of supply, however, measures change in quantity supplied of one commodity (say, wheat) when the price of another commodity (say, paddy) changes. It can be expressed as under:

$$Esc = \frac{\text{Proportionate (percentage) change in quantity supplied of wheat}}{\text{Proportionate (percentage) change in price of paddy}}$$

Here, E_{sc} is the elasticity co-efficient. It is always negative connoting that a rise in the price of one good will lead to a fall in the quantity supplied of alternative good. For example, a rise in the price of paddy by 1 per cent may reduce the quantity supplied of wheat by 0.22 per cent. In actual life, the concept of cross elasticity of supply is quite significant. The concept finds its application greatly in case of agricultural commodities. Since land is a scarce factor, farmers have to be conscious about its use. For instance, if price of paddy goes up, land will be diverted from wheat production causing fall in quantity of wheat supplied.

Supply Increase and Decrease

'Increase' and 'Decrease' in supply would imply a change in quantity supplied without any change in price. This, therefore, implies a shift in supply schedule to the right implying increase in supply and to the left implying decrease in supply. An increase in supply comprising willingness to make and sell more at each price may be caused by (i) improvements in technology, (ii) decreases in the prices of other commodities or (iii) decreases in the prices of factors of production used in making the commodity concerned. A decrease in supply involving reluctance on the part of sellers to sell as much as before at each price may be because of : (i) increase in the prices of other commodities or (ii) increase in the prices of factors of production used in making the concerned commodity.

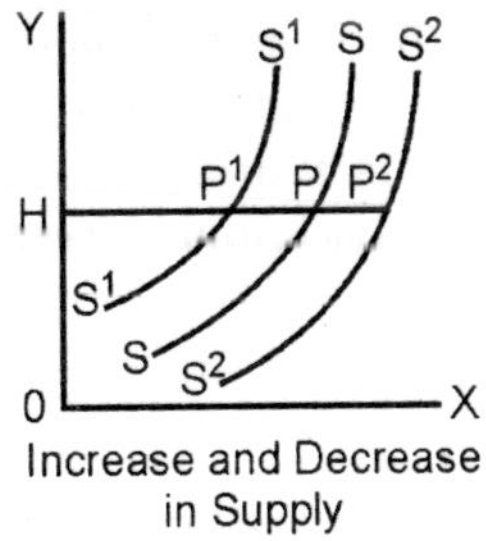

FIG. 3

If Figure 3, SS is the supply curve before the change, S′S′ displays a decrease in supply because at the same price, less is offered for sale. One must clearly distinguish between the increase in quantity supplied and increase in supply.

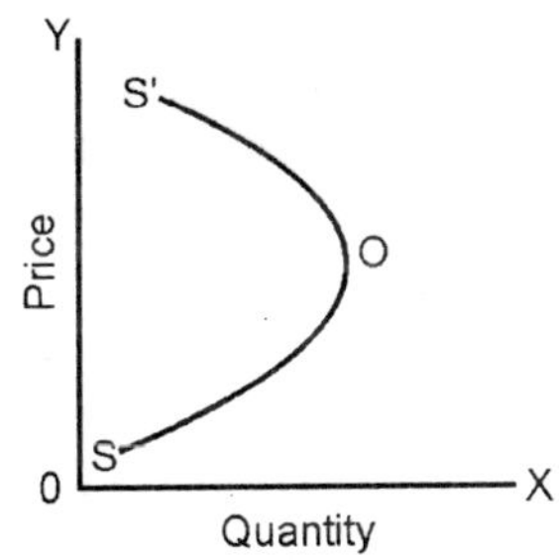

FIG. 4

Increase in supply means that the entire supply curve has shifted to a new position to the right. It is a new curve completely whereas increase in the quantity supplied means that more is being offered at a higher price. The supply curve is the same. A movement along the same supply curve simply connotes changes in quantities offered as an outcome of a change in price. It does not represent any change in the supply schedule.

Backward-Sloping Supply Curve

Ordinarily, the law of supply states that more will be supplied at a higher price. But it sometimes happens that this holds good only up to a point and thereafter less is offered at a higher price. The supply curve, therefore, begins sloping backward towards left as will be seen in Fig. 4. A familiar illustration of this can be found in the case of supply of labour. Rising wages induce more work, but after a point, leisure is preferred to labour and hence higher wages induce workers to work less and even have holiday.

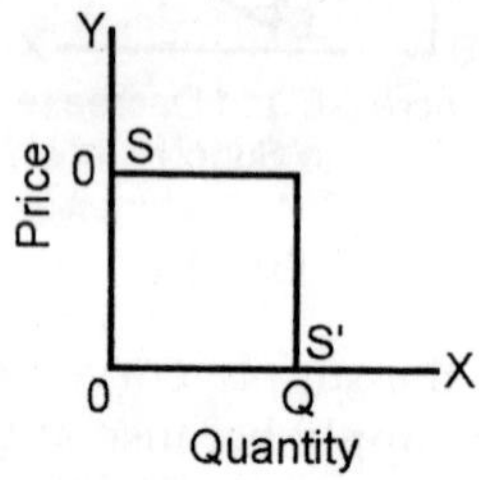

FIG. 5

A Special Supply Curve

Fig. 5 depicts a special supply curve. Suppose the government supplies electricity at a constant rate. The supply curve will look like SS1 curve in the graph. This displays that at price OP, the quantity supplied is OQ and no more. The supply curve under the quota system also looks like SS curve.

Composite and Joint Supply

When we supply two or more than two commodities together, it is joint supply e.g., wheat and husk, hides and bones. Here, when one is produced, the production of the other also takes place naturally.

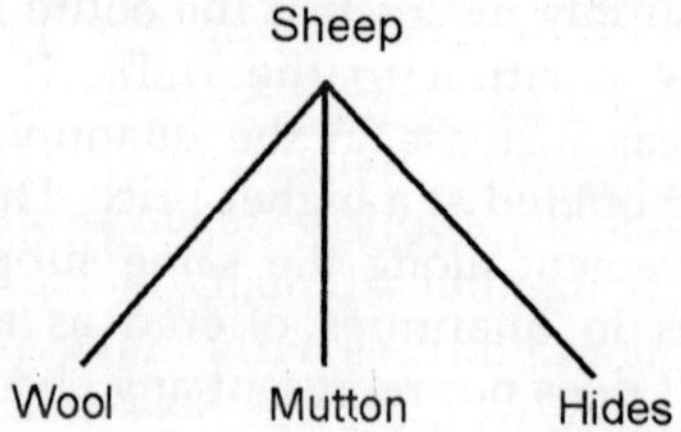

FIG. 6

When a single commodity is supplied by various sources, it is known as composite supply. For example, energy can be supplied by electricity, gas, oil.

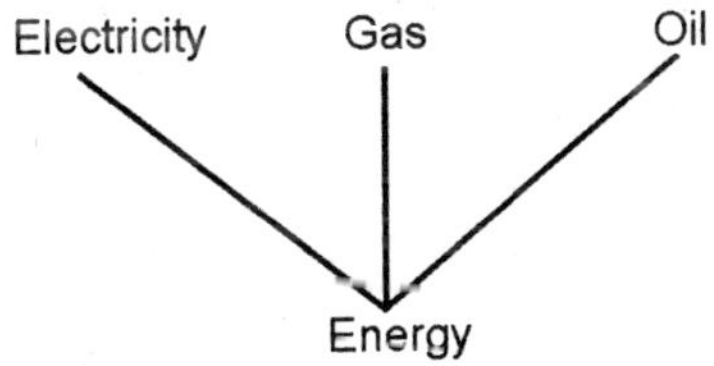

FIG. 7

VARIOUS FACTORS WHICH INFLUENCE SUPPLY

Different factors influencing supply are as follows :

(i) A commodity's supply depends upon the goals of firms. If drug companies prefer to engage in the production of medicines rather than rat poison because it makes them feel more significant in society, we hope more medicines and less rat poison to be produced than if producers held all commodities in equal quantities. If producers of some commodity want to sell as much as feasible, even if it costs them some profit to do so, more will be sold of that commodity than if they wanted to make maximum profits. If producers are reluctant to take risks, we would expect smaller production of goods whose production is risky.

(ii) A commodity's supply depends upon the price of that commodity. Ceteris paribus, the higher the price of the commodity, the more profitable it will be to make that commodity. One expects, therefore, that the higher the price, the greater will be the supply.

(iii) A commodity's supply depends upon the prices of all other commodities. Usually, an increase in the price of other commodities will make production of the commodity whose price does not rise relatively less attractive than it was earlier. We thus aspire that ceteris paribus, the supply of one commodity would fall as the price of other commodities rises.

(iv) A commodity's supply depends upon the prices of factors of production. A rise in the price of one factor of production will cause a large increase in the costs of making those goods which use a great deal of that factor and only a small increase in the cost of producing those commodities which use a tiny amount of the factor. For instance, a rise in the price of land will have a large effect on the cost of producing wheat and only a very small effect on the costs of producing motor vehicles. Thus, a change in the price of one factor of production will lead to changes in the relative profitability of different lines of production and this will cause producers to shift from one line to another, and so cause changes in the supplies of different commodities.

(v) A commodity's supply depends upon the state of technology. The enormous increase in production per worker that has been going on in industrial societies for about 200 years, is very largely because of improved method of production. These, in turn, have been heavily influenced by the advantages of science. But the Industrial Revolution is more than a historical event, it is a present day reality. Discoveries in chemistry have led to lower costs of products made of plastics and synthetic fibres. The new electronics industry rests upon transistors and other small devices that are revolutionising production in television, high-fidelity equipment, computers and guidance-control systems. Atomic energy will one day be used to build canals and to extract fresh water from the sea. At any time, what is produced and how it is produced depends upon what is known. Over time, knowledge changes and so do the supplies of individual commodities.

(vi) Time factor can also determines elasticity of supply. Time can be broadly divided into three categories:

(a) Market period is the one where supply is fixed as no factor of production can be altered.

(b) Small period is the time period when it is feasible to adjust supply only by changing the variable factors like raw-material, labour, etc., and

(c) Long period where supply can be changed at will because all the factors can be changed. Naturally, in the market period, where the supply is fixed, the elasticity of supply will be zero. The elasticity will be higher in the long run than in the short run as the feasibility of changing output is limited in the short-run but not in the long run.

(vii) Supply may be consciously decreased by agreement among the producers, for instance, agreement among oil producing countries to cut back oil output.

(viii) Supply may also be destroyed to raise price. For instance, in Brazil, coffee was thrown into the sea.

(ix) Supply may also be affected by taxation on output or imports. Government may also restrict production of certain commodities on grounds of health (e.g., opium in India).

(x) Political disturbances or war may also create scarcity of some goods.

Some other important factors affecting supply are as under :

(a) Natural factors like failure of monsoons, floods, plant disease or pests, which are likely to affect production, may also influence the decision of stockholders.

(b) Expectations about the future level of prices may affect the willingness of the suppliers to sell the stocks or withhold them.

(c) When the trader intends to finish the old stock before having new stock, he will sell more commodity by reducing prices.

(d) Government procurement or other Government controls may also influence supply.

(e) The supply of some commodities depends on the price at sometime in the past rather than on the current price. For instance, in India, jute acreage and production has been found to depend on jute/rice price parity in the preceding year.

(f) When a particular trader is interested in changing place or trade, he sells more of the commodity by lowering the price so that he frees himself at an early date.

(g) At a time when prices of a commodity in international market are falling rapidly in comparison to the domestic market, sales in domestic market will grow despite price fall. This happened in case of coffee sales growing in the Indian retail market with international coffee prices dropping faster.

(h) Seldom, the objective of the firm is not to maximize profits but maximize sales. In that case, the quantity supplied may be increased even by lowering the price.

In the long run, supply is affected by cost of production. If costs are rising, some of the existing producers may withdraw from the field and new entrepreneurs may be scared of entering the field.

The central authority in a planned economy decides, for instance, how many pairs of shoes are to be produced and also how many pairs each of the different shoe-making enterprises should produce. Further, the central authority must ensure that each shoe factory receives appropriate quantities of raw materials and semi-finished products. The overall plan, then, must be so detailed that each enterprise will, at the right time, in the right quantity and in the right quality, receive the amount of inputs that are required. Only then, the enterprise will be able to fulfill its role in producing the quantity stipulated by the plan. In addition, the central authority must decide on any purchase of new machinery and on when and whether worn-out machinery should be replaced, that is to say, it decides what investments must be made. If a shoe manufacturer is needed to make 3,000 pairs of shoes per month, he must have enough leather, thread, plastic, rubber, buckles, etc., to make such production feasible. These materials must be delivered by other enterprises. Since the central authorities will often have a planning horizon of one year, it will be difficult to change the planned figures during this period. This problem will be exacerbated by the fact that a change in the planned figures for the shoe factory would result in a need to change the planned figures for everyone who supplied raw materials to this enterprise. In a planned economy, therefore, it is natural to expect the supply curve to be vertical. It is very difficult for an enterprise to increase production in the short term (see Figure 8).

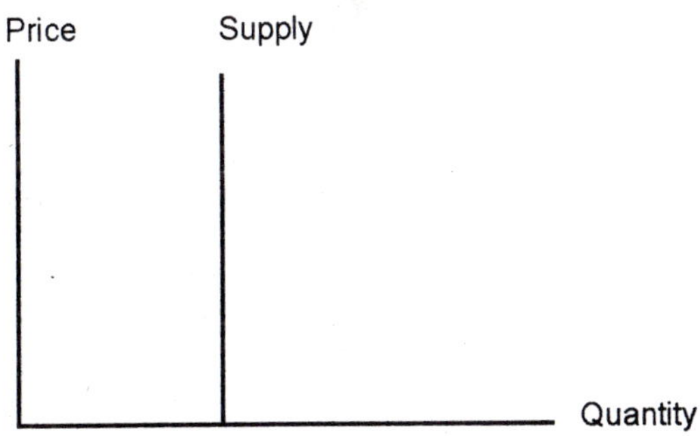

The supply curve in a planned economy

FIG. 8

The plan stipulates total production for the period. Thus, clearly planned figure remains firm, independent of the price of the product. The supply curve in a planned economy is therefore, vertical.

QUESTIONS

1. What do you know about Supply Analysis?
2. Describe in brief the Law of Supply.
3. What is Supply Function? Explain in detail various factors affecting supply.
4. Explain in brief Elasticity of Supply?

CHAPTER

4

Theory of Consumer Choice

CONSUMER EQUILIBRIUM

With the help of the law of marginal utility consumer's equilibrium is explained. The consumer with a given outlay of money, has to spend on different goods and services. Now, the question is, how he should allocate the given money among different goods. Supposing he has to buy only one commodity, he will attain equilibrium at a point of units of the commodity where the marginal utility equals price. In case of more than one commodity, the same principle is extended. It means the marginal utilities of goods and their prices should be equal. This is known as the Law of Equimarginal Utility.

The Law of Equimarginal Utility states that the consumer would distribute his money income between the goods in such a way that the utility derived from the last rupee spent on each good is equal. In other words, a consumer attains equilibrium when marginal utility of money expenditure on all the good is the same. In other words,

$$\frac{\text{Marginal utility of 'X' commodity}}{\text{Price of that commodity}} = \frac{\text{Marginal utility of 'Y' commodity}}{\text{Price of 'Y' commodity}}$$

According to Dr. Marshall, "If a person has a thing which he can put to several uses, he will distribute it among these uses in such a way that it has the same marginal utility in all."

Let us take the following example in order to understand this principle clearly.

TABLE I

Marginal Utility of X and Y Goods

Units	*Marginal utility of X Commodity*	*Marginal utility of Y Commodity*
1	20	24
2	18	21
3	16	18
4	14	15
5	12	9
6	10	3

Let us assume that price of X commodity is Rs. 2 per unit and that of Y is Rs. 3 per unit. Reconstructing the above table by dividing them with price, the reconstructed table will be as under:

Units	*Mu of X Commodity / Price of X*	*Mu of Y Commodity / Price of Y*
1	10	8
2	9	7
3	8	6
4	7	5
5	6	3
6	5	1

Now, with a given money income, i.e. he allots Rs. 19 to buy these goods, he will purchase 5 units of X commodity and 3 units of Y commodity and attains equilibrium. At 5th

$\frac{\text{mu of X}}{\text{price of X}}$ unit of X commodity, is equal to $\frac{\text{mu of Y}}{\text{price of Y}}$ of 3rd unit of Y commodity.

The diagrammatic expression of the theory of consumer's equilibrium is as under:

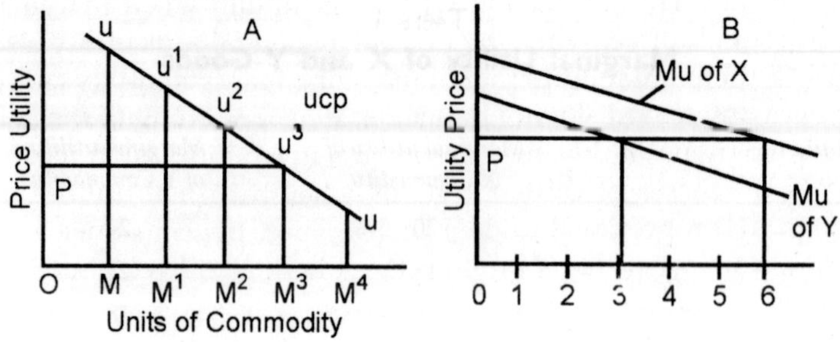

FIG. 1

In case of one commodity, the consumers buy (A) 4 units of X. commodity because the price is equal to utility of the 4th unit. In the 'B' diagram, consumer purchases two commodities X and Y. He purchases 6 units of X and 3 units of Y commodity and attains equilibrium.

UTILITY ANALYSIS : ITS SIGNIFICANCE

> *"A consumer is in equilibrium when he regards his actual behavior as the best possible under the circumstances and feels no urge to change his behavior as long as circumstances remain unchanged."*
>
> —Tiber Scitovosky.

Utility analysis is the basis of demand theory. With the help of law of diminishing marginal utility, the law of demand is formulated. As said above, the law of demand or demand curve displays the relationship between the price of the commodity and its quantity demanded. Marshall derived the demand curve for a commodity from its utility function. The law of demand can be derived in two ways: firstly, with the aid of law of diminishing marginal utility and secondly, with the help of equimarginal utility. The law of marginal utility states that as the quantity of a commodity increases, its marginal utility falls. In other words, marginal utility curve is downward sloping. Now the consumer goes on purchasing goods but the marginal utility of goods becomes equal to its price. He will be at equilibrium. His satisfaction will be maximum when marginal utility equals price. When the price of a good falls, its utility also falls. It, therefore follows that diminishing marginal utility curve implies downward sloping demand curve. According to the law of equimarginal utility, the consumer is in equilibrium in regard to his purchases of different goods when marginal utilities of goods are proportional to their prices. Thus, the consumer is in equilibrium when he is buying the quantities of two goods in such a way that it satisfies the following rule of proportion.

$$\frac{\text{mu of X}}{\text{price of X}} = \frac{\text{mu of Y}}{\text{price of Y}} \text{ etc.}$$

where Mu stands for marginal utility of the commodity.

The consumer will be in equilibrium when he equalises marginal utility of money expectations with the ratio of marginal utility and the price of each commodity. Supposing the price of X commodity falls and price of Y commodity and consumer's money income remain the same, then the equilibrium position also is disturbed. With the lower price, $\frac{\text{Mu X}}{\text{P X}}$ will be greater than $\frac{\text{Mu X}}{\text{P X}}$. In order to restore equilibrium, marginal utility of X must be reduced by buying more of X goods. It is thus clear that when the price of a good falls, the quantity demanded of that commodity rises.

DEMAND SCHEDULE

The demand curve displays the inverse relationship between the price and quantity demanded, i.e., how different quantities of a commodity can be sold at separate prices assuming other things like tastes and preferences, prices of the concerned goods and consumer's money income remaining constant. Classical economists were quite aware that price is not the sole factor determining sales and changes in other things may change the demand schedule. The effect of changes in demand consequent on changes in other things is known as shift in demand schedule. It means that quantity sold at each price will be different because incomes are greater or lower.

Some factors that affect the demand schedule are as—tastes and preferences of the customers, people's income, change in the prices of related goods, the number of consumers in the market, changes in the propensity to consume, consumer's expectation with regard to future prices, income distribution.

Some explanations to the above factors are:

Consumers Tastes and Preferences : Whenever the changes arise in fashion, because of the pressure of advertisements in mass media, it will affect the demand. In the sixties of the present century, when Pepsi was introduced to the market, the demand was very conservative. Even though the price of Pepsi was low, the demand was not high. But now, people's taste for Pepsi has undergone tremendous changes. Even though its price is high, demand is high. In economics, we would say that the demand curve for Pepsi has shifted upwards. On the contrary, when any goods go out of fashion, the demand for them decreases. Then the demand curve shifts downward.

People's Income: The demand for a commodity also depends upon the money incomes of the people. When their money earnings are high, their demand for goods and services also will be high. For instance, after planning was introduced in India, money earnings of the people have started increasing and consequently, the demand is rising even where prices are rising. Then the demand curve shifts upward.

Changes in the prices of the related goods : The concerned goods are complements and substitutes. When the price of a substitute good falls, the demand for it also falls and vice-versa. For instance, if the price of tea falls, demand for it also falls but demand for the substitute, the price of which has not changed, rises. Then the demand for coffee increases. The same things happen in the case of complementary goods. For instance, when the price of cars falls, the demand for them would increase, which in turn will increase the demand for petrol.

Customer's number in the market : In a country such as India and China, the number of consumers is vastly increasing owing to an alarming increase in population. Consequently, the demand for inevitable goods is also high. It is also easy for the sellers to find market for their goods in such thickly populated countries. Thus, the greater the number of buyers for a product, the greater the market demand for it.

Propensity to consume: Propensity to consume is another significant factor in determining the demand for a commodity. During the period of inflation, propensity to consume is high. Consequently, the demand for goods is also high. During depression, the propensity is low owing to fall in income and gloom about the future. Then the demand curve shifts downward. Changes in propensity to consume will bring about changes in the demand schedule.

Expectation of Consumer's about future prices of goods : This is another significant factor which affects demand. If because of some reason, the future prices would rise, the demand for many goods also will rise. During inflation, people expect the future prices will be high and start buying larger quantities at the prevailing prices. Then the demand curve shifts upward and vice-versa.

Distribution of Income: Income distribution implies the equitable distribution of income among people by Government's tax and public expenditure policies. When distribution of income is equal among the people, then the propensity to consume by the society as a whole increases and consequently the demand will be high. For instance, if progressive taxes are levied on high income groups of people and the same revenue is spent on the betterment of poor people, their incomes rise, which in turn increases the demand for goods and services.

If the growth of wealth and income is concentrated in the hands of the rich people, their number being small in a society, the purchasing power of a large percentage of the people will remain low and the demand for goods also will be low. Then the demand curve shifts downward. The increase and decrease in demand are displayed in the shifting of demand schedules. In the following diagram, the changes in demand schedules are shown.

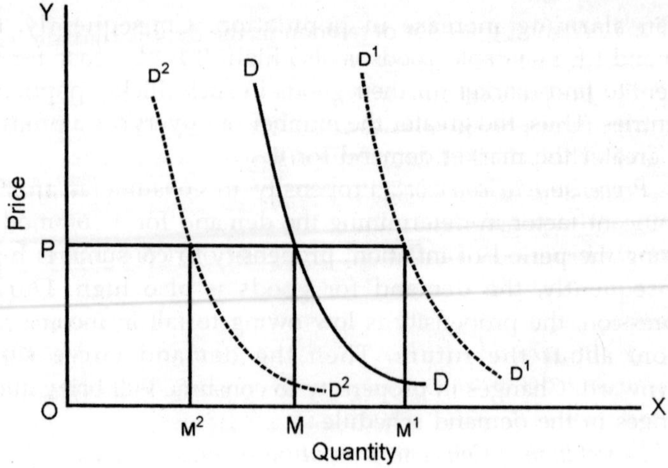

FIG. 2

In the beginning, DD is the demand curve. If there are favourable changes in the factors determining demand, the demand curve (DD) shifts upward to D^1D^1. At price OP, the consumers will buy more, i.e. from OM to OM^1. When the other factors become unfavourable, the demand curve shifts downward to D^2D^2. Then the demand falls to OM^2.

The increase in demand occurs because of the following factors :

(i) The fashion for goods changes or people's tastes and preference become more favourable for goods.
(ii) Income of consumers increases.
(iii) Price of substitutes of a commodity in question rises.
(iv) Price of complementary goods have declined.
(v) Propensity of the consumption of people increases
(vi) Increase in the number of consumers owing to increase in population.
(vii) Transfer of income in favour of middle and low-income groups of people.

In all the above cases, the demand curve shifts upwards. Decrease in demand occurs when the following situations arise:

(i) A good goes out of fashion or the people may develop distaste for the goods.
(ii) People's income falls.
(iii) Prices of substitutes fall.
(iv) The prices of complements rise.
(v) There arises decline in the propensity to consume by the people, and
(vi) Income is transferred in favour of rich people.

Essence

On the ground of above analysis, it becomes explicit that increase and decrease in demand arises when the assumptions change. This is also known as shifts in demand. The determinants of demand depend upon the product and on the demand situations like income, sales promotion, product improvement and the price.

CARDINAL UTILITY

Do you remember cardinal and ordinal numbers from school? Cardinal numbers are numbers like 1, 2, 3 and so on. Ordinal numbers are numbers like first, second, third and so on. In other words, in the case of ordinal numbers, the ranking alone is important. Beyond that, the numbers carry no special significance. Let us take a case where a teacher desires to rank the students in a class. Instead of calling the top student first, the teacher can be quirky and decide to call him second. This makes no difference, as long as the student who would otherwise have been second, is now called third. Indifference curve analysis is based on such ordinal rankings.

Cardinal utility, however, goes beyond mere rankings. The levels of utility have significance in Marshallian cardinal utility analysis. Thus, Marshallian analysis requires more stringent assumptions about measurement of utility. In addition, it requires the assumption that the marginal utility of money is constant.

Suppose I am comparing two competing theories. How will I decide which theory is better? One can, of course, test both theories to see whether their predictions are empirically satisfied or not. But suppose that testing is not a valid criterion.

Each theory operates on the basis of some assumptions. If both theories explain the same phenomena, then the theory with fewer assumptions ought to be superior. If both theories have the same assumptions, then the theory which explains more phenomena ought to be better.

CRITICISM OF CARDINAL UTILITY ANALYSIS

Economists like Edgeworth, Hicks, Samuelson etc. have criticized cardinal utility analysis on the following grounds:

1. Utility is subjective
2. Cardinal measurement of utility is not possible
3. Every commodity is not an independent commodity
4. Marginal utility cannot be estimated in all conditions
5. Marginal utility of money doesn't remain constant
6. Too many assumptions
7. No division of price effect between income effect and substitution effect
8. Consumer is regarded as a computer
9. Utility analysis breaks down in an under-developed planned economy
10. It doesn't explain Giffen's paradox.

The Indifference Curve Approach

The utility analysis has some shortcomings. It assumes that utility is measurable cardinally, i.e., it can be assigned definite numbers. Since utility is a mental concept, it cannot be measured cardinally. Instead we can have ordinal measure which means that satisfaction can be compared and say that it is more or less. Further, marginal utility analysis boasts too much and explains too little. Thus, an alternative analysis was propounded by Prof. Hicks and Allen, called *'Indifference Curve Analysis'*. In indifference curve analysis, the consumer compares the satisfactions obtained from varied combinations of goods. If different combinations are marked A, B, C, D and E, the consumer can tell whether he prefers A to B, B to C and so on. Similarly, he can indicate his preference or indifference between any other combinations. The concept of ordinal utility implies that the consumer cannot go beyond stating his preference or indifference.

Indifference Curves

It represents satisfaction of a consumer from two or more combinations of commodities. As all combinations of two commodities give the consumer equal satisfaction, he will be indifferent between them, that is, he will not bother about the specific combination. He is prepared to accept any combination so long as all combinations provide the consumer equal satisfaction. Let us begin the analysis by considering that the consumer purchases two commodities, namely apples and mangoes. He does not make the purchase of these two goods arbitrarily. If he purchases six apples, he does not buy any mangoes. If he purchases five apples, he purchases two mangoes. If he purchases three apples, he purchases six mangoes and so on. It is only in this way of selecting combination of goods, the consumer derives equal satisfaction. If he purchases more units of these two combinations, he derives higher satisfaction.

In the words of *Leftwitch*, "A single indifference curve shows the different combinations of X and Y that yield equal satisfaction to the consumers."

In the words of *Ferguson*, "An indifference curve is a combination of goods, each of which yield the same level of total utility to which consumer is indifferent."

Let us have an indifference schedule.

Combination	*Apples*	*Mangoes*
1	15	0
2	11	2
3	8	3
4	6	4
5	5	5

When the schedule of indifference analysis is depicted in the form of a diagram, it will be as under :

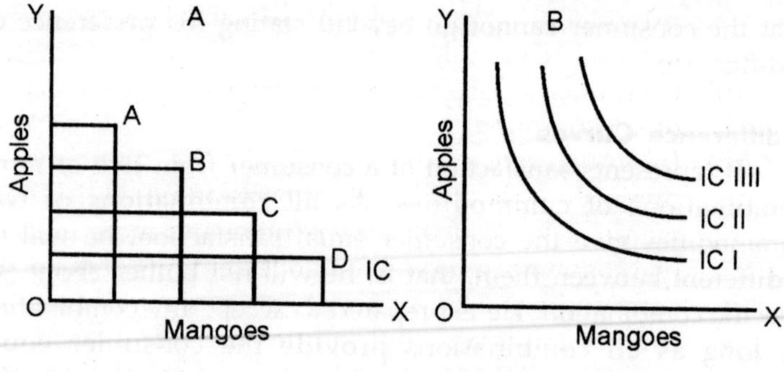

FIG. 3

In the diagram A, there are four combinations of two commodities. All these combinations give the consumer equal satisfaction. IC is an indifference curve with several combinations showing equal satisfaction.

In the diagram B, there are three indifference curves. No doubt, an indifference curve represents a level of satisfaction obtained by the consumption of these two commodities. The three indifference curves represent three levels of satisfaction. IC_1 represents a lower level of satisfaction while IC_3 represents higher level of satisfaction. Indifference curves remind us of a weather map showing lines of equal pressure of the contour lines on a topographical map. A set of indifference curves in a diagram is known as an indifference map. In other words, a higher indifference curve represents a higher level of satisfaction than a lower indifference curve but how much higher cannot be indicated. This is because the indifference curve system is based upon the concept of Ordinal Utility, according to which the consumer is able to state only the qualitative difference in his different levels of satisfaction.

An indifference map of a consumer portrays consumer's scale of preferences.

Let us now understand the properties or attributes of indifference curves. The assumptions made in this technique are as under :

(i) It is assumed that consumer will always prefer large amount of goods to a smaller amount of goods provided that the amount of other goods at his disposal remain the same.

(ii) Consumer's tastes remain the same during the period of consumption.

(iii) In indifference curve analysis, the principle of diminishing rate of substitution is assumed. In other words, if a consumer prefers more and more units of one commodity, he will forego fewer units of the other commodity. The concept of marginal rate of substitution is a tool of indifference curve technique and is parallel to the concept of marginal utility in the Marshallian analysis of demand.

INDIFFERENCE CURVES : ITS PROPERTIES

(i) Indifference curves slope downward to the right. This property implies that an indifference curve has a negative slope. When the indifference curve being downward sloping means that when the amount of one good in the combination is increased, the amount of other is reduced. This must be so, if the level of satisfaction is to remain on the same indifference curve. The diagram A in the previous page makes this point very clear.

(ii)

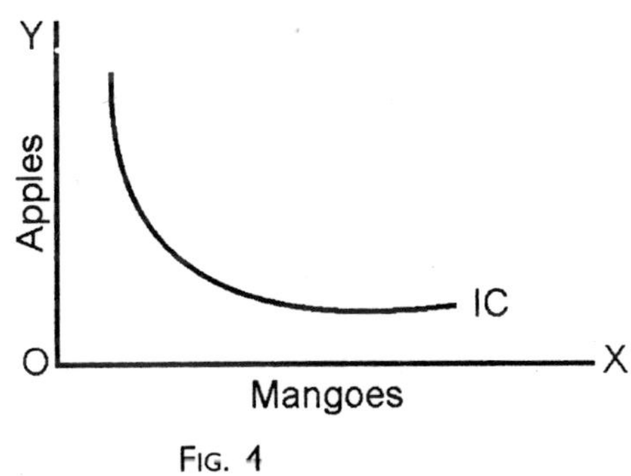

FIG. 4

(ii) *Indifference curves are convex to the origin.* The implication of this rule is that if one has more and more of X goods, he takes less and less of Y goods. The marginal rate of substitution goes on falling. In the third combination, he sacrifices 3 apples to one more mango. Like this, the rate of substitution between apples and mangoes goes on falling with the movement from one combination to another combination. Thus, the normal shape of the indifference curve is convex to the origin as displayed in the diagram A. The curvature of the indifference curves reflects the degree of substitutability between the two commodities. If the indifference curve is flat or straight, it indicates that the two commodities are perfect substitutes. In the case of perfect substitutes, the indifference curves are, downward sloping straight line (as displayed in the diagram C.) If the consumer is not willing to substitute one commodity for another, the indifference curve will either be vertical or horizontal as displayed in the diagrams D and E.

Goods which can be substituted are represented by the indifference curve which is convex to the origin.

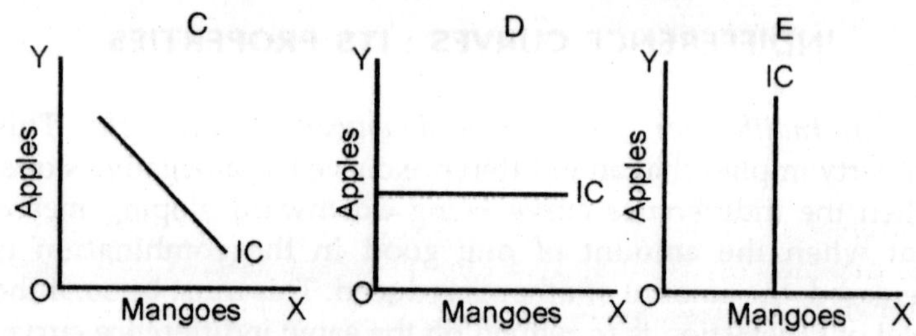

FIG. 5

(iii) Indifference curves cannot intersect each other. In other words, only one indifference curve will pass through a point in the indifference map. This property follows from the assumption 1 and 2. Supposing two indifferences intersect each other, then the whole theory becomes absurd. Let us study the following diagram keeping in mind the qualification of indifference curve.

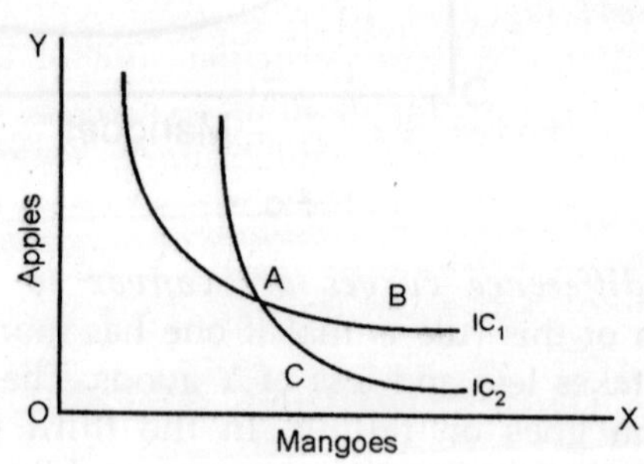

FIG. 6

Indifference curves represent varied levels of satisfaction. IC_1 is higher than IC_2 in the above diagram. The two indifference curves cut each other at the point A. At the point B, the consumer is on the higher indifference curve and at the point C, he is on the lower indifference curve. The point A is on both the indifference curves, which in turn means that A is at once equal to B and C which as seen, represent two indifference curves. Then the question arises whether higher indifference curve (IC_1) is equal to lower indifference curve (IC_2). As such, a thing cannot be and as such two indifference curves cannot intersect each other. Further, indifference curves can neither touch nor be tangent to each other.

(iv) Indifference curve touches neither X-axis nor Y-axis: it is assumed in the indifference curve analysis that a consumer buys combinations of different quantities of two goods. Hence, an indifference curve touches neither OX-axis nor OY-axis.

(v) Indifference curve need not be parallel to each other: Indifference curves may or may not be parallel to each other. It all depends on the marginal rate of substitution of two curves shown in the indifference map.

(vi) Indifference curves become complex in case of more than two commodities: When a consumer desires to have combination of more than two commodities, say, three commodities, then we will have to draw three dimensional indifference curves which are quite complex. If the consumer wants a combination comprising more than three goods then such a combination cannot be expressed in the form of a diagram. In that case, we will have to take recourse to algebra.

As we know that, the consumer will attain equilibrium when the utility from a particular unit of the commodity is equal to its price. (marginal utility = price), In indifference curve analysis, the procedure of equilibrium is somewhat different. In order to find out the equilibrium position of the consumer, we have to draw the price line. The price line is also known as the budget line or outlay line.

UNDERSTANDING OF PRICE LINE

In the words of *Ferguson*, "The price line shows the

combination of goods that can be purchased if the entire money income is spent."

Understanding of price line is very important for understanding the theory of consumer's equilibrium. The indifference curve is formed out of several combinations of the goods which give the consumer the equal level of satisfaction. Supposing as displayed in the diagram 7 there are four combinations of two commodities which are giving the consumer same level of satisfaction. It is because of this, he is indifferent to any of the combination. But there is one particular combination which gives him maximum level of satisfaction. To find out that combination, understanding of price line is very significant.

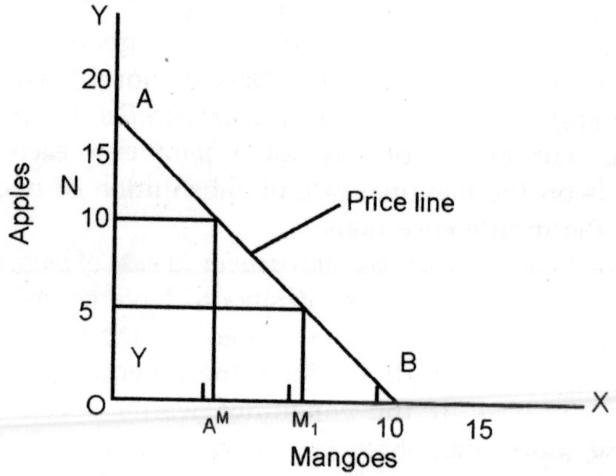

FIG. 7

For the determination of the price line, we have to know the prices of the two commodities and the money outlay to buy these goods. Supposing the consumer has set apart Rs. 30 from his total income to buy these two commodities.

If we assume that the price of apple is Rs. 2 and that of the mango is Rs. 3 and if he spends Rs. 30 on apples and on mangoes. These points are displayed in the following diagram. AB points in the diagram are connected by a line and this is known as price line. This line displays all the feasible combinations of two goods that the consumer can buy if he spends the whole of his outlay, prices being the same.

Supposing he purchases ON of apples, he has to buy OM of mangoes. If he prefers to buy OM of mangoes, he has to buy ON^1 of apples.

PRICE LINE SHIFTING

If the prices of the two goods remained the same and his income or outlay increases, then the new price line will be parallel to the old price line. Supposing the price of apples remain the same and that of mangoes fall, then the price line changes. These aspects are displayed in the following diagrams.

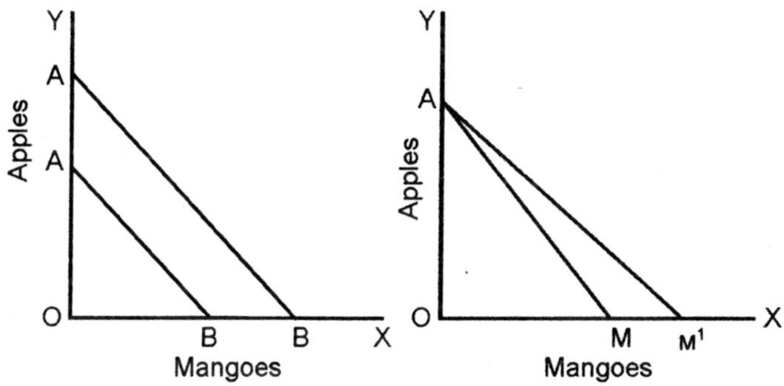

FIG. 8

The diagram 'X' indicates change in money outlay (income) while the prices of the two goods remain the same. In the Y diagram, the money outlay remains the same. The price of apples is the same and the price of mangoes falls. In the case of change in money income, a new price line parallel to the original price line comes into being. In the case of price line where the price of one commodity is constant and the price of the other commodity changes, the slope of the price line changes. The concept of price line helps in the determination of consumer's equilibrium.

Now we are in a position to explain with the help of price line, how a consumer reaches equilibrium position. A consumer is said to be in equilibrium when he is buying such a combination of goods which leaves him with no tendency to rearrange his purchases of goods. He is then in a balance position regarding the allocation of money on different goods.

In the indifference curve analysis, the consumer's equilibrium is determined in respect of the purchases of two goods only. The consumer has before him the indifference map showing three or four indifference curves. He has also a price line before him. In the diagram below, the process of consumer's equilibrium is explained.

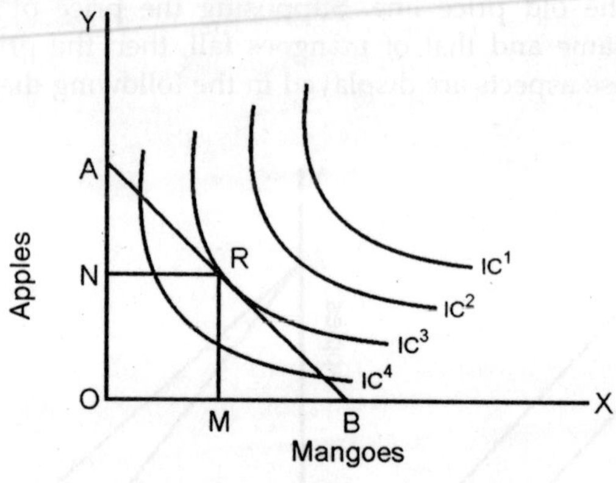

FIG. 9

There are four indifference curves displaying different levels of satisfaction. Price line AB represents the money expenditure on two goods. The price line AB contains all the feasible opportunities of combining the two goods that are open to the consumer. Any point of the indifference curve lying on the price line is the combination of two goods which provide the consumer maximum satisfaction. This is known as equilibrium position. Any point not lying on the price line cannot be an equilibrium point. The consumer will be in equilibrium at a point R, i.e., he will be buying OM of mangoes and ON of apples. Thus, it can be said that the consumer will maximise his satisfaction and be in equilibrium at a point where the price line is tangent to an indifference curve. In the above diagram, the price line AB is tangent to indifference curve 3 at the point R. Any combination of two goods other than the above cannot give the consumer maximum satisfaction and equilibrium.

EQUILIBRIUM'S CONDITION

It can be said that the condition for equilibrium arises when the given price line is tangent to the indifference curve. The same may be stated as equality between marginal rate of substitution and the ratio between the prices of these two goods. This is undoubtedly an essential condition for equilibrium. For attaining equilibrium, there is another condition which must be fulfilled. That is at the point of equilibrium, the marginal rate of substitution must be falling. It implies that indifference curve is convex to origin. If the indifference curve is convex to the origin at the point of equilibrium, it means that at that point, the marginal rate of substitution of mangoes for apples is falling.

In conclusion, we can say that the point of consumer's equilibrium may he defined by the condition that the marginal rate of substitution between any pair of two commodities will be equal to the ratio of the prices of the two commodities. In other words, the marginal rate of substitution of money for any commodity must be equal to the price of that commodity. The slope of the price line and that of indifference curve must coincide.

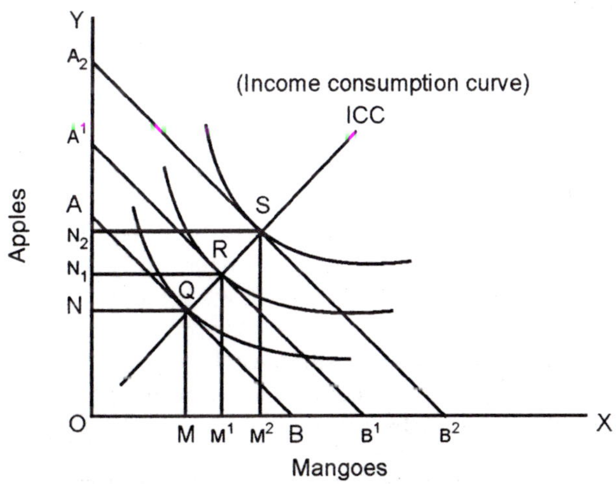

FIG. 10

INCOME EFFECT OR INCOME CONSUMPTION CURVE

In the above analysis, we have made two assumptions, namely the money income of the consumer is given and the prices of the two goods in combinations are also constant. Normally, either the money income of the consumer changes or prices of these goods change. The consequences of such changes are studied here under. Let us now take up the effect of consumer's change in money income on consumer's equilibrium. Whenever his money income rises, prices of goods and tastes of the consumer remaining the same, he will buy more quantities of these goods. This is known as income effect. Income effect displays this reaction of the consumer.

The income effect means the change in consumer's purchases of the goods as a result of increase in his money income.

With given money income and prices of the two commodities as indicated in the price line AB, the consumer will be in equilibrium at a point Q on the indifference curve (IC_1), buying ON of apples and OM of mangoes. Now his money income increases. The prices of the two goods are remaining the same. Then a new price line A^1B^1 comes into being. As a result of this change in money income and buying more units of the two goods, he goes to a higher indifference curve namely IC_2. The price line A^1B^1 is tangent to new indifference curve IC_2 at R. As a result of his increase in income, he purchases ON^1 of apples and OM of mangoes. If his income increases still further, then the price line moves further up to A^2B^2. He goes to a higher indifference curve IC_3. The consumer will be in equilibrium at point of S where the price line A^2B^2 is tangent to IC_3 at a point S. If the points Q, R and S are connected, we get a line called the income consumption line. The income consumption curve is the locus of equilibrium points at different levels of consumer's income. Income consumption curve traces out the income effect on the quantity consumed by the people.

INCOME EFFECT : ITS VARIOUS KINDS

Majority of the income consumption curves slope upwards to the right. This means as income increases, consumer purchases more of each of any of the two goods he is consuming. This is the usual shape of the income consumption curve. The effect of income consumption curve may be positive or negative. If the consumption of goods rises with the increase in income, the income effect for the goods is positive. For instance, if the income of wage earned i.e. factory workers increases, their consumption of superior goods rises. This is the positive effect of the income consumption curve.

However, for the same goods, the income effect is negative. Income effect for goods is said to be negative where, with the increase in income, the consumer reduces his consumption of goods. Such goods for which income effect is negative are called inferior goods. This is because the goods whose consumption falls as income increases are considered to be inferior goods by the consumer and he substitutes superior goods for them. Thus, with increase in income, consumption of superior goods rises while the consumption of inferior goods falls. When the people are poor, they consume coarse grains like jowar, maize, bajra, etc. When they become richer, they buy superior grains like wheat, rice, etc. In the case of inferior goods, the income consumption curve slopes backwards to the left. If the income effect is positive, it slopes upwards to the right.

PRICE EFFECT

Here we will explain how the consumer reacts to changes in the price of goods, his money income, the price of other goods and his taste remaining the same. Price effect displays the reaction of the consumer, whenever the price of one commodity falls. When the price of a commodity changes, the consumer would be better off or worse off than before, depending upon whether the price falls or rises. In other words, as a result of change in the price of the goods, his equilibrium position would also change. Let us study the Figure 11.

AB is the original price line and is tangent to IC_1 at Q. The consumer is in equilibrium buying ON of apples and OM of mangoes. The price of mangoes falls while the price of apples remain the same. As a result of this, the new price line AB_1 is formed. Since the consumer gets more units of mangoes for the same money expenditure, he goes to a higher indifference curve.

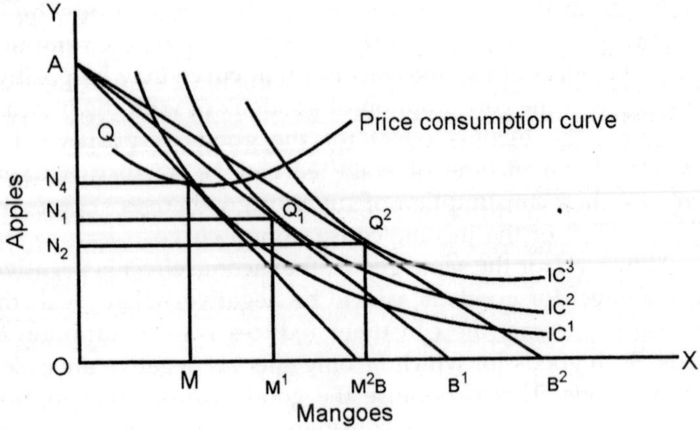

FIG. 11

The new price line AB_1 is tangent to IC_2 at Q,' and the consumer is in equilibrium buying ON_1 of apples and OM_1 of mangoes. He has thus become better off, i.e., his level of satisfaction has increased as a result of fall in the price of mangoes. Suppose the price of mangoes falls still further so that AB_2 is now the relevant price line, the consumer will be in equilibrium at Q, on the indifference curve IC_2 where he has OM_2 of mangoes and ON_2 of apples. When all the equilibrium points Q, Q_1, and Q_2 are joined together, we get what is known as price consumption curve. Price consumption curve traces the effect of change in the price of a commodity. It displays how the changes in the price of mangoes will affect the consumer's purchases of mangoes, price of apples, his tastes and money income remaining constant. The price consumption curve is downward sloping. It connotes as price of a commodity falls, more units of that commodity are bought.

PRICE EFFECT : ITS TWO COMPONENTS

In the case of falling prices of a good, the consumer feels better off. There is an increase in the potential purchasing power of the consumer's income following a comparative fall in the price of one commodity. This is known as income effect. It is as if his income has increased and the prices of both the goods have remained the same. The income effect is the first component of the price effect. The consumer is moving along the income consumption curve. The income effect will lead to the purchase of a better commodity. This is known as substitution effect. Since the price of X has fallen, it becomes cheaper. Since the price of Y has remained the same, it becomes dearer. So, a tendency arises in the mind of the consumer to buy more units of a commodity for which the price has not fallen. In other words, he will substitute cheaper goods for the dearer one. Thus, the second component of price effect is the substitution effect. The following diagram illustrates the two components of price effect. In the beginning, the consumer is in equilibrium, price line AB is tangent to the indifference curve 1. With a fall in price of X goods, a new price line comes into existence.

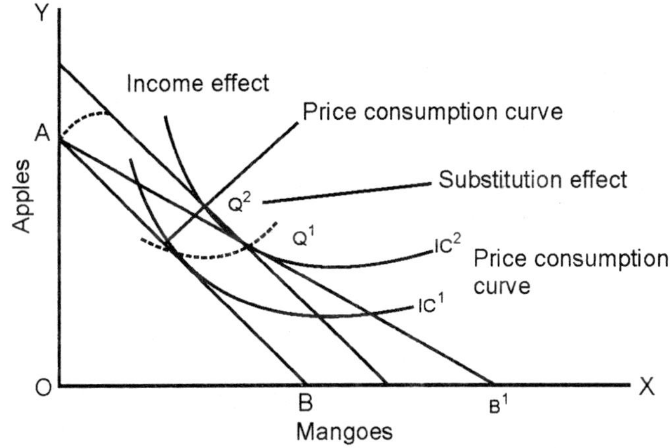

FIG. 12

Income effect and substitution effect of the fall in the price of one commodity differs while the price of other commodity is remaining the same. The splitting up of price effect into income effect and substitution effect is advantageous in bringing out explicitly the response of a consumer to a change in price of a commodity. The response to a change in price of a commodity will disclose in terms of income effect and substitution effect. In cases of most of the goods, the income effect and substitution effect will work in the same direction. But, in some cases, they operate in a different directions. The direction of substitution effect is very certain. A fall in the relative price of goods always leads to an increase in the quantity demanded of the goods. In other words, substitution effect always induces the consumer to purchase more of the cheaper goods. But the direction of income effect is not certain.

With a rise in income, the individual will generally buy more of goods. But with the rise in income, the individual will buy less of goods if it happens to be inferior goods for him, since he will use better or superior substitutes in place of inferior goods when his income rises. Thus, the income effect may be either positive or negative. In the case of superior goods, income effect is positive while it is negative in the case of inferior goods. Substitution effect is always positive. That is, if the price of goods falls, more of it will be purchased and substituted for other goods whose prices have not fallen. If the substitution effect is positive, the income effect is negative. It implies that the demand for the commodity, whose price has fallen may not increase much or it may diminish as in the case of Giffen Goods.

GIFFEN GOODS

Giffen goods are inferior goods. In the case of Giffen goods, the income effect is negative.

EFFECT OF CHANGE ON QUANTITY DEMAND

The price consumption curve traces the effect of a change on the quantity demanded of a good. The price consumption curve does not directly relate price with quantity demanded. In the indifference curve diagram, price is not displayed on the Y axis. On the other hand, demand curve directly relates to price and quantity demanded, price being displayed on the Y axis and quantity being displayed on the X axis. The demand curve can be drawn from the price consumption curve. For this, we have to assume price othe Y axis. Then the downward sloping demand curve comes into existence.

STUDY OF DEMAND ANALYSIS

Demand analysis is studied for specific purposes. The chief objective is for the business reasons. Business people have to make a thorough study of demand analysis with a view to solve business problems and to make business decisions. The business people have to produce goods which have great demand 'in the market. In order to study the demand potential for goods, they are divided into several types. They are as—producers' goods and consumer goods, durable and non-durable goods, derived demand and autonomous demand, industry demand and company demand, short run demand and long term demand, short term demand fluctuations and long term demand trends, market demand and market segments.

Distinction between Producers Goods and Consumers Goods: Producers' goods are those goods which are used in the production of goods which may be consumer goods or producers' goods. Instances are machines, tools and implements, ships, locomotives etc. Consumers' goods are those goods which are in use in the final consumption. Examples of consumer goods are any type of food items, readymade clothes, utensils and so on.

There are intermediate goods like steel to produce machinery for weaving yarn to produce cloth, which are producer goods. There are single use goods and durable goods. Manufactured food items are single use consumption goods. Sewing machines are a single use, durable goods. A car, a refrigerator are consumer durable goods. The reasons for the demand for producers' goods are—Buyers of produce goods are professionals. They are experts and they can make discrimination pricewise, quality wise and are sensitive to substitutes. Their motive is purely profit. Products are bought not for the product sake but for making profits. Their purchases are not at all influenced by advertisement, but are more sensitive to price differences, demand for producers' goods fluctuate more dramatically than consumer goods. The distinction between consumer goods and producers' goods, though serves a useful purpose, is purely arbitrary. Whether goods are producers' goods or consumers' goods, is based on (i) who purchases (ii) why he buys. For instance, if coal is used for cooking, it is a consumers' good, if the same coal is used in a railway engine, it is a producers' good. If the car is used by a retired executive, it is a consumers' good and if the same car is used by a marketing executive, it is a producers' good.

Distinction between Durable Goods and Perishable Goods: Durable goods are those which satisfy their owners for a long time to come if they are maintained properly, perishable goods or non-durable goods are goods which can be consumed only once. In other words, perishable goods are themselves consumed, while in durable goods, the services are consumed. Durable products present more complex problems of demand analysis than the non-durable goods or perishable goods. Sale of perishable goods are made to meet the current demand which depends upon current conditions while the sale of durable goods add to the stock of existing goods which are still serviceable. Therefore, it is necessary to segregate current demand for durable goods with that of existing goods. One feature of demand for durable goods is the volatile relation to business conditions, since the current production of durable goods is only a fraction of the products which are in current use. For instance, normal production of automobiles is used (i) to replace 10 per cent of the existing cars and (ii) to expand car production by 5 per cent, then a 3 per cent increase in demand for cars will raise the new car demand by 20 percent. To put it more clearly, let us assume that there are 20,000 cars in use. The replacement demand at the rate of 10% means 2000 cars. (Supposing there is expansion in demand for cars by 5%, it means 1500. Then the existing total production would be 3000. If there is an extra 3% rise, then it means 600 additional cars, i.e. 20% of the existing production of 3000 cars). Demand analysis for durable goods is not simple. Both replacement and expansion have manifold sets of demand determinants. Replacement demand depends on the value of existing car relative to their scrap value.

When the existing demand rises all of a sudden, the prices of used cars go up higher than the scrap value, as a result, the scrapping rate falls (replacement demand falls). If the expansion demand falls, the scrap rate will be higher than the level of new car production. The most significant determinant for replacement is obsolescence because of technological developments. Obsolescence is pervasive and strategic in American economy in determining the level of business activity.

Physical deterioration is rarely a deciding factor in replacement of durable goods. For durable goods, both consumers' and producers' goods style, convenience and income play a dominant role in determining demand. Occasionally, technological upheaval can produce a blast of obsolescence that wipes out any distinction between expansion and replacement. For such innovation, demand depends upon cultural tags, financial agencies and rivalry of alternate investments. While buying durable goods, the buyers, besides their incomes and current prices of the products, look into other things like maintenance and operating costs in relation to their future income and other demands. They may look into the future sale prices of these products. They consider carefully whether to buy now or postpone the purchase. Thus, for durable goods, not only present prices and incomes, but their current trends and states of optimism are proper variables to be included in demand functions. Expectation of proper improved designs are also significant.

Distinction between Derived Demand and Autonomous Demand : When the demand for a product is tied with another product, it is known as derived demand. For instance, demand for steel is related to the production of machinery. Demand for all producer's goods, raw-materials and components is derived demand. Demand for building materials like doors and windows, cement, sand etc. is derived from demand for houses. It is not easy to find those products whose demand is all demand.

In fact, independent demand is derived. There is no autonomous demand. Derived demand is supposed to have less price elasticity than autonomous demand, assuming that substitutes are equally available. For a 10% cut in the price of steel would cause only one percent cut in the cost of a car, assuming prices of all other components are the same. Some products are tied to others in their uses and they have no independent demand, for instance, television antennas. If a commodity has a number of uses, it is not easy to tie demand down to parent products. Derived demand facilitates forecasting when proportions of the two products are fixed.

In some cases, demand may not provide a very reliable basis. For instance, demand for looms in Cotton Textile Industry would normally be determined by the demand for cotton textiles. Yet, it may not give the current indicator as the looms may be used in double or triple shifts and the number of looms needed may be reduced by half or one third. The recession in motor car industry forced tyre manufacturers to cut production and reduce stocks. When the proportion between the parent and dependent goods is not fixed it is very difficult to determine demand for dependent goods on the basis of the demand for parent goods. If the number of uses to which a certain product can be put fluctuates, it is difficult to estimate the derived demand on the basis of the demand for the parent product. Electric motors and sulphuric acid are good examples for they can be used in any number of industries.

Distinction between Industry Demand and Company Demand: Industry demand implies the demand for the products used by all firms in a particular industry. For instance, total demand for jute, cotton, steel etc. in an economy. Industry is composed of a group of closely associated firms, All firms manufacturing cloth are put together in order to form a cotton textile industry.

The firms in the cotton textile industry are buying the same product namely yarn and selling the product (cloth) which are close substitutes. When there is considerable product differentiation within the industry and substitutes compete with other industries, then the concept of industry demand becomes irrelevant. For instance, jaggery and sugar are distant substitutes excluded in the sugar industry. An industry demand schedule represents the relation of the price of the product to the quantity that will be bought by all firms. It has a clear meaning that when the firms are producing close substitutes, the products produced by the firms may have different markets. Adding President and Premier cars and averaging their prices does not produce a meaningful demand schedule. Industry's demand schedule can be divided into customers groupwise. For instance, steel needed for building construction and manufacture of machinery, etc. From the managerial point of view, mere industry's demand does not serve any purpose. What is to be recognised is to know the company's share in the industry's demand. Company demand implies the demand for the products of a particular company. Demand for Ambassador cars implies the demand for the product of that company, while demand for cars implies the total demand for cars of all firms put together. In order to understand the relation between company demand and industry demand, it is essential to know the characteristics of different market structures. There are different market structures, like monopoly, perfect competition, monopolistic competition and oligopoly. In the case of monopoly, there is a single firm and hence there is no difference between company demand and industry demand. In other words, company demand curve would be the same as the industry demand curve. In case of perfect competition, the industry demand curve is totally divorced from company demand curve. The company in this market situation has no independent price since all firms are selling the identical product. In case of company, the demand curve is a horizontal straight line, while the industry demand curve is negative sloped. In the case of oligopoly, there are two types-one is homogeneous oligopoly and the other is differentiated oligopoly.

In the case of homogenous oligopoly, sellers are few and their products are standardised, the business is highly transferable among themselves. Example: aluminium, steel and cement. There is competition among rivals. The company's own demand curve is uncertain, for it depends on the rivals. What is usually done is that the sellers charge the same price to stay on in the market, since the product produced by all firms is identical. If a firm would reduce the price, this would lead to a chain of reactions in the industry. In several manufacturing industries, a few large firms dominate and account for great portions of the industry's output. But most of the products are not uniform and hence there is a small price variation. There is differentiated oligopoly-few sellers with differentiated products (for example, motor cars, refrigerators, television sets, etc.). The products of the rival companies differ physically, the company's demand is less closely inter-dependent on industry's demand, since the consumers express their own preferences.

The individual companies have got more leeway in manipulating their prices. The company may have an independent demand function, depending upon the superiority of the product and advertisement effect. In the case of monopolistic competition, the individual companies have their own demand curves and the industry demand curve has no meaning. The products of different firms are considered as different products and so for each product, there is a demand curve as in monopoly. It differs from the monopolist in that, company demand may be affected by the competitions of the rivals. Hence the demand curve of the firm in monopolistic competition is more price elastic.

Market Share Concept or Demand Analysis : The market share concept of company demand is now being utilised in demand analysis. The market demand for a product may be 10 million tonnes of steel. But a company's output may be 2 million tonnes. Then the company's share in the market demand is 20 per cent. It is said that some companies control 60 to 70 per cent of the product market, which are known as dominant companies. The concept of market share becomes significant because of the entire demand being the result of vast impersonal economic forces and is usually beyond the capacity of an individual company to control it. For instance, an X company which produced say 60 per cent of the market share, cannot control the whole market but the market share enjoyed by it can be manipulated. Market share information may help in persuading people to buy the product of that company. This concept of demand indirectly is useful for the company either to increase its market share or try to retain it at least for which the company has to improve the product or change the market strategy. The factors that determine the market share are (1) The price differentials, (2) Promotional expenditure and (3) Product improvement. The price differential or price spread for product in the market determines the market share of the company. If a company's price is lower than the price charged by other companies, then that company would be able to capture a greater market share. If there is still competition in the market, a company may resort to increased promotional campaign, or it may take up product improvement by using latest technology. Thus, market share concept influences the individual companies to improve their respective positions in the market. In this cultural setting, market share objectives are often defensive.

Demand of Short Run Demand and Long Run: Short run

demand implies present or current demand. Further, there is an immediate reaction to price changes, income fluctuations, etc. whereas long-term demand implies demand which ultimately exists because of changes in prices or promotion of product improvement. For instance, a cut in price of electricity will induce the existing users of electrical appliances to make greater use of them. This is short term change in demand. In the long run more people will be induced to buy them, ultimately leading to a greater demand for electricity.

Thus, a temporary price cut cannot be viewed in the same light as one that is expected to stick for a longer period. Competition among the producers will result in cut in the prices in the short run. This will lead to the entry of new competitors and exploration of substitutes in the long run. Factors that cause this distinction are (1) Cultural lags in information and experience, (2) Capital investments needed on the part of consumers to change their consumption patterns. A price change today will result in a chain of adjustments in customer's attitudes and competitor's prices. There may be delayed action on the part of the buyers in response to price changes, because in practice, the consumers' use patterns are sticky. In case of new products, price changes may not induce the buyers to buy more. In the long run, price cuts may accelerate growth considerably, because by that time, there will have been adjustments in the use patterns. Another factor is with regard to the new investments that will have to be made in order to take advantage of price cuts. In order to buy electrical appliances like refrigerators, TV sets, washing machines, etc., a huge investment will have to be made, which may not be feasible for many people. Thus, long run growth is not entirely dependent on price-cuts. Yet, price cuts influence the increase in demand considerably.

Fluctuations in Demand : Fluctuations in demand cause more problems to producers since demand shifts with the passage of time. There are several types of time patterns like of day, month, seasonal and cyclical trends. Forecasting brief of time patterns does not pose serious problems to businessmen. But the forecasting as to how sales fluctuate from year to year and projecting long term trends in demand pose difficulties. In year to year fluctuations, much of the setting namely competitive structure, market position, quality and even prices remain constant. For long term, the trend is different, for everything is uncertain. There might be changes in tastes, technology and way of life. Forecasts of year to year changes provide for programming firm's production plans, such as, man-power requirement, raw materials requirement, inventory, cash etc. Projection of long range demand trends are useful for planning investments, choosing location, etc. Joel Dean observes that in the atomic age, long run forecast is necessarily a speculation.

Entire Market and Market Segment : Total market for a product implies its total demand. When the total market for toilet soaps is referred, it includes all the brands or substitutes of toilet soaps.

Market segment implies the part of the total market like foreign market, local market, regional market and national market Market segment may also be carved out by sub-products, the uses of products, sensitivity to price, etc. When demand is divided into different segments, this gives rise to the market segment. Total market includes all segments. When demand forecasting is to be made, total market has to be taken into consideration. When pricing, distribution and promotion is to be taken up, their market segment is preferred. Each of these market segments may differ in prices, packaging, promotion etc. For manipulating price, promotion, production and distribution, a segment concept of demand is appropriate.

ESTIMATION OF FORECASTING

Forecasting is a prediction about a future event which is most likely to happen under given conditions. Demand forecasting means estimate of expected future demand conditions. Kotler remarked that 'forecasting is like trying to drive a car blindfolded on following directions given by a person who is looking out the back window'. Looking into the future which is uncertain, is really a difficult task but it has been so in the experience of mankind. Assuming that future would be bright, every man takes some risks in life and tries to advance further. In the business field, there was lack of forecasting in the past. It was only after the depression in 1930s, that systematic forecasting was realised as a tool of management.

Forecasting is defined as a study with scientific prediction in regard to an event which may have future demand for goods, services either at the micro level or at the macro level. Forecasting deals with the likely shape of future events, that is a scientific guesswork.

Forecasting is useful for managerial decision making, effective and efficient planning. It helps to assess the probable demand for goods and services in different periods of time. Demand forecasting translates the demand functions into quantitative guesses. A theoretical demand function seeks to include all the forces that influence sales. If these are to be translated into actuality, some of the demand determinants have to be selected and a formula for forecasting sales has to be evolved. This is the function of demand forecasting. Since the management operates under conditions of uncertainty, a probable guess about the future demand for the products is absolutely essential. This helps in reducing the risk of uncertainty to the absolute minimum. Forecasting is required in all areas of the enterprise. Since future is uncertain, no forecast is hundred percent certain. However, it is necessary for every firm to make forecast as correct as possible. Henry Fayol was the first to lay emphasis on forecasting as an important function of business management. A good forecast reduces the scope of uncertainty to the barest minimum.

QUESTIONS

1. Describe about Consumer Equilibirium.
2. What is Cardinal Utility Approach? Explain it in detail.
3. What do you know about Indifference Curve Approach?
4. Explain Estimation of Forecasting.

CHAPTER

5

Production Theory

PRODUCTION ANALYSIS

Production Function: The Concept

A producer uses inputs to produce outputs. Perhaps the producer uses two inputs, capital (K) and labour (L) to produce the output (Q). If the producer uses 10 units of K and 10 units of L, how much of output is he going to get? (By the way, as in the case of a consumer, the use of he for a producer means no male chauvinism.) With 10 units of K and 10 units of L, how much of output the producer is going to get, is beyond the control of the producer. It is given from outside, the producer has to accept this as exogenously determined. For instance, if 10 units of K and 10 units of L yield 100 units of output Q, this 100 is determined by the state of technological knowledge. The producer cannot influence this. Obviously, this presumes that the producer is operating efficiently. For instance, technology might imply that 10 units of K and 10 units of L should produce 100 units of Q. But there is an inefficient producer who only manages to produce 75 units of output. We are not concerned with such inefficient producers. The functional relationship that links inputs to outputs is called production function. We can write Q = Q (K, L). Given any combination of K and L used, the production function tells us how much of Q can be produced. It is this that is technologically determined. More precisely, the production function we have just written down is known as the explicit form of a production function. A production function can also be written in implicit form as f (Q, K, L) = 0.

Production Function, according to Watson is "The relation between a firm's physical production (output) and the material factors of production (input)". According to Koutsoyianis, " The production is purely a technical relation which connects factor inputs and output".

Suppose for example, that two different outputs Q_1 and Q_2 are simultaneously through the' production process. If you like, one output is a byproduct. This sort of situation is known as one that involves joint products. If there are joint products, it is evident that a production function can never be written in explicit form. We will have to be content with an implicit production function like f (Q_1, Q_2, K, L) = 0. But without joint products, the production function can always be written down in explicit form and it is this sort of statement that we will stick to, throughout this unit. The production function Q = Q (K, L) that we have just stated is a general statement. It only states that inputs and outputs are linked through a functional relationship. In fact, the functional relationship is too general for anything further to be said. Therefore, quite often, one needs to refer to specific forms of production functions. A production function that is commonly used is the following:

$Q = A K^a L^b$. A, a and b are constants, with $0 < a, b < 1$.

This is called the Cobb-Douglas production function. Not very surprisingly, it is named after two economists named Cobb and Douglas. In fact, what we have just stated is called the unrestricted form of the Cobb-Douglas production function. A CobbDouglas production function in restricted form is written as $Q = A K^a L^{1-a}$. What is the difference between the two forms? Not much. In the restricted case, we have obviously assumed that a + b = 1. The unrestricted version is thus more general than the restricted one. The Cobb-Douglas production function is actually one of the simplest production functions that one can think of. More complicated production functions can, be thought of. The following is an example.

$Q = y\ [dK{-}p + (I{-}d)\ L^{-P}]^{-1/P}$. This is called a constant elasticity of substitution (CES) production function. Sometimes, this production function is also referred to as the ACMS production function, after the names of four economists-Arrow, Chenery, Minhas and Solow. The Cobb-Douglas production function is a special case of the CES production function. There is yet another production function called as the variable elasticity of substitution (VES) production function. We will skip the expression for the VES production function, as it is still more complicated. The CES production function is a special case of the VES production function. It is no one's case that a production process has to involve only two inputs. Several inputs (n in number) are feasible and the production function accordingly has to be generalised. For instance, if there are n inputs L_1, L_2,..., L_n, the Cobb-Douglas production function can be generalised in the following form. However, in what follows, we will assume that there are only two inputs, K and L. This is purely for the purpose of simplicity.

THE SHORT RUN

In the short run, some inputs are fixed and some inputs are variable. It is therefore convenient to break up costs into a fixed component and a variable component. Let FC stand for fixed costs and VC stand for variable costs. Since C is total cost, C = FC + VC. Fixed costs are also known as overhead or indirect costs. Variable costs are also known as prime or direct costs. Is FC a function of Q? Not quite. That is, FC does not depend on the level of Q. This is because fixed costs are because of fixed inputs and in the short run, fixed inputs cannot vary. Therefore, fixed costs are also the same. If we plot FC as a function of Q, we will get a completely horizontal straight line. Let us now define AFC as average fixed costs. AFC = FC/Q. What will the AFC curve look like? When Q is zero, AFC is infinitely high. Thereafter, AFC steadily comes down as Q increases. In Figure 1, we have also plotted the AFC curve as a function of Q and you can see that. the curve is downward sloping. Can we say anything more about the shape of the AFC curve? Indeed, yes. The AFC curve will be a rectangular hyperbola. This becomes obvious if we write AFC.Q FC. The right hand side is constant. The left hand side, AFC.Q, will therefore also be a constant. Since we have plotted AFC along the Y-axis and Q along the X-axis, the resultant curve is naturally a rectangular hyperbola. Let us now define MFC as marginal fixed costs. MFC = AFC/AQ. Since FC is the same, it is clear that although we have defined MFC, MFC is a meaningless concept in the sense that MFC is definitely zero. Having talked about fixed costs, one needs to turn to variable costs. VC has been used to denote variable costs.

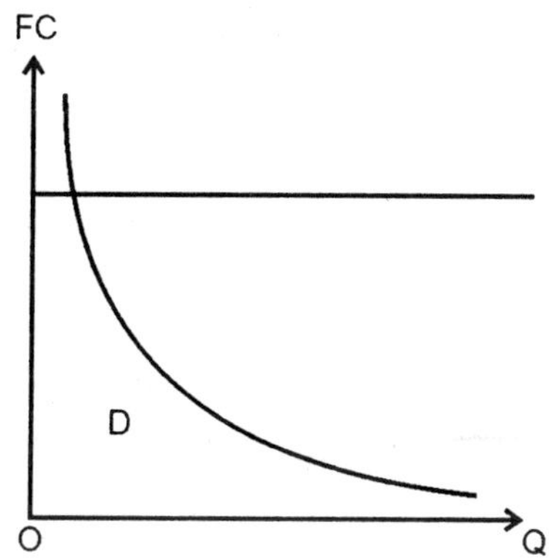

FIG. 1

The average variable cost can be written as AVC and defined as AVC = VC/Q. The marginal variable cost can be written as MVC and defined as DVC/DQ. Let's use the notations AC for average total costs and MC for marginal total costs. Note the following simple relationships. C = FC + VC. Dividing both sides by Q, C/Q = (FC/Q) + (VC/Q).

AC = AFC + AVC.
DC/DQ = (DFC/DQ) + (DVC/DQ). Since DFC
= 0, MC = MVC.

If we want to know what the AC curve looks like, we need to know the shapes of the AFC and AVC curves. We already know the shape of the AFC curve. Therefore, let's focus on the

AVC curve. Take the case of two inputs, K and L. K is fixed in the short run. The variable input is labour, L. If PL is the price that has to be paid for one unit of labour, the total variable cost (with L units of labour used), will be P_L. L. Thus, AVC = $P_L L/Q$. Go back and read the definition of the average product of labour. Once you have done this, you will realise that the relationship can be written as AVC = P_L/AP_L. If the amount of labour hired by the producer does not affect the price at which labour can be hired, P_L will be constant. The average variable cost (AVC) will then be inversely related to the average product of labour. To determine the shape of the AVC curve, we need to know the shape of the AP_L curve.

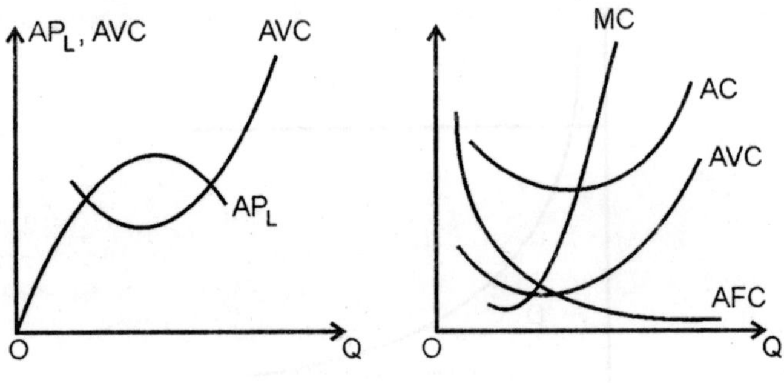

FIG. 2

There is no way one can prove what the shape of the APL curve will be like. Because of successive stretches of increasing returns, constant returns and diminishing returns, the AP_L curve will have a reverse U-shape. This is reproduced yet again in the first panel of Figure 2. Given the inverse relationship between the AVC curve and the AP_L curve, the AVC curve will then have the U-shape displayed in the first panel of Figure 2. The peak of the AP_L curve will correspond to the trough of the AVC curve. What does the trough of the AVC curve mean? This is the output level at which the average cost per unit is the lowest. In a sense, this is the optimum level of output if one is trying to minimize the average variable cost of production. The way we have drawn Figure 3, there is only a single trough in the AVC curve. However, if the AP_L curve has a flat segment at the peak (instead of a single peak), the AVC curve will also have a flat segment at the trough. At all these different levels of output, the average variable cost will be the lowest. Such an AVC curve is said to have a saucer shape. We now need to splice the AVC curve with AFC curve and this is done in the second panel of Figure 3. Since AC = AVC + AFC, the AC curve is a vertical sum of the AVC and AFC curves. Note the following. The AFC curve always declines. The AVC curve initially declines, and rises thereafter. When both curves decline,. they reinforce each other. When AVC rises and AFC declines, the two pulls neutralise each other. As the second panel of Figure 2 shows, the AC curve will also have a U-shape. Having said all this about average costs, let us turn to marginal costs.

Since AFC = 0, MC = MVC. Marginal variable cost is identical to marginal total cost. Thus, one can simply say marginal cost. What shape will the MC curve have? Take the case where there are only two inputs, K and L. The capital input is fixed in the short run. With PL standing for the price of labour, it is clear that $MC = P_L/MP_L$. MP_L stands for the marginal product of labour. Variations in the quantity of labour hired by the producer do not lead to changes in the price of labour. PL is therefore fixed and MC is inversely related to MP_L. There is no way to prove what the shape of the MPL curve will be. If there exists successive stretches of increasing returns, constant returns, and diminishing returns, the MP_L curve will have a reverse U-shape. The MC curve will accordingly have a U-shape. This explains the depiction of the MC curve in the second panel of Figure 2. (The way we have drawn the diagram, we have assumed a very small stretch of increasing returns.) Please do note that the marginal cost curve intersects both the average variable cost and the average cost curves at their minimum points. Have you understood why this must always be the case?

THE LONG RUN

Having discussed the short run, we can now turn to the long run. As you have been told earlier, the long run is a situation where all inputs are variable. There are no fixed inputs whatsoever. The treatment of the long run is a little more messy, although the basic idea is quite simple. In the short run, capital is fixed. In the long run, capital can be varied. However, varying capital input is tantamount to varying the size of the plant. To get an idea of what is involved, take a look at the first panel of Figure 3. Along the Y-axis, we have plotted average cost. Along the X-axis, is plotted the quantity of output. The panel displays three different short run average cost curves, labelled SAC_1, SAC_2 and SAC_3. Each short run average cost curve corresponds to a given level of capital and therefore, to a given plant size. In the short run, since capital is fixed, the producer has to operate along the short run average cost curve that corresponds to that fixed level of capital input. However, in the long run, the producer can also vary the capital input and this is equivalent to his being able to choose which particular short run average cost curve he would like to operate along. A natural objective for the producer is to try and reduce the average cost of production. Thus, if the intention is to produce OQ_1 units of output, the producer will not choose a capital input that corresponds to the curve SAC_2. He will instead choose a plant size that corresponds to the curve SAC_1.

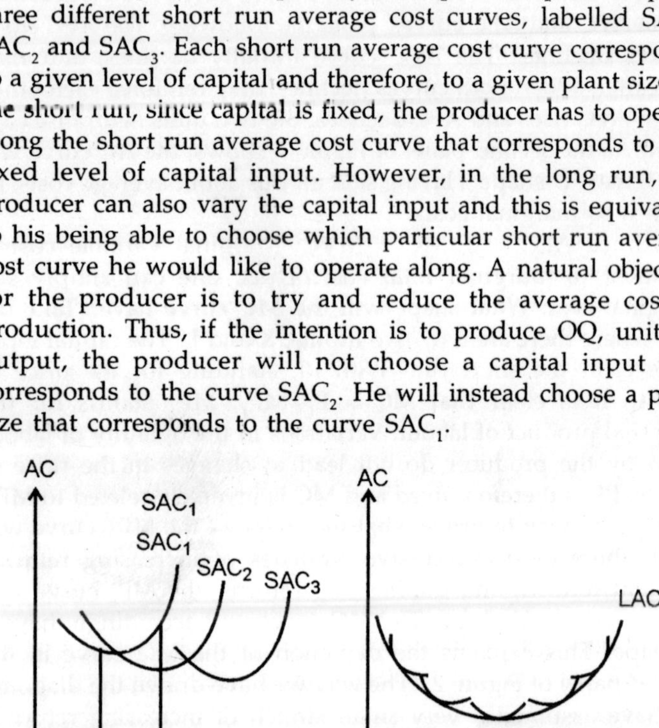

FIG. 3

However, if the desired level of Output is OQ_2, the plant size corresponding to SAC_2 will be preferred to the plant size corresponding to SAC_1. This idea now generalizes. The first panel of Figure 3 only has three short run average cost curves. However, if capital is infinitely divisible, there will be an infinite number of such short run average cost curves. In the long run, since the producer can choose the quantum of capital input, he will choose to operate along the short run average cost curve that ensures the lowest average cost. The long run average cost curve is in this sense a curve that bounds the short run average cost curves from below. The expression used is actually an envelope. Thus, the long run average cost (LAC) curve is an envelope of the short run average cost curves from below. This is displayed in the second panel of Figure 3. The word envelope is not very precise. What does it mean? Look at it like this. We must draw a curve (the long run average cost curve) that touches all the short run average cost curves from below. Stated differently, each point on the LAC curve will be a point of tangency with some SAC curve and the locus of all such tangency points is nothing but the LAC curve. Note a significant point. The LAC curve is not necessarily tangential to SAC curves at the minimum points of the SAC curves. In fact, if you take a look at the second panel of Figure 4 again, you will notice that the LAC curve is tangential at the minimum point of a SAC curve only for the output level OQ_1. Nowhere else, the LAC curve drawn in Figure 4 has a U-shape.

In fact, it has a rather neat U-shape, with a single minimum point. The output level that corresponds to this unique minimum point is OQ_1. Since this level of output is obtained at the lowest average cost feasible, this is known as the optimal level of output. At this level of output, the LAC curve is tangential to a SAC curve. Not only is it tangential to a SAC curve, it is tangential to this particular SAC curve at the minimum point of the SAC curve.

The average cost is minimum along the SAC curve as well. The plant size that corresponds to this SAC curve is known as the optimal plant size. This optimal plant size will naturally vary from sector to sector. For instance, no one can argue that the optimal plant size in the automobile industry is identical to the optimal plant size in leather manufactures. The LAC curve need not always have a neat U-shape. First, note that if there are constant returns to scale, the LAC curve will always be perfectly flat and horizontal. The average cost will be fixed, regardless of the level of output. The reason for this is simple and can be easily understood in the case of two inputs, capital (K), and labour (L). If the price of K is denoted by P K and the price of L is denoted by PL cost (C) can be written as $C = P_K K + P_L L$. Accordingly, average cost is $C/Q = (P_K K + P_L Q/Q)$. In the long run, both K and L can be varied. Since one has constant returns to scale, if K and L are multiplied by a factor, Q gets multiplied by exactly the same factor. But this means that C/Q will be the same, even though one is varying L and the plant size (K). If one has constant returns to scale, the LAC curve will accordingly be horizontal. One draws a U-shaped LAC curve because one does not believe that constant returns to scale always exist.

For instance, as output is initially expanded, one often obtains increasing returns to scale. This may happen if inputs like capital are not perfectly divisible and come in lumpy investments. Incidentally, increasing returns to scale is also referred to as internal economies of scale. (The reason for using the word internal will become clear in a short while.) Beyond a point, constant returns to scale sets in. If constant returns to scale continue for a stretch, the LAC curve will not have a unique minimum point. Instead, the minimum stretch will extend over a flat segment and the LAC curve will have the shape of a saucer. Beyond this stretch, decreasing returns to scale sets in and the LAC curve begins to rise. The concept of returns to scale is a situation where all inputs are varied. The standard explanation for decreasing returns to scale is that, no matter how hard one tries, all inputs can never be increased. Therefore, average costs begin to rise. Incidentally, decreasing returns to scale is also referred to as internal diseconomies of scale. Many empirical studies display LAC curves that have L-shapes, that is, the average cost continues to fall, even though the rate at which the average cost falls, may decline.

In other words, the forces that lead to decreasing returns to scale are effectively neutralised. Two types of reasons are advanced to explain L-shaped LAC curves. First, each LAC curve is drawn with a given state of technological knowledge. If continuous technological progress takes place so that costs are brought down, this may more than neutralise the forces that lead to decreasing returns to scale. Second, there is a phenomenon that economists refer to as learning by doing. This simply means that the more one does of some thing, the better one gets at it. Thus, even if nothing else changes, if one produced more output, one would be able to bring down average costs because one learns in the process. Learning by doing can also neutralise the forces that lead to decreasing returns to scale. You were told that increasing returns to scale is referred to as internal economies of scale and decreasing returns to scale is referred to as internal diseconomies of scale. The adjective internal implies the fact that these changes in costs take place when the producer changes his own output level. However, the producer's costs may also be affected by changes in the output level of the industry, that is, by changes in the output levels of other producers. These are called externalities. The effect on the producer's costs need not always be favourable. If the effects are favourable, that is, if the producer's average costs are brought down in the process, one implies external economies of scale. External economies of scale are also known as positive externalities. Instances of positive externalities are cheaper materials, capital equipment and skilled labour, or better infrastructural facilities. Positive externalities serve to lower SAC and LAC curves. If the effects are unfavourable, that is, if the producer's average costs go up in the process, one implies external diseconomies of scale. External diseconomies of scale are also known as negative externalities. Examples of negative externalities are hikes in the prices of inputs used. Negative externalities serve to raise SAC and LAC curves.

MARGINAL RATE OF TECHNICAL SUBSTITUTION

The point worth noting is that the law does not state that each and every increase in the amount of the variable factor employed in the production process will yield diminishing marginal returns. It is feasible that initial increases in the amount of variable factor employed in the production process may yield increasing marginal returns. However, in increasing the amount of the variable factor employed, a point will be reached where the marginal increases in total output will begin declining or marginal return will begin declining.

RETURNS TO SCALE AND RETURNS TO FACTORS

We now want to define a mathematical concept, known as that of a homogeneous function. Take the following functional relationship, p = p (x, y z). This simply states that p is the dependent variable and depends on the values of three independent variables, x, y and z. We have taken three independent variables for purposes of simplicity, one can have as many independent variables, as one wants. Let us suppose that all three independent variables are now multiplied by a factor of t, t is positive. The function is then said to be homogeneous of degrees if the following holds.

$p(tx, ty, tz) = t^s p$. That is, when all the independent variables are multiplied by a factor of t, the dependent variable is multiplied by a factor of t^s.

It is easy to translate this concept to the case of a production function Q = Q (K, L). The production function is homogeneous of degree s if $Q(tK, tL) = t^sQ$. Two inputs are used for purposes of simplicity. The concept generalises to the case where there are more than two inputs.

Make sure you have understood what this means. Initially, output was Q and the inputs used were K and L. If $t > 1$, both inputs have now been increased by a factor of t. (If $t < 1$, one is talking about a decrease in inputs by a factor of t.) Since both inputs have been increased by the same factor t, the K/L ratio remains the same. Q (t K, t L) is the value of the new output. If the production function is homogeneous of degree, the value of the new output is t^s times the value of the old output. That is all this fancy notation means.

Take the case where $s > 1$. What does this mean? The inputs have been increased by a factor of t. But output has increased by a factor of more than t. Labour and capital inputs may have doubled, but output has more than doubled. Output increases more than proportionately. This is known as a situation of increasing returns to scale. Stated differently, the production function is homogeneous of degree more than one.

Take the case where $s = 1$. What does this mean? The inputs have been increased by a factor of t. Output has also increased by a factor of t. Labour and capital inputs may have doubled, and output has also doubled. Output increases proportionately. This is known as a situation of constant returns to scale. Stated differently, the production function is homogeneous of degree one. Sometimes one says, the production function is linearly homogeneous.

Take the case where $s < 1$. What does this mean? The inputs have been increased by a factor of t. But output has increased by a factor of less than t. Labour and capital inputs may have doubled, but output has less than doubled. Output increases less than proportionately. This is known as a situation of decreasing returns to scale. Stated differently, the production function is homogeneous of degree less than one.

Please appreciate that a production function need not exhibit the same sort of returns to scale uniformly. In other words, the same production function can have stretches of increasing returns to scale, stretches of constant returns to scale and stretches of decreasing returns to scale.

Consider the Cobb-Douglas production function $Q = A K^a L^b$. What sort of returns to scale does this have? It is simple to check that for this production function, returns to scale will be given by the expression $a + b$. If $a + b > 1$, one will have increasing returns to scale. If $a + b = 1$, one will have constant returns to scale. And if $a + b < 1$, one will have decreasing returns to scale,

The restricted Cobb-Douglas production function $Q = A K^a L^{1-a}$ has constant returns to scale. It is restricted in the sense that constant returns to scale have been assumed. No such assumption characterizes the unrestricted Cobb-Douglas production function.

Perhaps a diagram will help to further explain the concept of returns to scale. Take a look at Figure 2. The figure has three panels. The first panel depicts increasing returns to scale, the second constant returns to scale and the third decreasing returns to scale. Take the first panel first. Originally, 10 units of K and 10 units of L are used to produce 100 units of Q. If 20 units of K and 20 units of L are used instead, the corresponding isoquant must have an output level of more than 200 units, if increasing returns to scale exist. Similarly, if 30 units of K and 30 units of L are used, the corresponding isoquant must have an output level of more than 300 units. If you have understood the depiction of increasing returns to scale, the depictions of constant returns to scale and decreasing returns to scale in the other two panels should be self-explanatory.

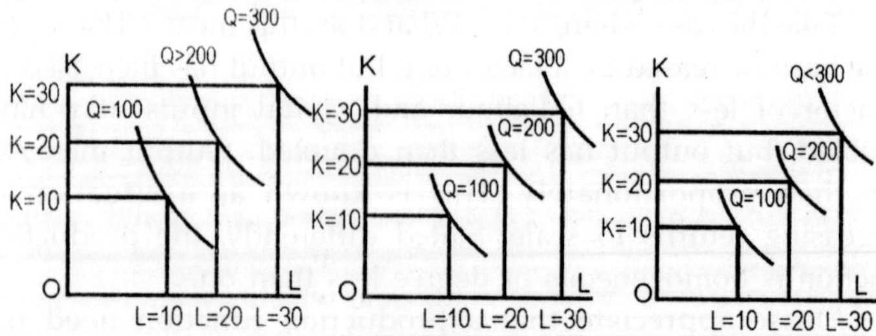

FIG. 4

There is another way to represent returns to scale. The two representations amount to the same thing, the second representation is displayed in Figure 5. In the first representation, we started with a given level of inputs, multiplied them by a given factor, and asked how much the output was going to be. For instance, under increasing returns to scale, with L = 20 and K = 20, Q was more than 200. Let us stick to increasing returns to scale, the first panel of Figure 5. In the second representation, we start with a given level of output (Q=100), multiply this by a factor (Q=200), and ask how much of inputs are required. Since this is increasing returns to scale, obviously the amount of K and L needed will be less than 20. Is the first panel of Figure 5 clear now? To put it differently, under increasing returns to scale, progressive isoquants (Q=100, 200, 300 and so on) tend to move closer together. As the second panel shows, under constant returns to scale, progressive isoquants are evenly spaced out. And under decreasing returns to scale, progressive isoquants are further and further apart.

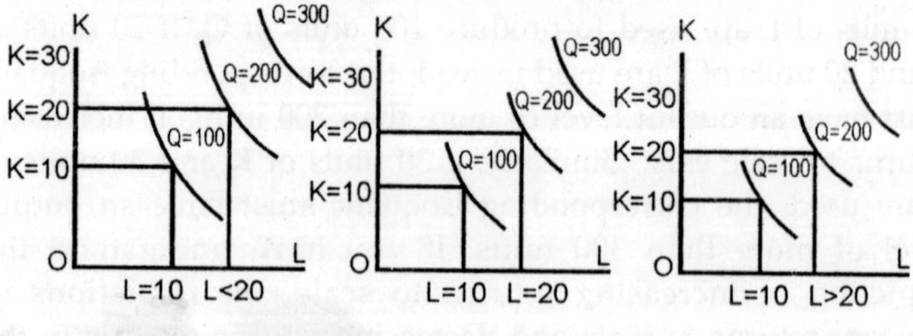

FIG. 5

ECONOMIES OF SCALE

Marshall classified the economies of large-scale production into two types—External Economies and Internal Economies.

External Economies: External Economies are available to all the firms in an industry, e.g., the construction of a railway-line in a certain region which would reduce transport cost for all the firms, the discovery of a new machine which can be purchased by all the firms, the emergence of repair industries, rise of industrialists utilising by-products, and the establishment of special technical schools for training skilled labour as research institutes etc. These economies arise from the expansion in the size of an industry, involving an increase in the number and size of the firms engaged in it.

Internal Economies: Internal Economies are the economies which are available to a particular firm and give it an advantage over other firms engaged in the industry. Internal economies arise from the expansion of the size of a particular firm. From the managerial point of view, internal economies are more important as they can be affected by managerial decisions of an individual firm to change its size or scale or otherwise.

QUESTIONS

1. Describe in brief the Production Analysis.
2. What is Production Function? Explain it in detail.
3. What are Returns to Scale?
4. Briefly explain about Marginal Rate of Technical Substitution.
5. What do you know about Economies of Scale?

CHAPTER

6

Cost Theory

Introduction: To produce a commodity, every firm employs factors of productions (Land, labor, capital) and pay them factor payments (Rent, Wages, Interest). All these factor payments are included in the cost of production. The type of cost concept used in a certain situation depends upon the business decisions that the management makes. An accountant will take into account only the payments and charges made by the manager to the suppliers of different productive inputs. But for the managerial economist the cost in a somewhat different form. The cost estimates made by conventional financial accounting are not appropriate for all managerial uses.

Therefore, it is essential to have a complete understanding of different cost concepts for clear business thinking. One way of getting clear-cut distinctions among different notions of cost is to up the many alternative bases of classifying costs and display the relevant set of each for various types of problems. The very objective of defining and distinguishing concepts of cost is to scout the fallacy that cost estimates produced by conventional financial accounting are appropriate for all managerial uses. Actually, they serve only the purpose of financial accounting. There is another objective, namely different business problems call for different types of costs. Cost concepts differ because of differences in view point. Various combinations of cost ingredients are significant for different types of management problems. Disparities take place from deletions, from additions, from recombination of elements, from price level adjustments and from the introduction of measurements which do not appear anywhere in the accounting records. Various cost concepts explained in our study are : Incremental costs vs. sunk costs, Actual cost and opportunity costs, Past vs. future costs, Short run vs. long run costs, Variable and constant costs or fixed costs, Traceable and common costs (direct and indirect cost), Historical and Replacement costs, Past and future costs.

Cost Function: Cost function describe the Functional Relationship between cost and Output

C= f(Q)

C = Cost of Production
F = Function
Q = Output

According to Prof Koutsoyannis states "Cost functions are derived functions. They derived from the production function"

CLASSIFICATION OF COST

(1) Money Costs

Money cost refers to the cost which is incurred by the producer in monetary terms.

According to *Prof Hanson* "The money cost of producing a certain output of a commodity is the sum of all the payments to the factors of production engaged in the production of that commodity"

Money cost includes Depreciation and Obsolesces charges, Wages and salaries, Cost of machinery, Interest on capital, Insurance capital, Transport cost etc.

(2) Explicit and Implicit Cost

(a) *Explicit cost:*Explicit cost includes all those expenses which are incurred to engage the outside factors of production. They are paid to outsiders like wages paid to labour, rent paid to land, interest paid to capital etc. They are also called "Absolute costs" or "Outlay cost" or "actual cost" or "Accounting cost" or "Historical cost"

According to *Leftwitch* "Explicit costs are those cash payments which firm makes to outsiders for their services and goods"

(b) *Implicit costs*: Implicit cost is the cost of an entrepreneur's own factors of production. They are paid by entrepreneur to him for using his own factors of production like rent for using own land, wages paid to himself, interest paid for using own capital. They are also called "Implied cost" or "Unnoticed cost"

According to *Leftwitch,* "Implicit costs are costs of self-owned and self-employed resources"

(3) Incremental cost and Sunk cost

(a) *Incremental cost :* Incremental costs are the added costs of a change in the level of production or the nature of activity. It may be, adding a new product, or changing distribution channel, or adding new machinery, etc. It seems to be resemble to marginal cost, but it is not marginal cost. Marginal cost implies the cost on the added unit of output.

(b) *Sunk costs*: Sunk costsare those costs which cannot be altered in any way. Sunk costs are the costs which have already been incurred. For instance, cost incurred in constructing a factory. When the factory building is constructed, cost has already been incurred. The building has to be used for which originally envisaged. It cannot be altered when operations are increased or decreased. Investment on machinery is an example of sunk cost.

The distinction between the sunk cost and the incremental cost is very significant in evaluating tile alternatives. Incremental cost will be different in the case of varied alternatives.

Hence, incremental cost is relevant to the management in decision-making. Sunk costs will remain the same irrespective of the alternative selected. The only costs that matter for the decision are the added costs. Each alternative marketing programme has its own set of incremental costs for equipment, delivery men, executive time and so forth. These are outlays that are relevant to the decision on the type of selling job to undertake as well as to the prior decision whether market expansion is preferable to increased advertising or new products. To the extent the existing operations are unaffected various programmes have the same types of sunk costs Incremental costs change.

(4) Actual Cost and Opportunity Cost

(a) *Actual costs*: Actual Costs are those costs that involve financial-expenditure incurred for acquiring inputs for producing a commodity. These expenditures are recorded in the books of accounts of the firm. The expenditure are wages paid, payment made for the purchase of raw materials, machinery, etc. These costs are known as actual costs or outlay costs.

(b) *Opportunity cost*: Opportunity cost is not the actual expenditure, but it is the revenue earned by employing that good or service in some other alternative uses. Opportunity cost is the cost of producing any commodity which is the next best alternative good that is sacrificed. Opportunity cost may also be called alternative cost. For instance, the inputs which are used for manufacturing a car may also be utilized in the production of a military equipment. Therefore, the opportunity cost of the production of a car is the output of the military equipment foregone or sacrificed, which could have been produced with the same amount of inputs, that have gone into making a car. Let us take another instance. A farmer who is producing paddy can also produce sugarcane with the same factors. Therefore, the opportunity cost of one quintal of paddy is the amount of sugarcane given up. Two points must be noted in the definition of opportunity cost. Firstly, the opportunity cost of any commodity is only the next best alternative foregone. Secondly, the next best alternative commodity could be produced with the same value of the factors, which are more or less the same. In managerial decision making, opportunity cost concept is very potent. The economic importance of opportunity cost is as under:

It helps in determining relative prices of factor inputs at different places. For instance, there are 100 building sites in a remote village and one building site in the heart of a city like Delhi, Chennai, etc. That one building site in the heart of Delhi is equal to 100 sites in a far off village. The opportunity cost of one site in the heart of the city is 100 sites of the villages which are foregone. In other words, opportunity cost is-the imputed cost. According to Joel Dean in business problems, the message of opportunity cost is that it is dangerous to confine cost knowledge to what the firm is doing. What the firm is not doing is frequently the critical cost consideration which is perilous but easy to ignore. Imputed costs which are not actually incurred but would have been incurred in the absence of employment of self-owned factors. In the case of a factory, where the owner is the manager, the cost of managerial function is ignored. It helps in determining the remuneration to service. For instance, a mechanical engineer is drawing a salary of Rs. 10,000 in a steel factory. It helps the manager to decide what he should produce in the factory. He can produce electric motors and telephone equipment. The opportunity cost of one electric motor is 20 telephones. The market price of one electric motor is Rs. 5,000 and the price of telephone is Rs. 200. Then it is profitable to produce electric motors.

CONCEPT OF OPPORTUNITY COST : ITS IMPORTANCE

When the company, with its limited resources, wants to make a choice between another layer of advertising in the established markets or some fundamental changes in the product line, it has to examine the opportunity costs of these two proposals. The profit that could be otherwise earned in these alternatives is the opportunity cost of using the funds. If the prospective earning from the expansion is less than the alternative earnings, there is a real loss. But the alternative earnings or opportunity costs can only be determined by comparing projected cash outlay costs and revenues which are thus the basic data for decision.

(I) Private and Social Cost

This is another important type of costs. This classification is one of the recent developed concept but of a great concern in the present time.

Private Cost: Private Cost are actual cost paid or incurred by the entrepreneur to purchase goods or services from the market. It includes both explicit and implicit costs. It is the total cost of the project to its entrepreneur.

Social Cost: This is the cost that bears by the society. This is a external cost that effect the whole society. Or in simple words the effect of the project on the different sections of society is a social cost. This is not paid by the entrepreneur but use of the common public and society treasures. E.g. Pollution, use of road drainage system etc.

(2) Past and Future Costs

(a) *Past costs* : Past Cost are those actual costs which have been incurred in the past. These costs are mentioned in the financial accounts.

(b) *Future costs* : Future costs are those costs which are to be incurred in the near future. This is only a forecast. Future costs matter for managerial decisions since, the management can evaluate the desirability of that expenditure.

Since the past costs are costs that have already been incurred, there is no scope for managerial decision. If the management finds out that the past costs are excessive, it cannot do anything to rectify it now. In the case of future costs, if the management considers them very high, it can either reduce them or postpone the use of them. For price policy, it is the future cost than the past cost that is needed. To the extent that costs are relevant at all, it is expectations that govern policy decisions and that should also guide the determination of specific prices. Though the future is not certain, it is essential to make explicit forecasts of future costs.

(3) Historical and Replacement Costs

Historical Cost is the actual cost incurred at the time of the purchase of machinery while, replacement cost is the cost which will have to be, incurred if machinery is purchased in place of the old machinery. The two costs differ because of the differences in prices during that period. For instance, a machine purchased in 1990 for Rs. 6 lakhs was Rs. 8 lakhs in 1995. For this, it may be concluded that replacement cost was higher than historical cost. During the period of substantial price changes, historical cost is a poor indicator of actual cost.

(4) Short Run vs Long Run Costs

Short run and long run cost is a time based classification of the cost. Short Cost are those costs which are associated with variation in the use of fixed plant or other facilities, whereas long run costs encompass changes in the size and kind of plant. Short run cost is relevant when a firm has to decide whether or not to produce more or less with the given plant and equipment. If the firm decides to expand the capacity of the plant, it must examine the long run cost. Long run cost is useful in making investment decisions. Land and Building, Plant and Machinery are some example of the fixed cost, as they can not be change immediately with the change in number of product produce. Where as salary, raw material, electricity are some of short run cost.

THEORIES OF COST

(a) Traditional Theory
(b) Modern Theory

Traditional Theory: Traditional Cost theory divides cost into two parts on the basis of time period i.e Short run cost and Long Run cost.

Short Run: ShortRunrefers to the time period in which certain factors of production are fixed and others are variable. In short run cost can be divided into three types (1) Total Cost (2) Marginal Cost (3) Average Cost

(1) *Total Cost: Total Cost* Refers to the all total money cost incurred by entrepreneur in process of production.

According to Dooley" Total cost of production is the sum of expenditure incurred in producing a given volume of output.

TC = TFC + TVC
TC = Total Cost
TFC = Total Fixed Cost
TVC = Total Variable Cost

Fixed and Variable Costs

Fixed Cost: Fixed cost refers to the cost which is fixed at the various level of production e.g. Rent of a building and land, Wages of permanent employees etc. They are also called Supplementary cost, Indirect cost, overhead cost.

According to Anatol Murad "Fixed cost are cost which do not change with change in the quantity of output".

Variable Cost : Variable cost refers to the cost which varies with level of production. The curve cost starts from origin. E.g. like wages, raw material, electricity charges etc. It is also called direct cost, Special cost.

According to Dooley "Variable cost are those cost which may vary as level of output varies".

There are some inputs which can be readily adjusted to the changes in the level of the output. Thus, a firm can soon employ labour and rawmaterial inputs without any delay if it wants to expand the output. Thus, labour, raw materials are the inputs which can be soon varied which change the quantity of the output. Such factors are known as variable factors. On the other hand, there are factors like capital equipment, factory buildings. and top management cannot be readily varied, with the change in output. It requires more time to make variations in them. It takes time to expand the factory building. Likewise, it takes more time to manufacture the machinery. These factors are known as fixed factors. The distinctions between fixed and variable costs is not a watertight one it is very difficult to decide which is fixed and which is variable at a situation.

Again, it may be noted that the variability of costs is regarding output and not to the time factor though in the long run, all costs tend to be variable. What is fixed at one level of output may vary at another level output. In between the fixed and variable costs, there are semi-variable costs which vary but not at the same rate by which production increases or decreases. For instance, a salesman may get a monthly salary as well as commission. Monthly salary is treated as fixed while commission is treated as variable cost, for it varies with the output. The distinction between fixed and variable costs is significant in forecasting the effect of short run changes in the volume upon costs and profits.

Difference between Fixed and Variable Cost

Short Run Fixed Cost and Variable Cost : The cost of production may be analysed from another stand point. Some costs vary more or less proportionately with the output while others are fixed and do not vary with the output. The former is known as prime costs while the latter is known as supplementary costs. The supplemented fixed costs are incurred even though production has been stopped temporarily. For instance, rent of the factory building, interests on capital invested on machinery, salary to the inevitable staff, etc. The prime costs on the other hand are variable costs. Variable costs vary with the output. They are incurred only when the factory is at work. Total cost is obtained by adding total fixed cost and total variable cost. Short run cost curves are displayed in the following diagram.

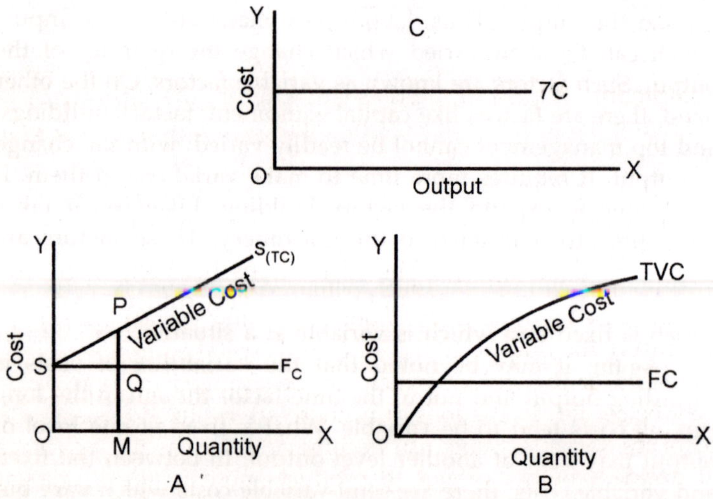

FIG. I

Diagram C displays the fixed cost curve. This is a straight line parallel to OX axis. This means that the total fixed cost remains constant whatever the level of output. Diagram B displays the total variable cost curve. TVC curve rises upward showing thereby, as the output is increased, the total variable cost (TVC) also rises. TVC starts from the origin which displays when the output is zero, the total variable cost also is zero. Diagram A displays the total cost curve, which is the aggregation of diagram C and B. TC indicates total fixed cost and total variable cost. For zero output, the fixed cost is OS and there is no variable cost. For OM output, the fixed cost is MQ = OS, while the variable cost is PQ and the total cost is MP. For zero output, the total cost is OS. As output rises, the total cost curve also rises. SS is displayed as the total cost curve.

Short Run and Long Run Costs: Traditional theory distinguishes between short run and long run. Short run is defined as a period in which the firm can vary its output by varying only the amount of variable factors like labour and raw-materials. In the short run, the quantifies of fixed factors such as capital equipment, buildings, top management cannot be varied. In other words in the short run, the firm cannot build a new plant or abandon an old plant. If the firm wants to increase production, it can do so only by increasing labour and raw material inputs. It has to overwork the existing capital equipment. It cannot increase output in the short run by enlarging the size of the existing plant or building a new plant of a large size.

Thus, short run is a period of time in which only quantities of the variable factors can be increased while fixed factors remain constant. Long run is defined as a period in which quantities of all factors can be increased. It implies that the firm can increase the quantities of both fixed and variable factors for increasing the output. In the long run, capital equipment can be increased or the size of which can be changed or a new plant may be set up. In the long run, there are no fixed costs, but all costs are variable. Short run becomes relevant when a firm has to decide whether or not to produce more in the immediate future. In this case, there is no need for setting up of a new plant. The firm manages with the given plant itself. Long run costs become relevant when the firm has to decide whether to establish a new plant. Long run costs help the businessman in running the best scale of plant or best size of the firm for his purposes.

Average Fixed Cost and Average Variable Cost : Average fixed cost is the total fixed costs divided by the number of units of output produced. Graphically, total fixed cost is displayed by a straight line parallel to OX axis. As output rises, the average fixed cost also decreases. AFC falls steadily as output rises. AFC curve slopes downwards throughout the length. For instance, a firm starts with a fixed cost of Rs. 50,000. When the output includes 100 units, AFC will be Rs. 500. When the output rises to 200 units, the AFC will be Rs. 250. When the output rises to 400 units, the AFC will be Rs. 125. Since the total fixed cost is a constant quantity, the average fixed cost will steadily fall as output rises.

Average variable cost is the total variable cost divided by the number of units of output produced. The average variable cost is the variable cost per unit of output. The average variable cost will usually fall as output rises from zerc to normal capacity output because of increasing returns. But, beyond the normal capacity output, the average cost vill rise steeply because of the operation of dimishing returns. The average fixed cost and average variable cost curves are displayed below :

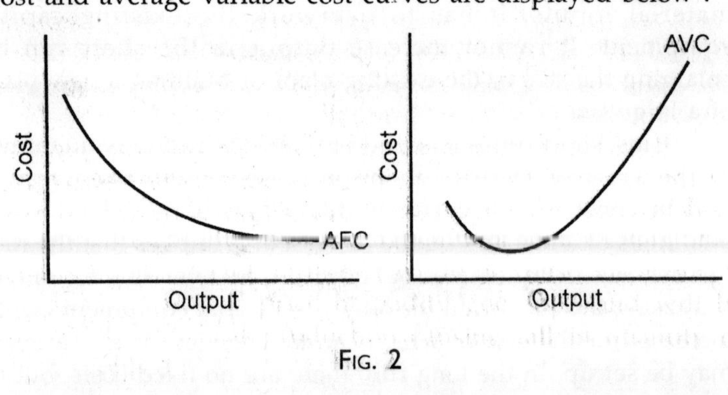

FIG. 2

Average Total Cost and Marginal Cost : The average total cost or what is known as average cost is, total cost divided by the number of units of the product. Average total cost is realised by adding average fixed cost and average variable cost. This can be proved as under:

ATC = Since TC = TVC + TFC
Therefore, ATC =
= AVC + AFC

Average cost is also known as unit cost, since it is the cost per unit of output. It follows from the above that the behaviour of ATC depends upon the behaviour of AFC and AVC curves. In the beginning, both the AVC and AFC curves fall. Then, the ATC curve also falls sharply in the beginning. When AVC curve begins rising, though AFC curve is falling, the ATC curve begins to rise. Afterwards, ATC rises steeply. Therefore, ATC curve falls first, reaches the minimum and rises afterwards. The ATC curve is thus U shaped. The U shape of both AVC and AFC reflects the law of variable proportions.

Marginal Cost : The concept of marginal cost is very significant in economic analysis. Marginal cost is the addition to the total cost caused by producing one more unit of the output. In other words, marginal cost is the addition to the total cost of producing n units instead of n-1 units (i.e., one less) where n given number. In symbolic language, it is stated as MC-TCn-1TCn-1 Suppose the production of 100 units of a product costs Rs. 1,000. If the increase in production to 101 units raises the total cost to Rs. 1,025, then the marginal cost of 101th unit of output is Rs. 25 (1025-1000 = 25). Marginal cost is derived from the total costs of two successive units. Marginal cost of any product closely follows the average cost of the product. When the average cost is falling, marginal cost is below it. When the average cost is rising, marginal cost rises above it more sharply than the average variable cost. The following diagram displays the average cost and marginal cost curves. Marginal cost is independent of the fixed cost. Since fixed cost does not change

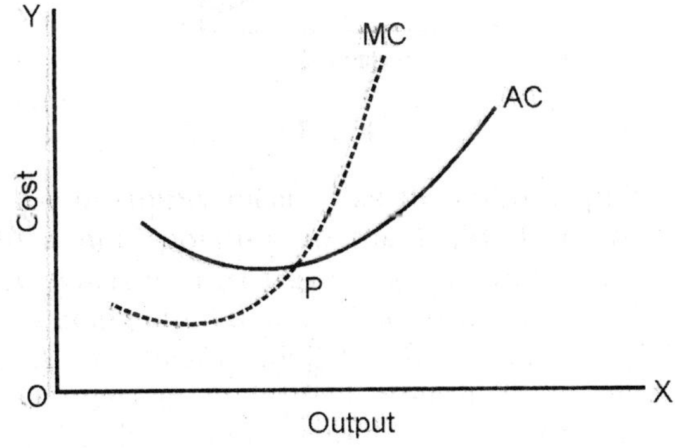

FIG. 3

with output, it then follows the average variable cost. It should be noted that the marginal cost of production is intimately related to the marginal product of the variable factor. Marginal cost varies inversely with the marginal product of the variable factor. The shape of the marginal cost is determined by the law of variable proportion, i.e., the behaviour of the marginal product of the variable factor.

Marginal cost concept, when taken with marginal revenue concept, helps the management in rational decision taking.

Through the illustration of the following diagram the cost-output relationships can be explained:

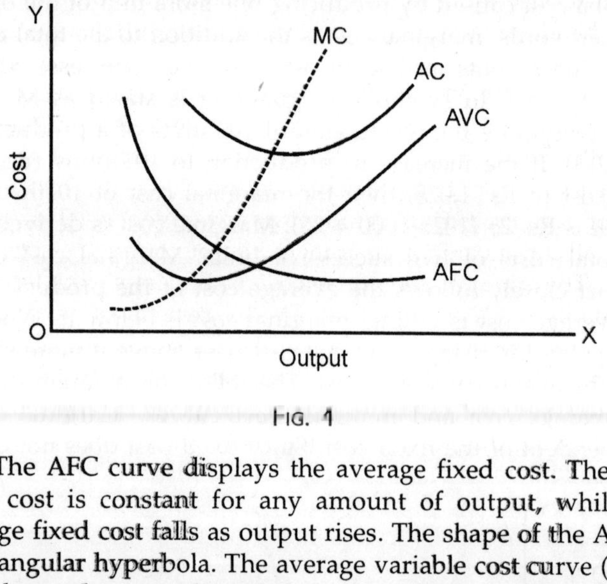

FIG. 1

The AFC curve displays the average fixed cost. The total fixed cost is constant for any amount of output, while the average fixed cost falls as output rises. The shape of the AFC is a rectangular hyperbola. The average variable cost curve (AVC) first slopes downwards and then rises slowly as output rises. The ATC curve displays the average total cost. Since ATC is the sum total of average fixed cost and the average variable cost, it is related to downward sloping of ATC and upward rising of the AVC. The MC curve displays that the marginal cost curve intersects both AVC and ATC curves at their lowest points. If marginal cost is less than average cost, it pulls average cost down. If MC is greater than AC, it will push up AC. If MC is equal to AC, equilibrium is restored. Therefore, MC will intersect AC at its lowest point.

Long Run Cost Output Relationship and Cost Curve: The long run is a period of time during which the firm can vary all its inputs. In the short run, some inputs are fixed, while in the long run, none of the factors are fixed. All are varied in order to increase the output. The long run production function has no fixed factors and the firm-has no fixed costs in the long run. It is conventional to regard the size or scale of plant as a typical fixed input.

The term plant implies input size of the plant which is fixed and it cannot be increased or decreased. That means, one cannot change the size of the capital equipment in the short period if one wants to increase or decrease the output. On the other hand, long run is a period of time sufficiently long to allow the changes in plant, that is, in capital equipment, machinery, land, etc. In the short run, the firm is tied with a given plant, but in the long run, the firm moves from one plant to another. If the firm wants to increase the output, it can make a large plant. The long run cost of production is the least feasible cost of combination of producing any given level of output when all inputs are variable including of course the size of the plant. The long run average cost is the long run total cost divided by the level of output. The long run average cost curve depicts the least feasible average cost for producing all feasible level of output. To derive the long run average cost curve, we have to take three short run average cost curves as displayed in the following diagram. The three short run average cost curves are also known as plant curves, and the three short run average cost curves display three different scales of production or three varied sizes of plants. In the short run, the firm is operating on any short run average cost curves given the size of output. For each of these scales, there is an optimum output. The producer would like to produce the optimum output, because his average cost is the least cost at that point. If the demand for the product increases, he wants to produce more by increasing the variable inputs. But, in the long run, the firm can choose among the three feasible sizes of plant as depicted by short run average cost curves. In the long run, the firm will examine which size of the plant or short run average curve is profitable to produce the given output at the minimum feasible cost.

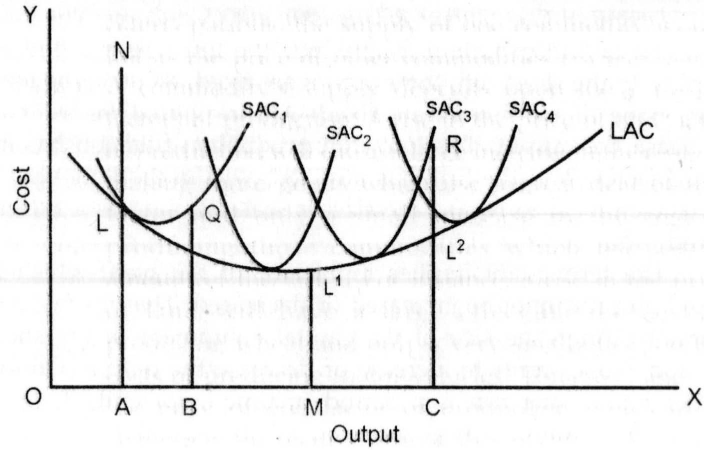

FIG. 5

In the above diagram, there are three feasible short run average cost curves depicting three different sizes of plant or scale of production. SAC_1, SAC_2, SAC_3 are short run average cost curves or three different plant sizes. The firm is producing under short term average cost curve SAC^1. The firm is producing OB output at lower cost. If it produces OA output, the average cost (AL) is lower than OB output. If it produces the same output in SAC_2 curve, it costs AN. Since AL is smaller than AN, the firm will produce with SAC^1 curve. Similarly, all other output levels up to OB can be produced with the smaller plant size of SAC^1 rather than SAC^1. In the long run, the firm will be producing OB output in the SAC^1 size of the plant. It will be seen that if more output could be produced in SAC_2, the average cost will be lower than SAC_1. If the output OM is produced, the average cost will be OL1, which is taken to be the lowest in the SAC_2 plant size. If the firm wants to increase output up to OC, it incurs CR cost which is higher than the cost of SAC_3 size. If it produces OC output, at SAC_3 plant size, the average cost CL_2 is lower than CR on the SAC_2 size. Therefore, for output larger than OC, the firm will employ a plant size corresponding to the short run average cost curve SAC_2. If the tangents of all the short run cost curves are added, a long run average cost is derived. This will be the LAC. It is also U shaped and it will be flatter than the short run average cost curves. The longer the period to which the curve relates, the less pronounced will be the U shape of LAC curve. Economists generally call this curve as envelope since it envelopes all the short run average cost curves. It is also known as the planning curve of the firm. The tendency for the long run average cost to fall as the firm expands its scale of operations is a reflection of cost economies available with the increase in size, while the ultimate rise in the long run cost curve is largely because of the setting up of the diseconomies of scale. It is significant to note that the long run average cost curve (LAC) is not tangent to the minimum points of the short run average cost curves. When the long run average cost curve is declining that is for the output less than OM, it is tangent to the falling portion of the short run average cost curve. This implies that if there is any output smaller than OM, it will not pay to operate the plant at the minimum average cost. If the output is produced at the lowest point of the short run cost curve, it means the average cost is higher in the short run than in the long run. If the firm expands the size to SAC_2 then the LAC is tangent to its lowest point. When the long run average cost is rising, it will be tangent to the rising portion of the short run average cost curve (SAC_3). This implies that the output larger than OM is produced more cheaply by constructing a plant With a given optimal capacity and operating it to produce larger than its capacity, i.e., using it to produce at more than its minimum unit cost of Production.

Importance of Long Run Average Cost curve : Long run average cost curve generally known as 'the planning curve'. It is because it helps a firm to plan to produce any output by choosing a plant on the long run average cost curve. The long run average cost curve reveals to the firm how large a plant should be for producing a certain output at the least cost. Thus, while making decisions regarding the choice of a plant, the firm has to look at its long run average cost curve enveloping a family of plant curves (short run cost curves). The long run average cost curve thus helps the firm to select the best size of the plant.

Optimum Scale (Plant)-Optimum Output-Optimum Firm : Optimum scale (plant) is the lowest scale of enterprise. It is not essentially the most profitable scale. In various cases, the market may not be big enough to absorb the whole output produced at the optimum scale. In such cases, a firm is needed to operate at lower costs per unit with a small plant than will a larger plant using only partial capacity. There are instances where firms to attain dominance, may over expand beyond the optimum scale disregarding profit.

Sometimes, out of the fear of the government action, the firm may not expand to reach the optimum point. In the interest of the economy, it is useful for the firm not to expand beyond the optimum size. The plant is said to be of optimum size, when it operates at the point of its minimum average cost of production. It is the plant, the minimum point of its whose short run average cost curve coincides with the minimum point of the long run average cost curve. In the above diagram, SA_2 is operated at its minimum cost of production for producing OM output. This plant size is being utilised to its full capacity to produce optimum output. Any size of the plant other than SAC_2 will be producing at higher average cost. In the diagram, OM is the output. It is optimum because it is the least cost output. If the output is smaller or bigger than OM, the cost of production is more than what it is at OM output. The firm is said to be optimum when it produces optimum output, i.e., the least cost output with the optimum plant. The optimum firm can also be defined as the firm which produces at the minimum point of the long run average cost curve. The optimum size of the firm varies a great deal in different industries. In agriculture, and extractive industries like mining, optimum size is comparatively small. That is, the minimum point of the long run average cost curve is reached at a relatively small output. On the other hand, optimum size of the firm in steel industry, automobile industry other heavy industries and public utilities, is comparatively very large, i.e., a minimum point of their long run average cost curve is reached at a relatively very large output.

COST ESTIMATION

There are three kinds of methods of estimating production. They are Engineering method, Statistical method and Accounting method. The Engineering method of cost estimation depends upon the knowledge of physical relationships.

Generally, the engineering estimate is built up in terms of physical units, like man-hours, and quantity of materials. In the Statistical method of cost estimation, statistical techniques are used. The objective is to find a functional relationship between changes in costs and the factors upon which the costs depend like output, rates, sales quantity, etc. Statistical method-has the advantage of isolating fixed cost elements from the total cost.

The Accounting method is based on historical data found in the account books of the firm. Its goal is to find the relationship between output levels and cost for similar cases to that for which the present estimate is needed. In this method, costs are divided into fixed, variable and semi-variable cost. Fixed costs are those which the accounts display to be the same in the monthly total regardless of the output rate. Variable costs are those which the accounts display to vary in direct proportion to the level of output. Semi-variable costs are neither perfectly variable nor absolutely fixed in relation to output. They change in the same direction as volume but not in direct proportion thereto. For instance, electricity bills often include both a fixed charge and a charge based on consumption. The benefit of accounting method is that it is very simple. It must be noted that the future may not be like the past records of the firm. Therefore, this method is used in cost estimation.

COST AWARENESS

The ability of the firm to earn sustained profits, the long run prosperity of the firm. The profits depend upon the selling price of the product and the cost of production of the product. Very often, the firm is not in a position to dictate the price of the product to the market. But, it has all the feasibility of controlling the cost.

The firm is needed to aim at doing at the minimum cost. If the firm wants to produce a certain amount of output during a given period, control must be exerted to ensure that the given output is produced at the minimum cost. This aspect of management is known as cost awareness. Cost awareness by management is a search for a better and efficient way of completing the production of the product. It means bringing down the cost of production as much as feasible. There are two ways of minimising cost : (1) Reduction in specific expenses; (2) Efficient use of the money spent. Cost control involves keeping the costs down than bringing the cost down. There is more profit in cost control when the business is good than when business is bad. Cost control helps a firm to improve its profitability and competitiveness. In the absence of control, despite large and increasing business, profits are bound to be reduced. A big sale will not indicate big profit. An increase in sales may create a false sense of prosperity while behind the scene increasing costs will eat up profits. Therefore, cost management is indispensable for stability of a firm.

Cost management tools : A control of any type depends upon comparing actual performance with some pre-determined criterion. The two criteria which are in use today are: (1) Standard cost and (2) Budgets.

Standard Costs: The techniques of standard costing has been developed to establish standards of performance for producing goods and services. These standards serve as a goal for attainment and basis of comparison with actual cost. The standard cost is a predetermined cost which determines what each product or service should cost under given situations.

Standard, costing starts with an estimate of what a product ought to cost during a future period, given reasonably efficient working. Once the standard costs have been worked out, then actual costs for the products have to be compared with them. If there is any adverse difference, cost control could be enforced. Standard costing makes it feasible to isolate the causes which have contributed to high costs. Standard cost need not be ideal cost or the best cost under ideal conditions, but a cost could be reached if it were operated efficiently. Standard cost is not rigid but can be revised from time to time. Standard costs provide a yardstick against what actual costs may be measured. Since standard cost is calculated under efficient operating situations, it is a good yardstick for measuring efficiency. If the standard cost is below the actual cost, there is a need for immediate investigation. Standard costs provide a valuable aid to management in determining pricing policies.

Budgets: A budget is a pre-determined statement of management policy during a given period which provides a standard for comparison with the results actually achieved.

Budgetary Control is a system of controlling costs which includes the preparation of budgets, coordinating the departments and establishing responsibilities and comparing actual performance with the budgeted one. Estimated cost of future operations is brought into use as standard against which actual costs are compared. Estimated future costs are determined from the past experience. Estimated costs are better than historical costs for it takes into consideration future development. In a business of rapidly changing situations, estimated costs are feasible for cost control purposes. Intangible operations like research and development, morale building, public relations, etc., are not subject to control by any other standard except estimated cost. Cost control even with budgets and standard cost remains unconvincing as they are not cent percent accurate. If the standards are set, they have to be adhered strictly. But normally, such adherence is not to be seen anywhere. However, a realistic standard has to be set up and managers must be encouraged to achieve them. For decision taking purposes, cost information is essential. If the cost information is given in an arbitrary way, then this misleads the managers. Therefore, realistic cost information is to be supplied to the managers to take timely action.

Cost Benefit Analysis : It is a method for assessing the desirability of projects when it is essential to take both a long and a wide view of the repercussions of a particular programme expenditure or policy change. Cost benefit analysis is being used in government undertakings in order to study the economic consequence of a project. It seeks to measure all economic imports of the project, direct as well as the side effects. As in the case of collective goods like defence, public health measures, educational facilities, it is not feasible to use market price to evaluate their benefits. These are not quantifiable and hence cannot be valued in any market sense.

Discount Rate : There is the question of ascertaining the present value of the future costs and benefits. This is known as discounting process. The rate of discount is very significant, because a higher rate may entirely switch investment priorities. Baumol has preferred the opportunity cost criterion for estimating social discount rate. This approach is based on the fact that resources invested in one sector might be withdrawn from that sector and invested elsewhere, which yields a higher return. For instance, if the resource can earn 10 percent in one sector, it should not be transferred to another sector unless it earns more than 10 percent.

IMPORTANT CONSTRAINTS

There are various kinds of constraints such as legal, physical, distributional and budgetary constraints. The most common physical constraint is the production function which relates to physical inputs and outputs of a project. This directly enters into the calculation of costs and benefits. If the supply of one input is inelastic, regulated pricing is to be made.

There are administrative and distributional constraints like constraints in the income distribution, etc. It is not feasible to make the gainers compensates the losers. The budgetary constraint is that the project should be completed within the budget allotment. The chief objective of the cost-benefit analysis is to select the project for investment or lay down the investment criteria. Where no projects are inter-dependent or mutually exclusive and where there are no constraints, the projects which maximize the present value of total benefits less total costs are to be selected. In those projects where the present value of the benefits exceeds the present value of costs, they are supposed to be good projects. Further, in those projects where the rate of return exceeds the chosen rate of discount, they are considered to be good.

*Cost Effectiveness:*It is not feasible to apply cost benefit analysis in those governmental activities such as defense, environmental protection, income distribution, etc. Cost effectiveness analysis may be utilized as an alternative strategy. Cost benefit analysis asks the question: What is the money value of programme costs and benefits and do the benefits exceed the costs to justify undertaking the programme? Cost effectiveness asks the question: Given that some prespecified objective is to be reached, what are the costs of different alternative means for reaching that objective? Cost effectiveness analysis is similar to cost benefit analysis. But the former is used in defence programmes while the latter is used in the civilian sector. There are many programmes where the output is abstract and hence not easy to evaluate in money terms. One such programme is pollution control. It is not easy to measure the pollutions being emitted in big factories and by motor vehicles, but it is not easy to evaluate the social benefit derivable from different levels of discharge reduction. In evaluating the programme, the most significant task to do is to find out whether the goal has been achieved. If the goal is achieved from the cost incurred for running the project, then it is considered as beneficial. While selecting projects for investments out of a number of technically possible alternatives, the most significant consideration is to weigh their costs and benefits and to select those which maximise the differences between costs and benefits.

The costs include capital cost, cost of rawmaterial, rent, salaries, wages, etc. and benefits refer to returns obtained from the sale proceeds of the output. The aim is to maximise the present value of all benefits less that of all costs. The purpose of cost-benefit analysis is to indicate whether a particular industrial project is worth starting. If there are alternative projects for investment, a correct choice is to be made for this purpose. The cost benefit analysis is thus useful. The alternative projects differ in type and also need so many labourers, raw-materials and their quantity and capital equipment, the period needed for completion and also the resultant revenue from such investments. The differences affect costs and benefits of these projects. A selection of a project requires valuation of costs and benefits.

The common principles of cost benefit analysis involve the following issues. They are:

(i) What costs and benefits are to be considered.
(ii) The ways of evaluating the costs benefits of the projects.
(iii) The rate of interest to be charged for the gestation period.
(iv) The constraints that are to be faced.

In this regard, it is essential to distinguish between social costssocial returns and private costs-private returns. Social cost means the opportunity cost. Social costs and benefits are different from accounting costs and returns. 'The costs and the benefits of a project are the time streams of consumption foregone and provided by that project.' It is essential to find out the opportunity cost of different alternative investment opportunities when benefits of a project are reinvested. Some of the funds used for the project would otherwise have been invested or it has been rendered impossible to invest these funds in some other mutually exclusive investment projects, because the cost has been used here in the sense of opportunity cost.

Costs and Benefits : In such cost-benefit analysis, usually direct and supplementary costs and benefits are to be considered. When an investment is made, there will be production of a commodity and the investing firm gets the revenue. Besides it, society also derives benefit. For instance, when an investment is made on road building, besides the total tax revenue the organisation gets; which is the primary benefit, others like road side restaurants, gas refuelling stations generate individual incomes. These are secondary benefits. The total benefit is to be imputed. The benefit which causes in the form of changes in land value and rents to land-lords also count in the calculation of benefit.

Costs and Benefits Valuation : If in the valuation of costs and benefits, they are expressed in money terms, we have to make adjustments to the expected prices of future inputs and outputs in order to make allowance for the anticipated changes in the relative prices of the concerned items, but not for the expected in the general price level.

The expected changes in the level of output are also to be noted. Some corrections will be required for the distortions resulting from the market imperfections. Social costs of materials, machinery and equipment should be calculated like labour. In the case of a material like sand, stones, the only social cost of labour is the use of labour for collecting and digging, etc. In the case of imported machinery, social cost is higher than the private accounting cost.

Cost Control and Cost Reduction : The business organisations aim at producing the product at the minimum cost. This is essential in order to achieve the goal of profit maximisation. The success of financial management is judged by the action of the executive in controlling cost. Modern business is not only very complicated but also competitive. The business organisations are incurring a large number of costs, all of which go to the production cost. If the cost of production is increasing, the firm has to sell the product at a higher price. It is then that the competitive capacity of the firm comes into being. If the firm fails to take note of cost control, its very survival is threatened.

COST DETERMINANTS

There are so many factors on which the cost of production of goods and service depend. These factors may differ from firm to firm within an industry and from one industry to another. The significant cost determinants are as under:

Output Level : With the larger output, the greater will be the production cost. For there will be larger use of different factors of production who shall get larger payments. Thus, total cost varies directly with output.

Input Factors Prices : A rise in factor prices also increases total production cost. The different factors of production, viz., land, labour, capital and organization get rent, wages, interest and salary respectively as their reward. Naturally larger payments will have to be made to the factors of production when their prices go up. Thus, the cost of production varies directly with the prices of factors of production.

Factor Productivity : It implies the output per unit of that factor. The higher the productivity of a factor of production, the lower the cost per unit of the input factor. Thus, an increase in factor productivities would reduce the total production cost for producing a given output. Productivity and efficiency are synonymous. Factor efficiency can increase in various ways like increasing the machine speed, raising the number of hours per day and/or month the machine is operated, and so on. Given a certain output, an increase in efficiency brings down the total production costs.

Plant Size : Plant size is yet another significant cost determinant. Production costs are usually lower in case of bigger plants than in smaller plants. This is so due to economies of large scale production. Notably, with a bigger size, although initial fixed costs are high variable costs tend to be low compared with a small with sized plant.

Stability of Output : Stability of output also leads to savings in different types of hidden costs of Interruption and learning. Overall costs are generally lower where output is stable and constant over a period of time. Production by sudden breaks and disruption is bound to be costly.

Size of Lot : It also affects production costs. Lot size here means the size of a single production job. In cases where the installation costs of machinery are considerable, the economy of large lots is significant. Besides, if it is feasible to process a bigger lot at one time, the total cost of operation and thereby the unit cost will be lower compared with a process in which only smaller lot sizes are produced.

Diminishing Returns Law : If the law of diminishing returns is operating, the cost will display a tendency to rise. The reverse will be the case when the law of increasing returns operates.

Capacity Utilization Level : In the short run, level of capacity utilization determines the cost. This particularly affects the per unit fixed cost. Thus, with higher capacity utilization, fixed cost per unit of output is bound to be low.

Consideration of Period : If one considers the short period, the cost curve will rise steeply. However, in case of long period, cost would not increase that steeply.

Technology : It is a significant cost determinant. Technological progress or improvement leads to an increase in the efficiency or productivity of factors of production. This in turn leads to a reduction in the cost of production. In other words, cost varies inversely with technological progress. Also, most technological innovations aim at reducing costs. A knowledge of the relationship between cost and technological progress is inevitable to forecast the cost. The change in technology generally changes the equipment, the size of the plant and the plant flexibility to output changes. A forecast of technology is also inevitable for the purpose of tackling the problem of equipment replacement. Here one has to determine the degree of obsolescence of the old machine to be replaced.

Learning Effect : It implies that in several activities costs decline as the activity is repeated an increasing number of times. As workers and management become more familiar with a production process or a certain product, there will be cost reductions. If there are substantial learning effects, there will be firstmover advantages by virtue of being the first to undertake an activity as against late-comers.

Breadth of Product Range : Costs are determined by the breadth of product range. Such cost benefits can occur when the processing of different goods can share inputs or where distribution and promotion can take place jointly.

Degree of Vertical Integration : Cost benefits can be had by increasing the degree of vertical integration within the firm, moving closer to the final customer (forward vertical integration) or to sources of supply (backward vertical integration).

Geographical Situation : Costs may be affected by geographical situation when factor prices, tax regimes and government incentives vary from place to place.

Institutional Factors : Institutional factors such as unionisation, local content/indigenisation rules and tariffs also affect costs.

*Autocratic Firm's Policies:*Costs also depend upon a wide range of firm's discretionary policies. The instances are: Nature and design of the product being manufactured; Level of service provided to customers; Package of human resources policies adopted regarding pay, incentive schemes, employee benefits, training, etc.

QUESTIONS

1. What do you know about Cost Concept? What are its determinants?
2. Describe Short and Long Run Cost Function.
3. What are Cost Curves?

CHAPTER

7

Markets

Price Determination under Different Market Condition

FEATURES OF DIFFERENT MARKET STRUCTURES

Product's price determination is a very important managerial function. Price affects profits through its effect both on revenue and cost. Total profit means the difference between total revenue and total cost. Total revenue is the sale proceeds of the firm at a single price or at different prices. The quantity sold varies with the price and the total revenue depends upon the total volume of the output produced. If the producer sets a high price for the product, he cannot sell more of it and as such his profit also is reduced. If the producer sets a low price, he can sell more of it, but he cannot make much profit. Hence, pricing occupies a significant place in economic analysis. However, all firms are not able to set prices for their products. There are some firms which are price takers while others are price makers, depending upon the market situations they face. The knowledge of market structure which a firm is to operate is useful in understanding the nature and extent of maneuverability which the firm has in deciding about the price and the quantity of the products.

The Market : There are different market structures. Market forms are based on the degree of competition prevailing in the market. Broadly, the market forms are divided into two kinds, (a) Perfectly competitive market. (b) Imperfectly competitive market. Before we begin to study the characteristic of market structure, let us understand what we mean by market. Market in economics implies, a meeting place of buyers and sellers directly or indirectly. Cournot, a French Economist, defines market as "Economists understand by the term market not any particular market place in which things are bought and sold, but the whole of any region in which buyers and sellers are in such a free intercourse with each other that the prices of the same goods tend to equality easily and quickly."

As Jevons says, "The word market has been generalised so as to mean any body of persons who are in intimate business relations and carry on extensive transactions in any commodity."

Benham explains the term market as "any area which buyers and sellers of a commodity are in close touch with each other either directly or indirectly that the price obtainable in one part of the market affects the prices paid in other part. 'Ely observes', market "as the general field within which the forces determining the price of particular product operate.

For Stonier and Hague the term market is "any organisation whereby buyers and sellers of goods are kept in close watch with each other... There is no need for a market to be in a single building... The only inevitable for a market is that all buyers and sellers should be in constant touch with each other either because they are in the same building or because they are able to talk to each other by telephone at a moment's notice."

If we go through the above definitions, we find that a market comprises of the following components:

Consumers : The product's buyers are known as consumers. The buyers of a product are identified by means of income, need, etc. If there are high income groups and they are concerned with trade and commerce or higher government administration, they need luxuries like motor cars, VCRs etc.

Sellers : In the market there should be manufacturers of a product. There must be industries manufacturing motor cars in a country. They form sellers in the market.

A Commodity : A market implies the buying and selling of a commodity. If there is no commodity, the market will not exist. Each commodity has a separate market, in the sense that every commodity has a separate set of buyers and sellers.

A Price : If the commodity is to be bought and sold, there must be a price for the product. The exchange of the product between buyers and sellers occur at a certain place. Thus, all the four components constitute a market.

MARKET : ITS DIVISION

Market is divided on the basis of an area, like regional markets, local market, national markets and international markets. On the basis of the nature of transactions, the market is divided into spot market and future market. Where goods are physically exchanged on the spot, the markets are known as spot markets. In the case of transactions involving agreements of future exchange of goods, such markets are known as future markets. Market is divided into wholesale market and retail market on the basis of the volume of business. Market is divided on the basis of time as very short period market, long Period market and very long period market or the secular market. On the basis of status of sellers, the market is divided into primary, secondary and terminal markets. The primary market comprises of manufacturers who produce and sell the product to the wholesalers. The wholesalers who sell the product to retailers comprise of the secondary market. The business involving the retailer who sells it to the ultimate consumers are known as terminal markets. Market is further divided into regulated market and unregulated market. If the government stipulates certain conditions and regulations for the sale and purchase of product then that market is known as regulated markets. These are absent in unregulated markets. Market is further divided on the basis of competition as perfectly monopoly market, competitive market, monpolistic competitive market, monopoly market, monopolistic competitive market, oligopoly market etc. If there is no competition for the product, then such a market is known as monopoly market. In a competitive market, several producers are manufacturing the product. The product is homogeneous. There are large number of buyers and sellers in the market. Such a market is known as perfectly competitive market.

(A) Price and Output Determination under Perfect Competition

Perfect Competition

The concept of *perfect competition* was first introduced by Adam Smith in his book "Wealth of Nations". Later on, it was improved by Edgeworth. However, it received its complete formation in Frank Kight's book "Risk, Uncertainty and Profit" (1921). Leftwitch has defined market competition in the following words:

> *"Prefect competition is a market in which there are many firms selling identical products with no firm large enough, relative to the entire market, to be able to influence market price".*

The main *conditions or features* of perfect competition are as under:

Features or Conditions for Perfect Competition

(1) *Large number of firms.* The basic condition of perfect competition is that there are large number of firms in an industry. Each firm in the industry is so small and its output so negligible that it exercises little influence over price of the commodity in the market. A single firm cannot influence the price of the product either by reducing or increasing its output. An individual firm takes the market price as given and adjusts its output accordingly. In a competitive market, supply and demand determine market price. The firm is price taker and output adjuster.

(2) *Large number of buyers.* In a perfect competitive market, there are large number of buyers of the product. If any consumer purchases more or purchases less, he is not in a

position to affect the market price of the commodity. His purchase in the total output is just like a drop in the ocean. He, therefore, too like the firm, is a price taker.

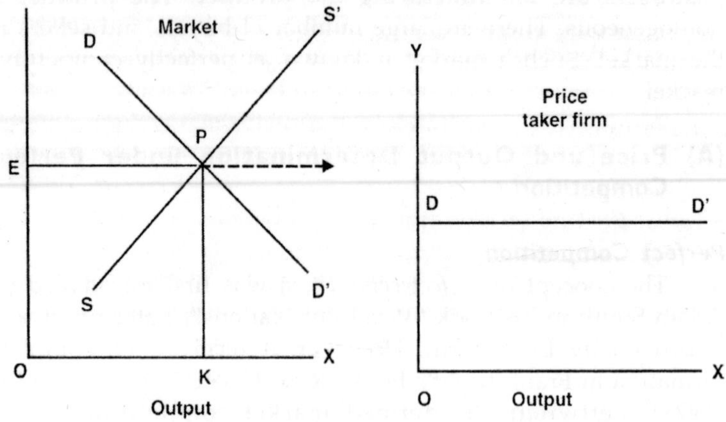

FIG. 1

(3) *The product is homogeneous.* Another provision of perfect competition is that the good produced by all the firms in the industry is identical. In the eyes, of the consumer, the product of one firm (seller) is identical to that of another seller. The buyers are indifferent as to the firms from which they purchase. In other words, the cross elasticity between the products of the firm is infinite.

(4) *No barriers to entry.* The firms in a competitive market have complete freedom of entering into the market or leaving the industry as and when they desire. There are no legal, social or technological barriers for the new firms (or new capital) to enter or leave the industry. Any new firm is free to start production if it so desires and stop production and leave the industry if it so wishes. The industry, thus, is characterized by freedom of entry and exit of firms.

(5) *Profit maximization.* For perfect competition to exist, the sole objective of the firm must be to get maximum profit.

Equilibrium of the Firm

MR = MC (Marginal Revenue = Marginal Cost) Rule:

A firm under perfect competition faces an infinitely elastic demand curve or we can say for an individual firm, the price of the commodity is given in the market. The firm while making changes in the amounts of variable factor evaluates the extra cost incurred on producing extra unit MC (Marginal Cost). It also examines the change in total receipts which results from the sale of extra unit of production MR (Marginal Revenue). So long as the additional revenue from the sale of an extra unit of product (MR) is greater than the additional cost (MC) which a firm has to incur on its production, it will be in the interest of the firm to increase production. In economic terminology, we can say, a firm will go on expanding its output so long as the marginal revenue of any unit is greater than its marginal cost. As production increases, marginal cost begins to increase after a certain point. When both marginal revenue and marginal cost are equal, the firm is in equilibrium. The firm at this equilibrium point is either ensuring maximum profit or minimizing losses.

Short Run Equilibrium of Firm

Definition of a Short Run

By *short run* is meant a length of time which is not enough to change the level of fixed inputs or the number of firms in the industry but long enough to change the level of output by changing variable inputs. In short period, a distinction is made of two types of costs (i) fixed cost and (ii) variable cost. The fixed cost in the form of fixed factors i.e., plant, machinery, building, etc. does not vary with the change in the output of the firm. If the firm is to increase or decrease its output, the change only takes place in the quantity of variable resources such as labor, raw material, etc. Further, in the *short-run*, the demand curve facing the firm is horizontal. No new firms enter or leave the industry. The number of firms in the industry, therefore, remain the same. Under perfect competition, the firm takes the price of the product as determined in the market. The firm sells all its output at the prevailing market price. The firm, in other words, is a price-taker.

Equilibrium of a Competitive Firm

The short-run equilibrium of a firm can be easily explained

with the help of marginal revenue = marginal cost approach or MR = MC rule. Marginal revenue is the change in total revenue that occurs in response to a one unit change in the quantity sold. Marginal cost is the addition to total cost resulting from the additional of marginal unit. Since price is given for the competitive firm, the average revenue curve of a price taker firm is identical to the marginal curve. Average revenue (AR) thus is equal to marginal revenue (MR) is equal to price (MR = AR = Price).

According to the marginal revenue and marginal cost approach or (MR = MC) rule, a price taker firm is in equilibrium at a point where marginal revenue (MR) or price is equal to marginal cost. The point where MR = MC = Price, the firm produces the best level of output. From this it may not be concluded that the perfectly competitive firm at the equilibrium level of output (MR = MC = Price) necessarily ensures maximum profit. The fact is that in the short period, a firm at the equilibrium level of output is faced with four types of product prices in the market which give rise to following results:

(i) A firm earns supernormal profits.
(ii) A firm earns normal profits.
(iii) A firm incurs losses but does not close down.
(iv) A firm minimizes losses by shutting down. All these short run cases of profits or losses are explained with the help of diagrams.

Determining Profit from a Graph

(I) Profit Maximizing Position

A firm in the short run earns abnormal profits when at the best level of output, the market price exceeds the short run average total cost (SATC). The short run profit maximizing position of a purely competitive firm is explained with the help of a diagram.

In Figure 2, output is measured along OX axis and revenue/cost on OY axis. We assume here that the market price is equal to OP. A price taker firm has to sell its entire output at this prevailing market price i.e. OP. The firm is in equilibrium at

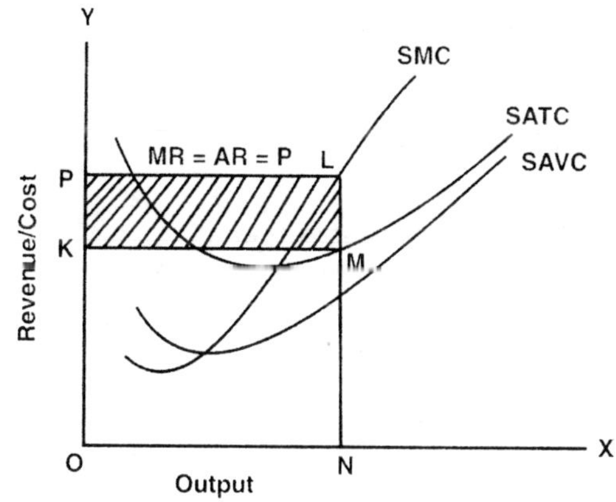

FIG. 2

point L. Where MC = MR. The inter section of MC and MR determine the quantity of the good the firm will produce.

After having determined the quantity, drop a vertical line down to the horizontal axis and see what the average total cost (ATC) is at that output level (point N). The competitive firm will produce ON quantity of output and sell at market price OP. The total revenue of the firm at the best level of output ON is equal to OPLN. Whereas the total cost of producing ON quantity of output is equal to OKMN. The firm is earning supernormal profits equal to the shaded rectangle KPLM. The per unit profit is indicated by the distance LM or PK.

It may here be noted that a firm would not produce more than ON units because producing another unit adds more to the cost than the firm would receive from the sale of the unit (MC > MR). The firm would not stop short of ON output because producing another unit adds more to the revenue than to cost (MR > MC). Hence, ON is the best level of output where profit of the firm is maximum.

(2) Zero Profit of a Firm

A firm, in the short run, may be making zero economic profit or normal economic profit. It may here be remembered that although economic profit is zero, all the resources including entrepreneurs are being paid their opportunity. So they are getting a normal profit the case of normal profits of a firms at break even price is explained with the help of the Figure 3.

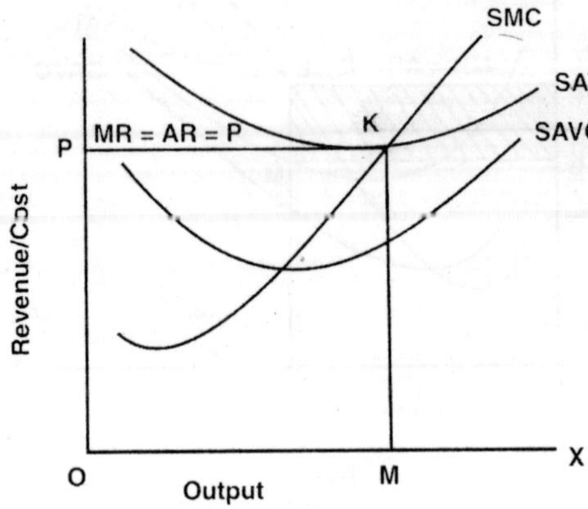

FIG. 3

We assume in the Figure 3 that OP is the prevailing market price and PK is the average revenue, marginal revenue curve. At point K, which is the break even price for a Competitive firm, the MR, MC and ATC are all equal. The firm produces OM output-and sells at market price OP. The total revenue of the firm to equal is the area OPKM. The total cost of producing OM output also equals the area OPKM. The firm is earning only normal profits. It is a situation in which the resources employed by the firm are earning just what they could-earn in some other alternative occupations.

(3) Loss Minimizing Case

The firm in the short rue is minimizing tosses if the market price is smaller than average total cost but larger than average variable cost. The loss minimizing position of a price taker firm is explained with the help of a figure.

We assume in the Figure 4 that the market price is QP. The firm is in equilibrium at point N where MR = MC. The firm's best level of output is OK which is sold at unit cost OP. The total revenue of the firm is equal to the area OPNK. The total cost of producing OK quantity of output is equal to OTSK. The firm is suffering a net loss equal to the shaded area PTSN.

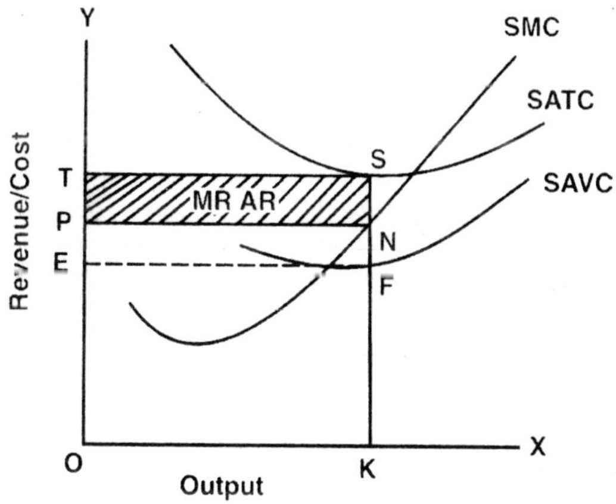

FIG. 4

The firm at price OP in the market is covering its full variable cost and a part of the fixed cost. The loss of part of fixed cost equal to the shaded area PTSN is less than, the firm would incur by closing down. In case of shut down, the firm has to bear the total fixed cost ETSF. The firm thus by producing OK output and selling at OP price is minimizing losses. Summing up, in the short run the firm will not go out of business for as long as the loss m staying the business is less than the loss from closing down.

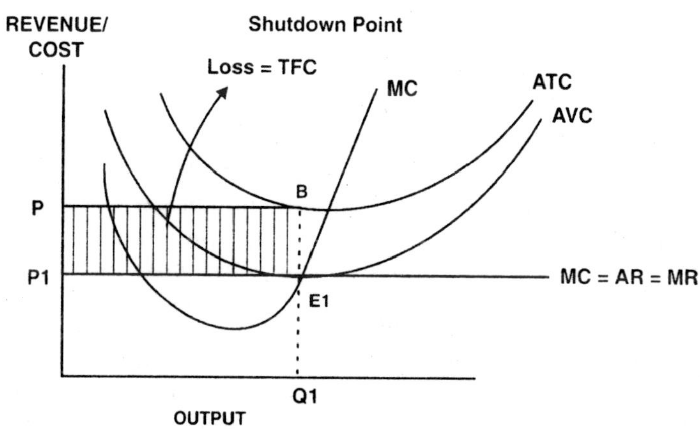

FIG. 5

(4) Short Run Shut Down

The price taker firm in the short-run minimizes losses by closing it down if the market price is less than average variable cost. The shut down position of a Competitive firm is explained with the help of a figure.

If the price falls below P^{sd}, the competitive firm will minimize its losses by closing down. There is no level of output which the firm can produce and realize a loss smaller than its fixed costs. It is therefore a *shut down point for the firm. Operate When Price is > average variable cost.*

Long Run Equilibrium of the Price Taker Firm

Definition

"All the firms in a competitive industry achieve long run equilibrium when market price or marginal revenue equals marginal cost equals minimum of average total cost."

Formula:

Price = Marginal Cost = Minimum Average Total Cost

Explanation:

The long run is a period of time during which the firms are able to adjust their outputs according to the changing conditions. If the demand for a product increases, all the firms have sufficient time to expand their plant capacities, train and engage more labor, use more raw material, replace old machines, purchase new equipments, etc., etc. If the demand for a product declines, the firms reduce the number of workers on the pay roll, use less raw material. In short, all inputs used by a firm are variable in the long run. It is assumed that all the firms in the competitive industry are producing homogeneous product and an individual firm cannot affect the market price. It takes the market price as given. It is also assumed that all the firms in a competitive industry have identical cost' curves. The industry it is assumed is, a constant cost industry. In the long run, it is for further assumed that all the firms in a competitive industry have access to the same technology.

When the period is long and profit level of the competitive industry is high, then new firms enter the industry. If the profit level is below the competitive level, the firm then leave the industry. When all the competitive firms earn normal profit, then there is no tendency for the new firms to enter or leave the industry. The firms are then in the long run equilibrium.

The case of long-run equilibrium of a firm can be easily explained with .the help of a diagram given below:

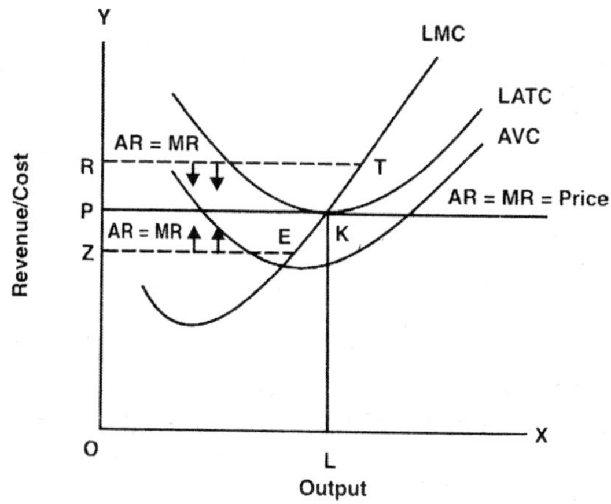

FIG. 6

In the figure 6, the firm is in the long run equilibrium at point K, where price or marginal revenue equals long-run marginal cost equals minimum of long run average cost. The average revenue per unit cost of the firm and its marginal revenue at price OP are the same. The firm at equilibrium point K, produces the best level of output OL and sells at price OP per unit. The total revenue of the firm is equal to the area OPKL.

The total cost of producing OL quantity of output is also equal to the area OPKL. The firm is earning only normal profits. At price OP, there is no tendency for the new firms to enter or leave the industry.

This can be proved by taking prices higher or lower price than OP. If the market price in the long run happens to be OR, the firm would be making more than normal profits. The new firms attracted by profit will enter the industry. The supply of the commodity will increase which derives the market price down to the OP level. The firm here makes only normal profits.

In case, a firm is faced with a market price OZ, the firm is then covering its full variable cost. As the firm is suffering a net loss at price OZ, it will leave the industry. So in the long run, price must be equal to OP which is the minimum average to cost of the firms.

At price OP, all the identical firms to the industry earn only normal profit. There is no tendency for the new firms to enter or leave the industry provided price equals marginal revenue equals marginal cost equals minimum average total cost of the firms.

Price = MR = MC = Minimum of LATC

Long Run Industry Equilibrium

Since all the competitive firms in the long run make normal profits, are of the optimum size and there is no tendency for the new firms to enter or leave the industry, they are, therefore, in equilibrium. When all the identical firms in the industry are in a state of full equilibrium equating price or marginal revenue, equating marginal cost equating minimum of average total cost, the industry itself is then in equilibrium.

When the industry is in the long run equilibrium, there is an optimum allocation of resources. The consumers get the. products at the lowest possible price as, the goods are produced at minimum price in the long run.

(B) Monopoly

Monopoly is from the Greek word meaning one seller. It is the polar opposite of perfect competition. *Monopoly* is a market structure in which one firm makes up the entire market. Monopoly and competition are at the two extremes. *Monopoly refers to a market where there is a single seller for a product and there is no close substitute of the commodity that is offered by the sole supplier to the buyers. The firm constitutes the entire industry.*

Explanation:

Monopoly, therefore, indicates a case where:

(i) There is only a single seller of a product or service in the market.
(ii) The goods produced by a sole seller has not close substitutes.
(iii) The entry of new firms into the industry is effectively barred by legal or natural barriers.
(iv) The firm being the sole supplier of a product constitutes industry. Firm and industry thus have single identity. Or we can say monopoly is a single firm identity.
(v) The single seller affects no other seller by its own action in the market. The other sellers too cannot affect the price and output of the monopoly
(vi) The demand curve facing the monopolist is negatively sloped. The monopolist being the only seller of the commodity in the market can increase the total sale by lowering the price and if, he raises the price, he would not lose all his sale. The demand curve facing a monopolist is less than perfectly elastic, i.e. it slopes downward from left to right.

For the monopoly to exist, it is not necessary that the size of a firm should be large. Even a small firm may have a monopoly. For instance, a local water company or a local electricity company, supplying water and electricity in the city possesses all the characteristics of a monopoly.

Short Run Equilibrium Price and Output Under Monopoly

Short Run Equilibrium of the Monopoly Firm

In the short period, the monopolist behaves like any other firm. A monopolist will maximize profit or minimize losses by producing that output for which marginal cost (MC) equals marginal revenue (MR). Whether a profit or loss is made or not depends upon the relation between price and average total cost (ATC). It may be made clear here that a monopolist does not necessarily makes profit. He may earn super profit or normal profit or even produce at a loss in the short ran.

(a) *Short run monopoly equilibrium with positive profit.* In the short period, if the demand for the product is high, a monopolist increase the price and the quantity of output. He can increase the, output by hiring more labor, using more raw material, increasing working hours etc. However, he cannot change his fixed plant and equipment. In case, the demand for the product falls, he then decreases the use of variable inputs, (like labor, material etc.). As regards the price, the monopolist is a price maker. There is a greater tendency for the monopolist to have a price which earns positive profits. This can only be possible if the price (AR) is higher than average total cost (ATC). The short run profit earned by the monopolist is now explained with the help of the Figure 7.

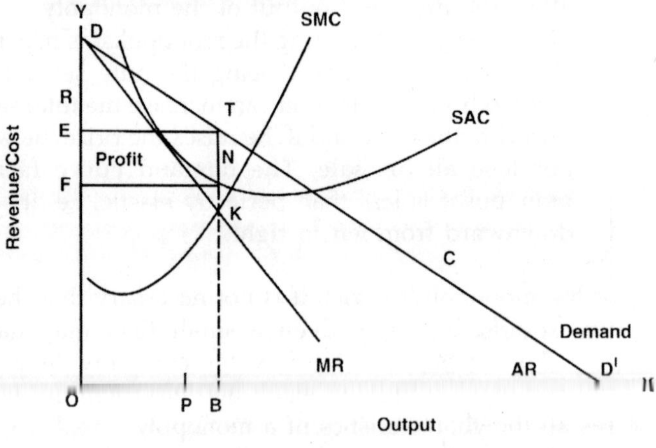

FIG. 7

In this diagram, the monopoly firm is in equilibrium at point K where SMC = MR. The short run marginal cost (SMC) curve cuts MR from below. At point K both the equilibrium conditions are fulfilled. As a result, therefore, OE is monopoly price and OB, the monopoly output. At the monopoly output OB, the average total cost OF = BN. The profit per unit is FE. The short run monopoly profit is ETNF, It is represented by the area of shaded rectangle in figure 3. At the output smaller than OB (say at point P) MR > SMC. Therefore, increased output up to B adds more to total receipts than to total costs. In case, the output is increased beyond OB, the MR < SMC. Hence, the increased outputs beyond OB adds more to total cost than to total receipts. This causes profits to decrease. So the best level of output for the monopolist firm is that where SMC curve cuts the MC curve from below.

(b) *Short run equilibrium with normal profit under monopoly.* There is a false impression regarding the powers of a monopolist. It is said that the monopolistic entrepreneur always earns profits. The fact, however, is that there is no guarantee for the monopolist to earn profit in the short run. If a monopolist firm produces a new commodity and attempts to change the taste pattern of the consumers through advertising campaigns etc., then the firm may operate at normal profit or even produce at a loss minimizing price in the short run (Covering variable cost only). The normal profit short run equilibrium of the monopoly firm is explained, in brief, with the help of the diagrams.

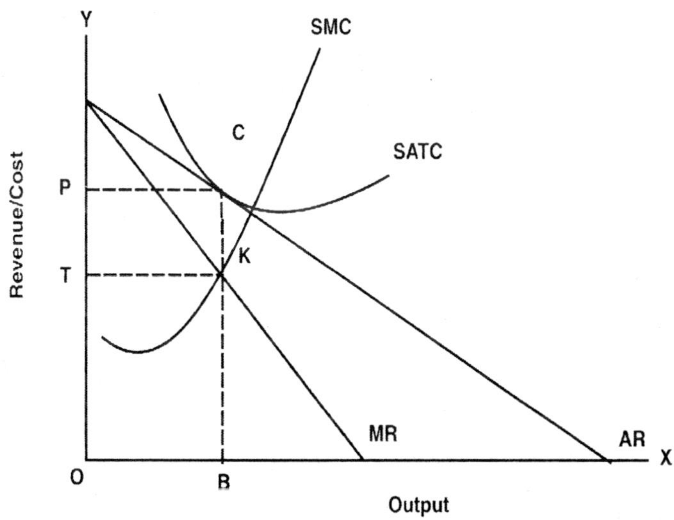

FIG. 8

In figure 8, a firm is in the short run equilibrium at point K, where SMC = MR. The price line is tangent to SAC at point C. The firm charges CB price per unit for units of output OB. The total revenue of the firm is equal to the area OPCB. The total cost of the firm is also equal to the area OPCB. The firm earns only normal profits and continues operating.

(c) *Short run equilibrium with losses under monopoly.* A monopolist also accepts short run losses provided the variable costs of the firm are fully covered. The loss minimizing short run equilibrium analysis is presented graphically.

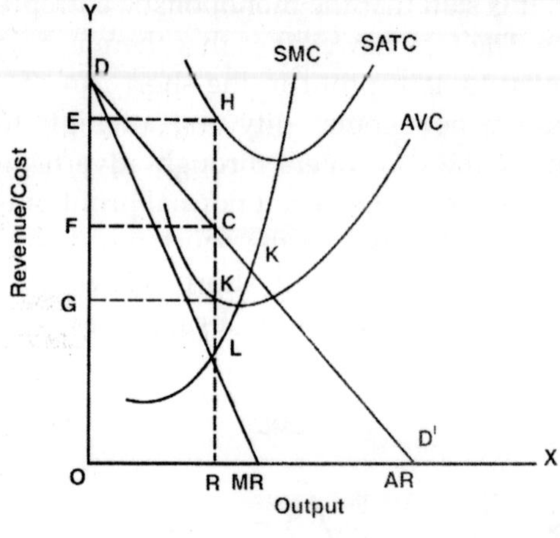

FIG. 9

In this figure 9, the best short run level of output is OB units which is given by the point L where MC = MR. A monopolist sells OB units of output at price CB. The total revenue of the firm is equal to OBCF. The total cost of producing OB units is OBHE. The monopoly firm suffers a net loss equal to the area FCHE. If the firm ceases production, it then has to bear to total fixed cost equal to GKHE. The firm in the short run prefers to operate and reduces its losses to FCHE only. In the long, if the loss continues, the firm shall have to close down.

Long Run Equilibrium Under Monopoly

The monopolist creates barriers of entry for the new firms into the industry. The entry into the industry is blocked by having control over the raw materials needed for the production of goods or he may hold full rights to the production of a certain good (patent) or the market of the good may be limited. If new firms try to enter in the field, it lowers the price of the good to such to the extent that it becomes unprofitable for new firms to continue production etc

When there is no threat of the entry of new firms into the industry, the monopoly firm makes long run adjustments in the scale of plant. In case, the demand for the product is limited, the monopolist can afford to produce output at sub optimum scale. If the market size is large and permits to expand output, then the monopolist would build an optimum scale of plant and would produce goods at the minimum cost per unit. However, the monopolist would not stay in the business, if he makes losses in the long period.

The *long run equilibrium of a monopoly* firm is now explained with the help of the following diagram.

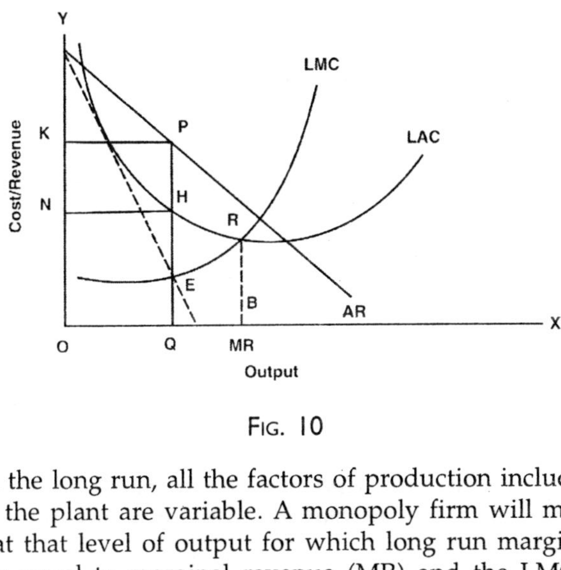

FIG. 10

In the long run, all the factors of production including the size of the plant are variable. A monopoly firm will maximize profit at that level of output for which long run marginal cost (MC) is equal to marginal revenue (MR) and the LMC curve intersects the MR curve from below. In the figure 10, the monopoly firm is in equilibrium at point E where LMC = MR and LMC cuts MR curve from below. QP is the equilibrium price and OQ is the equilibrium output. At OQ level of output, the cost per unit is QH (LAC), whereas the price per unit of the good is QP. HP represents the per unit super normal profit. The total super normal profit is equal to KPHN. It may here be noted that at the equilibrium output OQ, the plant is not being fully utilized. The long run average cost (LAC) is not minimum at this level of output OQ. The firm will build an optimum scale of plant only if the demand for the product increases.

Monopoly Competitive

We know that, monopoly implies that there is a single producer of the good or service concerned. This is a definition of monopoly that you are already familiar with. However, a market structure characterised by monopoly must satisfy two other conditions as well. First, there must be barriers to entry. Otherwise, other firms will enter the industry and the monopoly will break down. Second, the good produced by the monopolist cannot have close substitutes that are produced by other producers. If this condition is violated, there is competition with other producers and it is meaningless to say that there is a monopoly., Stated differently, the cross price elasticity of demand between the goods produced by our monopolist and goods produced by other producers must be close to zero, even if the elasticity is not actually zero. Since there is a single firm, under monopoly, there is no difference between the market demand curve and the demand curve faced by the monopolist. The two are identical. This is a crucial difference between the analysis of perfect competition and the analysis of monopoly. Under perfect competition, the market demand curve was downward sloping.

However, the demand curve faced by an individual firm was perfectly horizontal. Under monopoly, the demand curve faced by the individual firm will also be downward sloping. The firm is the same as the industry. This has an implication for the behaviour of the firm. Under perfect competition, the price is given to the firm from outside. The firm has no control or influence over the price.

Given the price, the firm chooses a level of output that maximizes its profit. Life is different under monopoly. The price is no longer given to the firm. Once the firm chooses a level of output, the price that corresponds to that output is determined from the demand curve. Thus, it is incorrect to say that a monopolist chooses a level of output that maximizes profits. A monopolist effectively chooses a price cum quantity combination. Naturally, both the price and the quantity are not decision variables for the monopolist. If he fixes the quantity, the price is determined from the demand curve. If he fixes the price, the quantity is determined from the demand curve. The first order condition for profit maximization was that marginal revenue must be equal to marginal cost. MR = MC.

This condition is irrespective of the market structure involved. Thus, even under monopoly, this must be the condition for profit maximization. For a firm under perfect competition, the marginal revenue was equal to average revenue (AR). This will no longer be true under monopoly. If e is the price elasticity of demand, then MR = AR (I-1./e). Since the average revenue is the same as the price (P), we can also write MR = P (I-1/e).

We can therefore write the monopolist's profit maximizing condition as under.

MR = P (I-1/e) = MC.

This equilibrium is depicted in Figure 11. Look at the first panel first. There is a downward sloping AR curve (market demand curve). The MR curve has also been drawn. There is an U shaped MC curve. The profit maximizing configuration is one where MR is equal to MC. That is, the monopolist fixes an output level of OQ and an accompanying price level of OP. (MR = MC can also happen along the declining segment of the MC curve). The monopolist's total revenue is OPBQ. His total cost is OACQ. Therefore, the monopolist makes a profit of APBC. This does not necessarily mean that the monopolist will always make a profit. It is feasible for a monopolist to make losses in the short run.

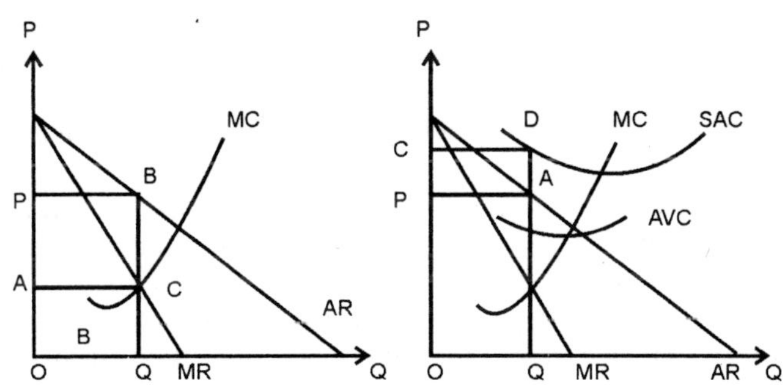

FIG. 11

In fact, we have talked about marginal cost without specifying whether we have short run marginal cost (SMC) or long run marginal cost (LMC) in mind. It can be both, depending on the time period. In either case, the principle of profit maximization remains the same. If it is the short run, SMC = MR. And if it is the long run, LMC MR. The second panel of Figure 1 now displays a situation where the monopolist incurs a loss in the short run. The panel is almost self-explanatory. The monopolist equates SMC with MR and chooses an output level of OQ.

The price is OP and the monopolist's revenue is OPAQ. Given the SAC (short run average cost) curve, the monopolist's costs are OCDQ and the monopolist incurs a loss of PCDA. The monopolist finds it worthwhile to produce because the price is greater than the average variable cost (AVC). By producing a positive level of output, the monopolist can neutralise some of the fixed costs. He is not exactly maximizing profits. He is minimizing losses, since losses have to be incurred in any case. In the very long run, such a monopolist will leave the industry. In the short run, a zero level of output will be produced only if the price is lower than the average variable cost. Go back to the equilibrium condition, MR = P (I - 1/e) = MC. If the marginal cost is positive, it follows that the marginal revenue must also be positive. But this means that the elasticity of demand (e) must be greater than 1. In such a case, it is obvious that MR will be smaller than the price (P). Since MR is equated to MC, it follows that P must be greater than MC.

As long as the marginal cost is positive, the price charged by monopolist will be greater than the marginal cost. This is an significant point that needs to be remembered. Stated differently, P = MC (e/(e - 1)). Thus, the price charged by a monopolist depends on marginal cost and on the price elasticity of demand.

Supply Curves

After analysing the profit maximization conditions for a competitive firm, we obtained a competitive firm's supply curve. The derivation of a supply curve is impossible for a monopolist, Definitionally, a supply curve gives the level of output that will be produced for any given price. The relationship between price and output supplied is one to one. This does not happen for a monopolist. The monopolist does not choose an output level, he chooses a price cum quantity combination. Figure 12 may help to explain this point.

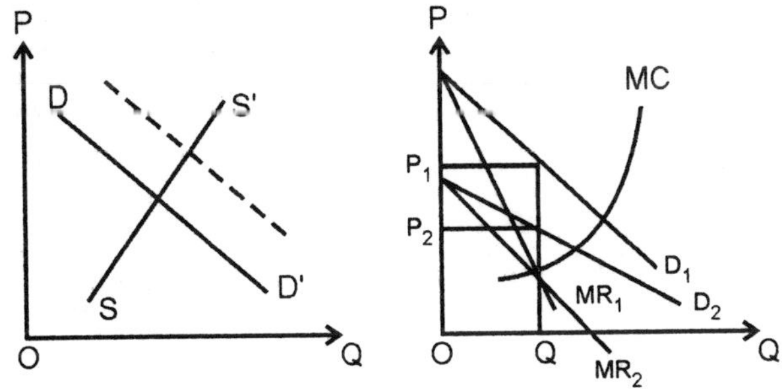

FIG. 12

The first panel depicts competitive conditions and we have a demand curve and a supply curve. This determines the equilibrium level of output and the equilibrium price. The demand curve now shifts and we have a new equilibrium level of output and a new equilibrium price. If you join these two points, you will find that you have traced out a segment of the supply curve. Thus, as the demand curve keeps shifting, one traces out a locus of all the equilibrium price and quantity combinations. And this locus is nothing but the supply curve. This will no longer happen under monopoly. Consider the second panel of Figure 12, depicting a condition of monopoly. Initially, the demand curve is DO the marginal revenue curve is MR, and the marginal cost curve is MC. The output level is OQ and the price level is OP_1. The demand curve now shifts to (ii) 2 and the marginal revenue curve shifts to MR_2. The output level continues to be OQ, although the price level is now OP_2. The same level of output can thus be associated with two or more completely different price levels. It is for reasons like this that it does not make sense to talk about a supply curve for a monopolist.

Inputs

We introduced concepts like the marginal revenue product (MRP), value of marginal product (VMP) and marginal factor cost (MFC). Those concepts can also be used to analyse the behaviour of a monopolist in the factor market. A monopolist implies that one does not have perfect competition in the product market. But does one have perfect competition in the factor market or not? Let us suppose that there is perfect competition in the factor market. This means that the marginal factor cost of any input will be identical to the price of the input. A profit maximizing firm equates the marginal revenue product with the price of the input. Let us consider the case of labour, for capital everything can be readily translated. For profit maximization, the condition for equilibrium is the following. If the marginal cost is positive, we have earlier argued that a monopolist's equilibrium will be at a point where the elasticity of demand is greater than one. Thus, MRP_L will be smaller than VMP_L. Under perfect competition, labour will be paid a wage rate (PL) that is equal to VMP_L-Under monopoly, labour will be paid a wage rate that is equal to MRP_L Since VMP_L is greater than MRP_L, the wage rate paid under monopoly will be smaller than the wage rate paid under perfect competition.

The Loss in Welfare

Compared to perfect competition, monopoly involves a loss in welfare. Consider the first panel of Figure 13. DD is the market demand curve for the industry. There are a large number of perfectly competitive producers. However, DD is the market demand curve and not the demand curve facing any one of them individually. SS is the market supply curve. Since there are a large number of perfectly competitive firms, SS should be interpreted as a horizontal summation of the supply curves of the individual firms. For any individual firm, the supply curve is the rising segment of the marginal cost curve. Life is in equilibrium. OQ_1 units of the output are produced and the price is OPV These competitive firms are now taken over by a monopolist.

Since existing competitive firms have been taken over, underlying demand and cost conditions do not change. The DD curve is the monopolist's AR curve now and we have drawn in the MR curve. To keep life simple, one can pretend that all the original firms were homogeneous. The SS curve is thus nothing but the monopolist's MC curve. The monopolist equates MR

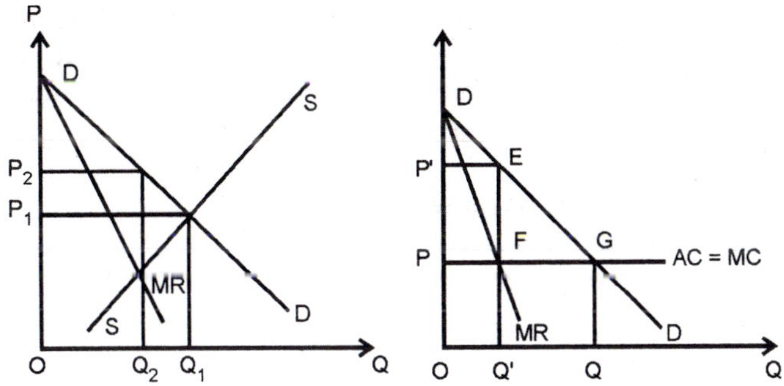

FIG. 13

and MC and fixes an output level of OQ_2. This involves a price level of OP_2. Thus, as compared to perfect competition, monopoly tends to have a smaller output and a higher price. You no doubt remember that in the very long run, perfect competition implies that the price is equal to the minimum average cost. In this sense, competitive firms tend to have an optimal economic size. But since output tends to be smaller under monopoly, a monopolist will usually have a suboptimal economic size. Now turn your attention to the second panel of Figure 13. DD is the market demand curve. For purposes of simplicity, let us assume that average cost (AC) is equal to marginal cost (MC) and that there are a large number of homogeneous competitive firms in the industry. Industry is in equilibrium when the price is equal to the marginal cost. The output level is OQ and the price level is OP. These competitive firms are now taken over by a monopolist who equates MR with MC. As before, the implicit assumption is that cost and demand conditions remain the same as a result of this takeover. Because we now have a monopolist, the output level falls to OQ^1 and the price level goes up to OP^1. Consider what has happened to consumer's surplus. As a result of the transition to monopoly, consumer's surplus has gone down by PP'EF + EFG. Since prices have gone up, the monopolist has extra profits to the tune of PP'EF. But EFG is a net welfare loss for which there is no compensation. Society has lost out 'on welfare and such a loss is known as a deadweight loss. There has accordingly been a deadweight loss because of the transition to monopoly. It is because of reasons like this that there often are government attempts to control or regulate monopolies. For instance, there may be price controls that specify the maximum price that can be charged by a monopolist.

Monopoly Power Measurement

Rare is the case when one has perfect monopoly, interpreted as a single seller who sells a product that has no substitutes. More commonly, there are different degrees of monopoly. Almost every market exhibits some characteristics of monopoly is there, therefore, any way to measure the degree of the monopoly power? Two types of measures have been used to assess the degree of monopoly power. The first of these uses the own price elasticity of demand, e. Under perfect competition, is infinitely large for an individual firm. Any deviation from this ideal accordingly ought to capture the degree of monopoly power. The smaller is e, the greater should be the monopoly power. The inverse of the own price elasticity of demand 1/e) is thus sometimes used as an indicator of the monopoly power. A measure allied to 1/e) is known as Lerner's measure of monopoly power. This captures the deviation of price (P) from marginal cost (MC) and defines an index of monopoly power as the ratio (P-MC)/P. Under perfect competition, the value of this index will be 0. And when marginal cost is zero, the value of this index will be 1. With profit maximization, MC MR and MR = P (1-1/e) If you now simplify, you will discover that with profit maximization, Lerner's index of monopoly power reduces to 1/e) In this sense, it is not a new measure. A second type of measure used to capture the degree of monopoly power, is the cross price elasticity of demand between a firm's goods and goods produced by other firms.

The smaller the cross price elasticity of demand', one can argue that the greater is the degree of monopoly power. This measure thus hinges on the extent to which substitutes for a product are available. If the cross price elasticity of demand is zero, one will have pure monopoly. If the cross price elasticity of demand is infinity, as will happen when homogeneous goods are produced by alternative producers, one will have the case of perfect competition.

Discriminating Monopoly

In our final section on monopoly, let us focus on the question of price discrimination across markets. An identical product may be sold in several different markets. Since this is an identical product, the marginal cost of producing the product is the same, regardless of which market it is sold in. Despite the marginal cost being the same, different prices are charged in different markets. The monopolist discriminates across different markets. Discrimination need not always be according to markets in a geographical sense. It can also be according to types of consumers. Power rates paid by farmers, as compared to power rates paid by industrial users, may be an example. The logic of price discrimination is quite simple. Let us suppose that there are two different markets. R_1 is the revenue the monopolist obtains from the first market and R_2 is the revenue the monopolist obtains from the second market. $R_1 + R_2 = R$. With C denoting costs, the monopolist's profits are R-C, or equivalently, $R_1 + R_2 - C$. Let MR_1 denote the marginal revenue obtained in the first market and let MR_2 denote the marginal revenue obtained in the second market. MC is the same for both markets, as the same product is being sold. The cost conditions do not vary from one market to another. We are already familiar with one condition for profit maximization, MR = MC. A little reflection will display that we must also have $MR_1 = MR_2$. Otherwise, the monopolist cannot possibly be maximizing profits. For instance, if marginal revenue in the first market is greater than marginal revenue in the second market, the monopolist can increase his profits by switching some sales from the second market to the first. Let us suppose that the elasticity of demand in the first market is e_1 and that the elasticity of demand in the second market is e_2 P_1 is the price at which the product is sold in the first market and P_2 is the price at which the product is sold in the second market. The following conditions then hold.

$MR_1 = P_1 (1\text{-}I/e_1)$ and $MR_2 = P_2 (1\text{-}I/e_2)$
But we also know that $MR_1 = MR_2$
Therefore, we must have $P_1 (1 - 1/e_1)\ P_1 (1 - 1e_2)$

Now go through the following steps.

If $e_1 > e_2'$ $1/e_1 < 1/e_2$
If $1/e_2 < 1e_2'$ 1 $e_1 > 1/e_2$
If $I/e_1 < 1/e_2'$ $-1/e_1 > -1/e_2$
If $I-1/e_1 > 1 - 1/e_2$ $P_1 < P_2$
If $e_1 > e_2'$ $P_1 < P_2$

Thus, a monopolist can increase his profits by charging different prices in the two markets. A higher price will be charged in the market that has a lower price elasticity of demand. And a lower price will be charged in the market that has a higher price elasticity of demand. There are a few points that need to be made about price discrimination. It is by no means essential that the price discrimination should be between only two markets. As long as different markets exhibit different elasticities of demand, the monopolist can discriminate between them. As long as different buyers exhibit different elasticities of demand, the monopolist can discriminate between them.. As long as different units of a commodity are sold at different elasticities of demand, the monopolist can discriminate between them. However, such fine shades of price discrimination are impossible to implement. That is the reason one normally talks about price discrimination between markets. For price discrimination between, markets to make sense, the elasticities in the two markets must differ.

In addition, for price discrimination to be feasible, the two markets must remain segmented. Buyers in one market cannot transfer themselves to the other market. Goods sold in one market cannot be diverted to the other market. These conditions are easy to ensure if there is some geographical distance between the markets. Manufacturers often charge a lower price in the export market than in the domestic market. For a country like India, the elasticity of demand in the world market is close to infinity. But the elasticity of demand in the domestic market is finite. The lower price in the export market can thus be explained in terms of price discrimination.

Price and Output Determination Under Discrimination Monopoly

Price discrimination takes place when a given product is sold by a monopolist at more than one price and these price differences are not justified by cost differences. The price discrimination is possible under the following conditions.

Conditions

(1) *Monopoly power.* The seller of a good must be a monopolist.
(2) *Segregation of market.* The monopolist must be able to segregate buyers into separate classes with different price elasticities.
(3) *No reselling.* There should be no possibility of reselling the good from a tow price market to a high price market.

Purpose of Price Discrimination

The purpose of price discrimination by a monopolist is two fold. Firstly, to increase his total revenue and profits and secondly, to produce a larger output than a non-practicing monopolist. Determination of price and output under monopolistic competition.

Price discrimination is possible and profitable when the monopolist is able to control the amount and distribution of supply and the buyers can be separated into different classes having a demand curve with different elasticities. Let us assume that the monopolist sells his total product in two sub-markets A and B. Sub-market A has low price elastic demand for the product and the sub-market B has high price elasticity of demand. The discriminating monopolist will sell a greater quantity of his product by making a price reduction in market B. He sells lesser commodity in market A at a price higher than in market B. The monopolist will then earn maximum profit by price discriminating as is illustrated with the help of Figure 14.

In this figure 14 market A and Market B have different elasticity of demand for the product of the monopolist. The slopes of the AR and MR curves in each market are different depending upon the elasticity of demand for the commodity. In market A, the elasticity of demand is relatively inelastic. The rise in price does not cause a much fall in demand. In market B, the demand for the monopolist product is relatively elastic. A reduction in price leads greater increase in the demand for the

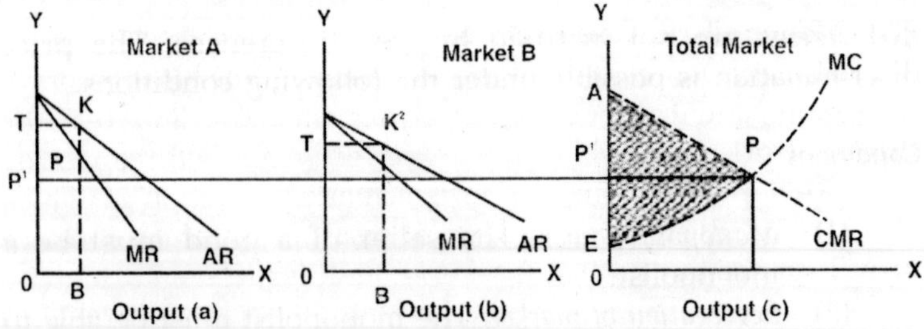

FIG. 14

product and adds more to the revenue. In figure, the combined marginal cost curve (MC) of the total output of the monopolist intersects the combined marginal revenue curve of the two markets A and B from below at point P. The best levels of output of the monopolist is OT given by the point P where MC curve cuts the AR curve from below. The monopolist Is to distribute this equilibrium output OT between the two markets A and B in such a way that the MR in each market is OP.

In market A, MR equates MC at point F. The monopolist sells output OB at price KB. In market B, where the demand is more elastic, the monopolist maximizes profit by selling output OB^2 at price K^2B^2 in market B, where the demand is more elastic, the price K^2B^2 is lower than in market A, the profit of the monopolist is maximum when he sells output of OB at price KB in market

A and output of OB^2 at price of K^2B^2 in market B. The monopolist total profit is shown in the shaded area APE in figure 14c.

Summing up, a discriminating monopolist can maximize profits only when:

(1) It is profitable for him to sell the output in different markets.

(2) The price is charged in different markets in such a way that the last unit of the commodity sold in market gives the same marginal revenue.

(3) The marginal revenue is equal to the marginal cost of total output.

(C) Monopolistic Competition

Monopolistic competition as the name signifies is a blend of monopoly and competition. It is a systematic and realistic theory of price analysis in this imperfectly competitive world.

Monopolistic competition is a market situation in which there are relatively large number of small firms which produce or sell similar but not identical commodities to the customers.

According to Leftwitch

"*Monopolistic competition* is a market situation in which there are many sellers of a particular product, but the product of each seller is in some way differentiated in the minds of consumers from the product of every other seller".

Characteristics of Monopolistic Competition

The main *characteristic or features of monopolistic competition* are as under:

(i) *A fairly large number of sellers:* The number of firms in monopolistic competition is fairly large. Each firm produces or sells a close substitute for the product of other firms in the product group or industry. Product differentiation is thus the hallmark of monopolistic competition.

(ii) *Differentiation in products:* Under monopolistic competition, the firms sell differentiated products. Product differentiation may be real or imaginary. Real differentiation is done through differences in the materials used, design, color, etc. Imaginary differences may be created through advertisement, brand name, trademarks etc. The firms producing similar products in .this imperfectly competitive world cannot raise the price of product much higher than their rivals. If they do so, they will lose much of their sale, but not all the sale. In case, they lower the price, the total sale can be increased to a certain extent. How much will the sale increase or decrease by lowering or raising the price will depend upon the product differentiation of the different firms. If the product of the various firms are very close substitutes of one another and no imaginary or real difference exists in the mind of the buyers, then a slight rise or fall in the price of the product of one firm will appreciably decrease or increase the demand for the product. If the product of one firm differs from that of other firm, (though the difference may be an imaginary one) a slight rise in the price of the product of one firm will not drive away all its customers. A few faithless buyers may be attracted by the low price of the other rival product but not all the buyers.

(iii) *Advertisement and propaganda:* Another very important characteristic of the monopolistic competition is that each firm tries to create difference in its product from the other by advertising, propaganda, attractive packing, nice smile, etc., etc. When it succeeds in its object, the firm occupies almost the position of a monopolist. It is, thus, in a position to raise-the price of the product without losing its customers.

(iv) *Nature of demand curve:* Since the existence of close substitutes limits the monopoly power, the demand curve faced by a monopolistically competitive firm is fairly elastic. The precise degree of elasticity will however, depend upon the number of firms in the group product or industry. If the number of firms is fairly large and the product of each firm is not very similar, the demand curve of a firm will be quite elastic. In case, there is close competition among the rival firms for the sale of similar products, the demand curve of a firm will be less elastic.

(v) *Freedom of entry and exit of firms:* The entry of new firms in the monopolistically competition industry is relatively easy. There are no barriers of the new firm to enter the product group or leave the industry in the long run.

(vi) *Sales efforts:* With heterogeneous products, the sale of the products by the firms can no longer be taken for granted sale depends upon sale efforts.

(vii) *Non-price competition:* In monopolistic competition, the firms make every effort to win over the customers.

Other than price cutting, the firms may offer after sale service, a gift scheme, discount not declared in the price list etc.

Short Run and Long Run Equilibrium

Short Run Equilibrium Under Monopolistic Competition

'Monopolistic competition refers to the market organization where there are a fairly large number of firms which sell somewhat differentiated products.

A single firm in the product group (industry) has little impact on the market price. However, if it reduces price, it can expect a considerable increase in its sales. The firm may also attract buyers away from other firms by creating imaginary or real difference through advertising, branding and through many other sales promotion measures (non-price competition). If the firm raises its price, it will not lose all its customers. This is because of the fact that the product is differentiated from competing firms due to price and non-price factors. The demand curve (AR curve) of the monopolistic firm is therefore, highly elastic and is downward sloping. As regards the marginal revenue curve, it slopes downward and lies below the demand curve because price is lowered of all the units to sell more output in the market

Firm's Equilibrium Price and Output

In the short-run, the number of firms in the 'product group' remains the same. The size of the plant of each firm remains unaltered. The firm whether operating under perfect competition, or monopoly wants to maximize profits. In order to achieve this objective, it goes on producing a commodity so long as the marginal revenue is greater than marginal cost. When MR = MC, it is then in equilibrium and produces the best level of output. If a firm produces less than or more than the MR = MC output, it will then not be making maximum of profits.

In the short-run, a monopolistically competitive firm may be realizing abnormal profits or suffering losses. If it is earning profits, no new firms can enter the industry in the short-run. In case, it is suffering, losses but covering full variable cost, the firm will continue operating so that the losses are minimized. If the full variable cost is not met, the firm will close down in the short-run.

Monopolistic can face three situation in short Run

(1) Super normal Profits
(2) Normal Profits
(3) Losses

Super Normal Profits

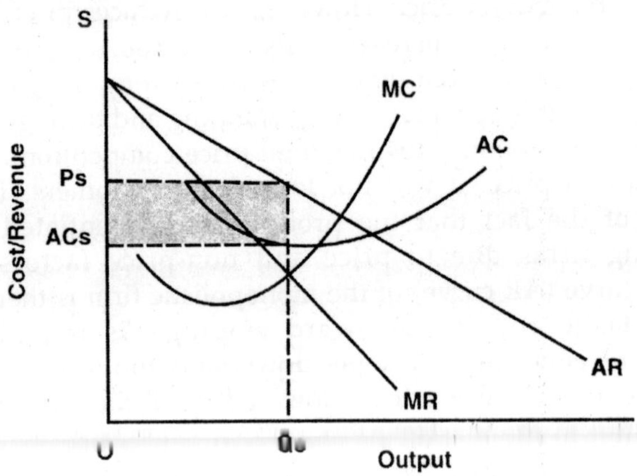

FIG. 15

In this Figure 15, the downward sloping demand curve (AR curve) is quite elastic. The MR curve lies below-the average curve. The SMC curve which includes advertising and sales promotional costs is drawn in the usual fashion. The SMC curve cuts the MR curve from below . The firm produces and sells an output Qs, as at this level of output MR = MC. The difference between the AR and AC is shown By Shaded area and this area represent abnormal profits in the short run.

Normal Profits

In Figure 16, when the output the firm is Q', the AR and AC are equal which represent Normal Profits to the firms.

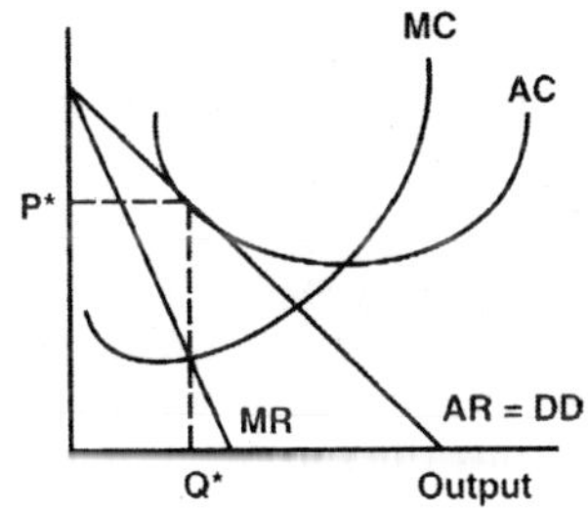

Fig. 16

Short Run Losses

If the demand and cost situations are not favorable in the market, a monopolistically competitive firm may incur losses in the short-run. The short-run equilibrium of the firm with losses is explained with the help of a Figure 17.

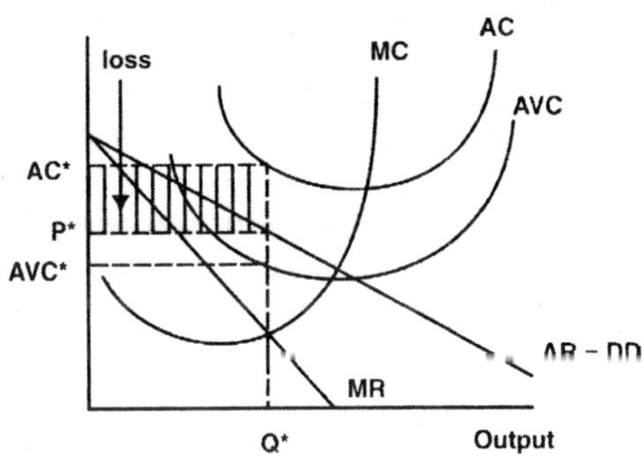

Fig. 17

In the Figure, marginal cost (SMC) equates marginal revenue MR curve from below at output Q^*. At this point firms AR is Less than AC at Price P^* so the shaded area represent loses to the monopolistic firm.

Equilibrium Price and Output in the Long Run Under Monopolistic Competition

Long Run Zero Economic Profits

In the long run, the firms are able to alter the scale of plant according to the changed conditions of demand for a product in the market. They can also leave or enter the industry. If the firms are earning abnormal profits in the short run, then new firm will enter the 'product group' (industry). The tendency of the new firms to enter the industry continues till the abnormal profits are competed away and the firms economic profits are zero. In case the monopolistically competitive firms realize losses in the short-run, then some of the firms will leave the industry. The exit of the firm continues till zero economic profits are restored with the operating firms.

In the long-run, there are no entry barriers for the new firms. The incoming firms install latest machinery and try to differentiate their products from those of the established firms. The old firms operating with .the used machinery try to match up with the new entrants by improved variety of products in their group. They increase expenditure on advertisement and on other sales promotional measures. They employ more qualified staff for. making technical improvement in their products. Since all the firms for their existence incur additional expenditure for improving the quality of the products, the cost curves of all the firms move up. Due to entry of new firms in the industry and higher costs of production, the output of each competing firm is reduced. There is, therefore, a waste in the economic resources of the country. The equilibrium price and output in the long-run is explained with the help of a Figure 18.

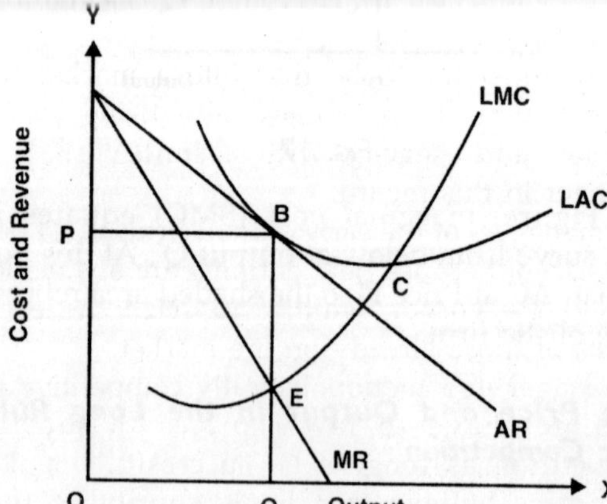

FIG. 18

In this figure at output OQ firms LMC=MR and LMC cuts MR at lowest Point i.e at E and here firms AR =LAC at point B. So in long run firm will earn only Normal Profits.

Perfect Competition and Monopolistic Competition : A Difference

(a) Under perfect competition, products are homogeneous; in monopolistic competition, products are differentiated.
(b) While perfect competition is a myth, monopolistic competition is fact of life.
(c) Advertisement does not help in perfect competition; It is rather essential to sustain monopolistic competition.
(d) Under perfect competition, the price prevailing in the market is the same for all producers; under monopolistic competition, there are various prices for differentiated products.

Important Lessons of Monopolistic Competition for Managers

(a) The manager must realize that a monopolistically competed market offers the opportunity for firms to compete not only by trying to be the lowest cost producer but also by effectively differentiating their products.
(b) A firm must try to be first into a market through differentiation: brand names, advertising, packaging, location and 'service with a smile', all help the manager in this regard.
(c) The managers of the early entrant firms must never be complacent because new entrants are always looking around the corner, waiting to seize the economic profits of those already on the market.
(d) A manager in a monopolistically competitive market need not have to lower prices in the face of competition as long as he successfully makes the customers believe that he is supplying the best product out of all competitors.

Outlet Differentiation

It is a market situation where sellers prefer one buyer or outlet over another is called "outlet differentiation". Many reasons can be given why sellers have preference for dealing with a buying firm:

(a) The buying agents of one firm may be more pleasant to deal with than those of another firm. They may be good tempered, liberal in approach and reasonable in dealings.
(b) The working conditions in one firm may be better than in others.
(c) Some buyers may be paying their bills more promptly than others and hence considered as "better customers".
(d) Dealings with some buyers may be considered a matter of "prestige".

Though outlet differentiation may occur wherever a product or service is sold, a potent example is that of the labour market. A labourer or an executive, for example, is very much concerned with the working conditions, nature of his boss, air and light at the place of work, the region and the community In which the job is located, and the like. Just as product differentiation allows a seller to charge a price higher than the competitive level, outlet differentiation induces him to agree to a price lower than the competitive level.

(D) Oligopolistic Competition and Competition at Short and Long Run

In our discussion of market structures, we have already analysed perfect competition and monopoly. Continuing in the same vein, in this unit, we will talk about oligopoly. Monopoly is relatively easy to analyse. But there are not too many real examples where one actually encounters a monopoly. Perfect competition is also relatively easy to analyse. But yet again, it is difficult to find real examples where one actually encounters perfect competition. Most real examples lie in the spectrum that lies between monopoly and perfect competition. One of the problems with analysing oligopoly is that there is no clear consensus about what it means. You may be surprised at this statement. Haven't we already defined oligopoly as a market structure where there are a few sellers who sell an undifferentiated or homogeneous product? Indeed we have. But not everyone agrees that this is an appropriate definition of oligopoly. For instance, oligopoly is sometimes defined as a market structure where a few sellers sell a differentiated product. Sometimes, this is referred to as oligopolistic competition, with the word oligopoly reserved for the homogeneous product case. In this unit, we will avoid unnecessary semantics and consider both oligopoly and oligopolistic competition. Yet another problem with analysing oligopoly is the interdependence among firms.

What happens to the objective function or profit function of a firm, depends not only on what the firm does, but also on what other firms do. A firm may therefore have to make reasonable assumptions about what other firms are likely to do. This interdependence does not exist for monopoly. And it is insignificant in the case of perfect competition or monopolistic competition. After all, there are many firms under perfect competition and monopolistic competition. Ile impact of one firm's decisions on another firm, is at best, expected to be marginal. Given the interdependence, it is also feasible for firms to collude among themselves. For instance, they can form cartels. A third problem lies with the behaviour rule that is stipulated for a firm. Profit maximization may be a reasonable assumption to make for perfect competition and monopoly and even for monopolistic competition. It is perhaps a less reasonable assumption to make for oligopoly. The upshot of all this is that there is no general theory of oligopoly. There cannot be. One can talk about the theory of monopoly or the theory of perfect competition, as there is only one theory for such market structures. That is no longer the case with oligopoly.

There are several different theories of oligopoly, each based on different assumptions. Therefore, one needs to talk about a theory of oligopoly. Each such theory focuses on one aspect of oligopoly that it regards as significant. Finally, this unit will club duopoly and oligopoly together. The inevitable analytical framework is the same. The only difference lies in whether the number of sellers is two or more.

Principle of Cournot

One of the earliest analyses of oligopoly goes back to the work of a French economist named Cournot. This was first published in 1838. More precisely, Cournot's analysis was restricted to duopoly, but it can readily be extended to situations of oligopoly. One must qualify this statement with the caveat that oligopoly in this case does not mean oligopolistic competition. That is, all sellers produce a homogeneous product. Let us stick to Cournot's original example. There are two identical mineral springs which are operated by two different owners. Since the mineral springs are identical, the water produced by them is identical and therefore one is talking about a homogeneous product. For simplicity, it is assumed that no costs are associated with extracting water from the mineral springs. This is purely a simplifying assumption and can be dispensed with, although that will make the analysis a bit more messy. The upshot of this assumption is that the marginal cost becomes zero. In the original Cournot framework, the demand curve is assumed to be linear. This helps to make the analysis tractable. Finally, each duopolist believes that regardless of what action he takes, the other duopolist will keep, his output the same.

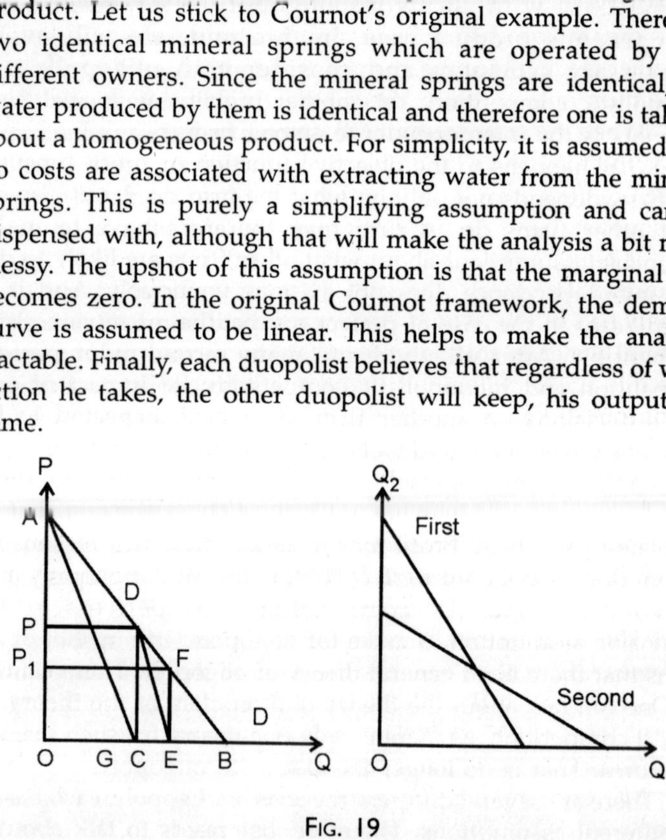

FIG. 19

That is, the other duopolist will continue to produce his present level of output. The second duopolist will not continue to produce the same level of output. As we will see, he will change his output depending on what the first duopolist does. But the first duopolist believes that the second duopolist will not change the level of his output. In other words, the Cournot framework ignores the problem of interdependence and this is one of its main drawbacks. Nevertheless, the Cournot model is significant as it highlights some of the problems that can arise in a situation of monopoly or oligopoly. Take a look at the first panel of Figure 19. The market demand curve that the producers of mineral water face is the linear demand curve AB. This is the AR (average revenue) curve. The MR (marginal revenue) curve is AC. We have implicitly assumed that the maximum output that can be produced from the two mineral springs taken together is OB. Since the springs are identical, each spring has a maximum output (daily say) of exactly half this amount.

When the entire output OB is produced, the market price is zero. Initially, there is only one duopolist in the picture. He therefore functions as a monopolist. Since he functions as a monopolist, he will equate MR with MC and produce a level of output equal to OC. MC is zero and profit maximization thus requires that MR also be zero. (I hope you realise that OC is exactly half of OB. Why?) This means that the price at which the mineral water is sold is OP = CD. The second duopolist now gets into the act. He notes that the first duopolist is producing an output of OC, although the market can absorb an output of OB. Under the assumption that the first duopolist will continue to produce an output level of OC, CB is the extent of demand that is not catered to. The second duopolist will therefore treat DB as the demand curve that he faces and draw the relevant MR curve (DE). He equates his MR with his MC and opts for an output level of CE. (I hope you realise that CE is exactly half CB.) The total output is now OC + CE and the market price becomes OP, = EF. Now it is the turn of the first duopolist to react. He notices that the second duopolist is producing an output level of CE = EB. The market demand that he can cater to, is thus OE. He equates MR with

MC and chooses an output level of OG, with OG being exactly half OE. The second duopolist reacts to this and the process goes on and on. We have not drawn any more lines as that will clutter up the diagram too much ' But we do need to ask, where will the process end? Let us argue in the following way. The maximum output feasible is Q (Q is equal to OB). In the first step, the first duopolist produces an output level of Q/

2. Since this leaves an unsatisfied demand of Q/2, the second duopolist initially produces an output level of Q/4. Since this leaves an unsatisfied demand of 3Q/4, the first duopolist alters his output level to 3Q/8. Since this leaves an unsatisfied demand of 5Q/8, the second duopolist alters his output level to 5Q/16. Since this leaves an unsatisfied demand of 11Q/16, the first duopolist alters his output level to 11Q/32. Since this leaves an unsatisfied demand of 21Q/32, the second duopolist alters his output level to 21Q/64. Note that the first duopolist began with an output level of Q/2. In each step, he reduces his earlier output level, with the absolute size of the reduction progressively becoming less and less. The second duopolist began with an output level of Q/4. In each step, he increases his earlier output Travel, with the absolute size of the increase progressively becoming less and less. This is all very fine, but where does the process terminate? It is feasible to carry out the argument verbally. However, it is convenient to use a little bit of mathematics. Let the first duopolist's output be denoted by Q_1 and the second duopolist's output be denoted by Q_2. If P is the price, with a linear demand curve, $P = a\text{-}b\ (Q_1 + Q_2)$. Notice that we used Q to signify the maximum feasible output. When this happens, $P = 0$ and therefore, $Q = a/b$. The first duopolist's profit is PQ_1, given that there are no costs. If we substitute for P, the first duopolist's profit is a Q_1 - $bQ_1 2\ bQ_1\ Q_2$. The first duopolist maximizes this with respect to Q_2, assuming that Q_2 is the same. This gives the relationship $a\text{-}2bQ_1\text{-}bQ_2 = 0$. In exactly the same way, for the second duopolist we have the relationship $a\text{-}2bQ_2\text{-}bQ_1 = 0$. If you solve these two equations, you will obtain the values' $Q_1 = Q_2 = a/3b$. Since $Q = a/b$, $Q, = Q_2 = (1/3)\ Q$. Each duopolist thus produces an output equal to one-third Q and the total output produced by the two duopolists is (2/3) Q. The equilibrium of Cournot duopoly is sometimes also expressed in the form of reaction curves and this is depicted in the second panel of Figure 19. We plot Q, along the Y-axis and Q, along the X-axis. The first duopolist's reaction curve is defined as the function relationship between the amount of output he will produce and the output produced by the second duopolist. It is therefore, the level of Q, the first duopolist chooses, given Q_2. Since we had the relationship a $2bQ_1\text{-}bQ_2 = 0$, this reaction curve is nothing but $Q_1 = (A/2b)\text{-}(I/2)Q_2$. The

relationship is a straight line and is plotted in the second panel of Figure 19. In exactly the same way, for the second duopolist, we had the relationship $a-2bQ_2-bQ_1 = 0$. This gives the second reaction curve as $Q_2 = (a/2b)-(I/2)\ Q_1$. This is also drawn-in the diagram. As is only to be expected, equilibrium occurs when the two reaction curves intersect each other. It is clear that this happens when the two duopolists produce an identical level of output.

Adjustment of Price

The Cournot model of duopoly is based on quantity adjustments. Assuming a certain level of output produced by the other duopolist, each duopolist chooses his own output level. Instead of quantity adjustments, price adjustments are also feasible. Assuming that a certain price will be charged by the other duopolist, each duopolist can choose the price that he will charge. One of the early models that used such price adjustments was because of Bertrand. One can argue out the contentions of the model verbally.

Apart from the assumption about price adjustments, the basic assumptions are identical to those in the Cournot model. Instead of assuming that the marginal cost of production is zero, one can assume that the marginal cost of production is constant and is thus equal to the average cost of production. The first duopolist sets up his business of selling mineral water first. Since he is the only producer, he behaves as if he were a monopolist and charges the price that would be charged by a monopolist. The second duopolist now arrives on the scene and thinks that the first duopolist will continue to charge the monopoly price. It is then logical for him to charge a slightly lower price than the monopoly price, because if he does this, all buyers will come to him and he will be able to capture the entire market. So he proceeds to do this. As a result, the first duopolist no longer has any sales. He decides that he should charge a price that is slightly lower than the price presently being charged by the second duopolist. The process goes on, with the duopolists under cutting each other in terms of price. There is however a limit to this price war, since no duopolist can afford to charge a price that is lower than the average cost of production, This is therefore the price at which an equilibrium is attained. No duopolist can afford to raise the price beyond this. And no duopolist can afford to lower the price below this. Since equilibrium is reached when the price is equal to the average cost of production, the Bertrand solution is identical to the solution one would have obtained under perfect competition. An equilibrium existed in the Bertrand framework.

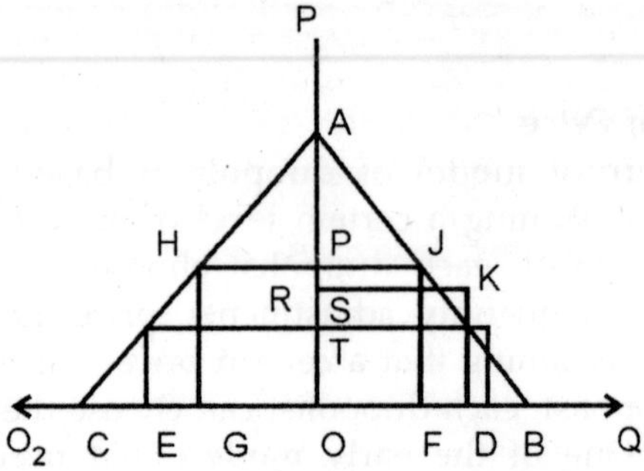

FIG. 20

However, a slight modification to the Bertrand framework makes equilibrium indeterminate and this analysis can be found in the work of Edgeworth, In the Bertrand framework, there was no limit to the quantity of output that could be produced by a duopolist. In Edgeworth's analysis, there is a ceiling on the quantity of output that a single duopolist can produce. Although not strictly inevitable for purposes of the analysis, let us continue to assume that the two duopolists are identical in every respect. We now have two quadrants. The first quadrant is used for the first duopolist and the second quadrant is used for the second duopolist. The two duopolists are identical in every respect and they sell a homogeneous product. Therefore, the market will be equally divided between the two, assuming that everything else is the same. AB is accordingly the demand curve that the first duopolist faces. Its mirror image, AC is the demand curve that the second duopolist faces. There is however a limit to the maximum level of output that the first duopolist can produce, displayed as OD. Its mirror image, OE, is the maximum level of output that the second duopolist can produce. For purposes of simplicity, let us suppose that the marginal cost is zero. If the two duopolists collude and act jointly as a monopolist, they will produce a, level of output such that the marginal revenue is zero.

This means that the first duopolist will produce an output that is equal to OF and the second duopolist will produce an output that is equal to OG. the resultant price will be GH = FJ = OP. Let us modify the assumption a little bit now, Both duopolists have been charging the monopoly price OP, but without any collusion taking place between them. The first duopolist thinks that the second duopolist will continue to charge a price OP. If that is the case, he can attract buyers by lowering the price slightly below OP. At present, he sells an output level of OF. But if he lowers the price marginally, he can sell his entire potential output of OD. Accordingly, he lowers the price slightly to OR. Consequently, his profits (assuming zero costs) go up from the earlier OPJF to ORKD. It is now the turn of the second duopolist to react, assuming that the first duopolist keeps the price at OR. The second duopolist therefore reduces the price to OS. The process of under cutting prices continues. When does it terminate? It will clearly terminate when the price charged is OT. This is the price at which either duopolist can sell the entire amount (OD and OE) that he can produce. There is no point in reducing the price further. Now comes the interesting bit. This situation is not an equilibrium. Let us look at the situation from the first duopolist's point of view. The second duopolist is charging a price of OT and selling an output of OE. He cannot expand his output beyond this level.

There are thus buyers who cannot be satisfied by the second duopolist. The first duopolist decides that he will tap this market. And in doing so, he can charge a price of OP, as the second duopolist is not in a position to attract away customers from him. Once the first duopolist has jacked up the price to OP, the second duopolist realises that he can make greater profits by charging a price that is slightly lower than OP, instead of charging a price of OT. The process continues ad nauseam, There is no equilibrium at all. The models we have so far described, are known as classical approaches to the problem of oligopoly. They recognised the problem of interdependence and highlighted the complexities that oligopoly leads to, but failed to find a satisfactory analysis for interdependence. It is, therefore, time to move on to more modern theories of oligopoly.

Recognition of Interdependence

In so far as modern theories of oligopoly are concerned, there are two books that you really ought to read. The first is known as The Economics of Imperfect Competition and is by Joan Robinson. The second is known as The Theory of Monopolistic Competition and is by Edward Chamberlin. For instance, within the Cournot framework, Chamberlin suggests a way of handling the problem of interdependence. There are two duopolists and the cost of production is zero. The product sold is homogeneous and the market demand curve is linear. Take a look at Figure 21. The market demand curve is AB. The first duopolist is the first one to enter the market and he behaves as if he were a monopolist. He accordingly produces an output level of OC and charges a price OP = CD. The second duopolist now arrives on the scene. He reckons that the demand curve he faces is DB. Therefore, he produces an output level of CE and charges a price OP'. Since the price has fallen from OP to OP, the first duopolist's profits decline. Now the analysis deviates from Cournot's. How will the first duopolist react to the arrival of a competitor?

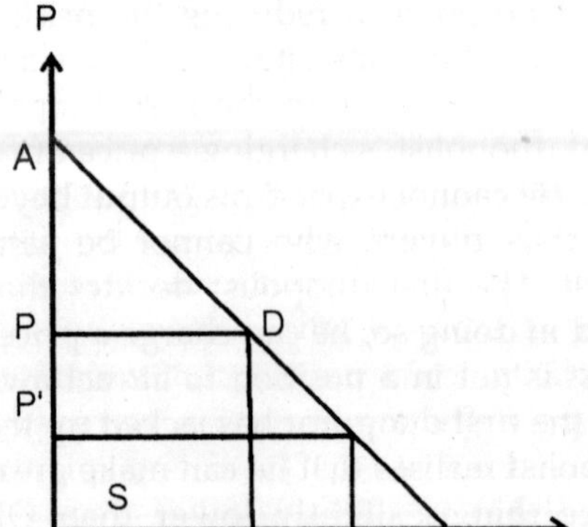

FIG. 21

He immediately recognises that there is mutual interdependence involved. The second duopolist produces an output level of CE and this is exactly half the monopoly output. The first duopolist, therefore, decides that he should also produce exactly half the monopoly output. The total output will then be the level of monopoly output OC and the price prevailing in the market will be OP. Once he does this, the second duopolist also realises what is happening and sees no reason to cause further problems. Equilibrium settles down at the monopoly level of output, although there has been no explicit collusion. What happens if there is explicit collusion? There is no ready answer, since collusion is a vague expression. What form does the collusion take? There can be cartels that decide on an uniform price that will be charged. Collusion ends with the setting of this common uniform price.

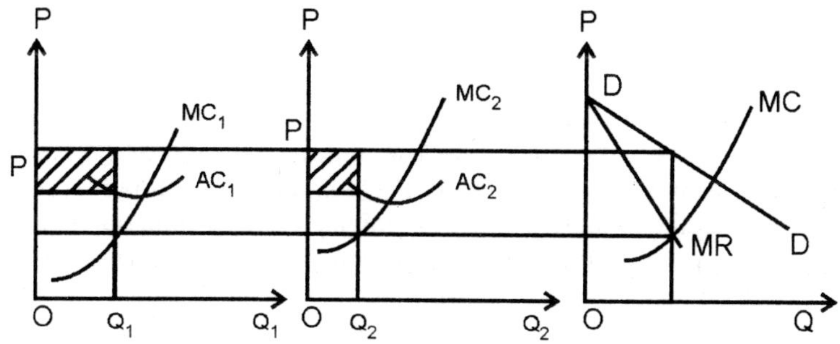

FIG. 22

There can be cartels that adopt market sharing arrangements. Collusion ends with such an apportioning out of markets. Complete collusion takes place when the firms decide to jointly maximize profits. De facto, they decide to function as a monopoly. Let us examine what happens in such a case. For purpose of simplicity, let us assume that we are dealing with a situation of duopoly. The argument can be readily generalised. The market demand curve is DD and is displayed in the third panel. Corresponding to this market demand curve, the marginal revenue curve is MR. To figure out conditions for joint maximization of profits, one needs to know what the aggregate marginal cost (MC) curve for the two duopolists taken together looks like. The two duopolists need not have identical cost conditions. The first panel displays the marginal cost curve for the first duopolist (MC_1). The second panel displays the marginal cost curve for the second duopolist (MC). The aggregate marginal cost curve will obviously be a horizontal summation of these two individual marginal cost curves. Once the aggregate marginal cost curve has been obtained, aggregate profits are maximized when MR is equal to MC. This means that total output will be OQ and the common price charged will be OP. All the cartel has decided on so far, is the total output OQ. This will now,have to be apportioned out among the two duopolists for production. Since the duopolists do not face identical cost conditions, it will not make sense for each of them to produce half the desired output. It should be fairly obvious that this allocation of output to the first duopolist (OQ_1) and the second duopolist (OQ_2) should be such that each duopolist has the same marginal cost of production. Is it clear that if the marginal costs differ, the allocation of production cannot be optimal? We have also drawn in the average cost curves AC_1 and AC_2. Given the price OP_1 the shaded regions display the profits that will be earned by the two duopolists. However, we are talking about joint profit maximization. So it is not the case that the two duopolists retain these profits. These profits go into a common pool. Which duopolist retains how much of the common profits, is a matter for negotiation and bargaining.

Concept of Price Leadership

There is a different form of collusion that is also feasible. In this type of collusion, the firms in the industry accept one producer as a price leader. So the leader sets the price and the other firms follow suit. The other firms function as followers. Since explicit price leadership agreements are sometimes prohibited by law, collusion through price leadership tends to be tacit or implicit. There are at least three different types of price leadership theories floating around.

First, one has the concept of price leadership by a low cost firm. Second, one has the concept of price leadership by a dominant firm, dominance being defined in terms of market shares. Third, one has the idea of barometric price leadership. Under this, an old or experienced firm accepts the role of leadership. We will concentrate on price leadership by a low cost firm and price leadership by a dominant firm. There are two firms in the industry and they sell an undifferentiated product. The first firm has an uniformly lower cost of

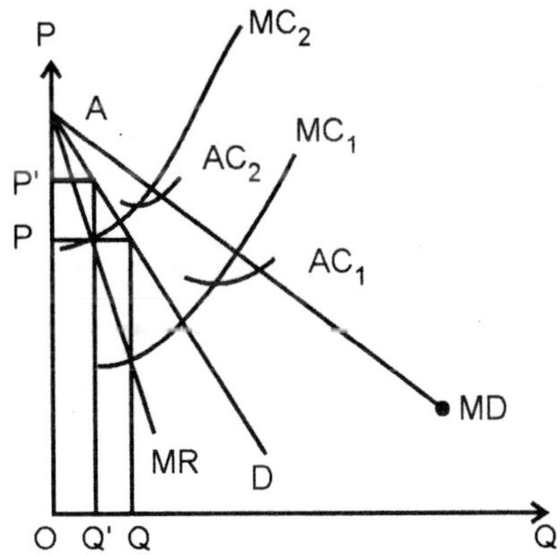

FIG. 23

production than the second firm. For purposes of simplicity, let us assume that each firm caters to exactly half the market. This means that each firm faces the same demand curve. In the diagram, the market demand curve is marked as AMD. The demand curve that each firm faces is marked as AD. Since the market is divided in a 50: 50 ratio, the AD curve is obtained by swivelling in the AMD curve inwards exactly half the way. The marginal revenue (MR) curve, which is also identical for both firms, is now drawn in. Superimposed on the diagram, we now have the cost curves of the two firms. MC_1 and AC_1 are respectively the marginal cost and average cost curves of the first firm, which has an uniformly lower cost of production. MC_2 and AC_2 are respectively the marginal cost and average cost curves of the second firm, which has uniformly a higher cost of production. The first firm (the price leader) will equate marginal revenue with marginal cost and fix a level of output OQ. At this level of output, the price in the market will be OP. The second firm would have liked to fix an output level of OQ′, with an associated price OP′. But because it is a higher cost producer, it doesn't want to get into a price war. It accepts the price leadership of the first firm. With a homogeneous product, there is no question of product being sold at two different prices. Therefore, having accepted the price of OP, the second firm also produces and sells an output level of OQ. Each has exactly half the market.

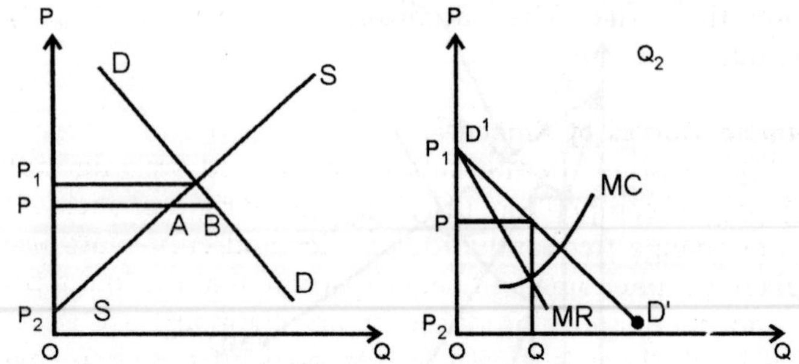

FIG. 24

The point is that the first firm will continue to maximize profits. But the profits of the second firm will be lower than the profits it would have obtained had it been able to equate its marginal revenue to its marginal cost. The next form of price leadership concerns price leadership by a dominant firm. The leader has a large chunk of the market. There are several other firms. But these other firms are all small firms. Therefore, even when taken together, they account for a small share of the market. The argument then proceeds as under, depicted in Figure 24. There are two panels in Figure 24. In the first panel, the market demand curve is displayed as DD. SS is the supply curve of all the small firms taken together. For any specific small firm, its supply curve will be its marginal cost curve. SS is the horizontal summation of all such individual supply curves. The dominant firm knows what SS looks like. In other words, it knows what the small firms will collectively supply for every conceivable market price. Using this information, the dominant firm can now draw the demand curve that it faces and this is displayed in the second panel of Figure 24. For instance, when the price is OP_1′ the small firms take care of the entire market and the demand that the dominant firm has to cater to, is zero. When the price level is OP_2, the small firms supply nothing and the entire market demand is catered to by the dominant firm. Accordingly, the demand curve faced by the dominant firm is displayed as D′D′ in the second panel. Based on this, the dominant firm draws its marginal revenue curve (MR). It equates marginal revenue with marginal cost and fixes a level of output OQ. At this output, the price is OP and the followers also accept this price. They accordingly collectively supply AP amounts of output.

Demand Curves of Kinked

Quite often, in markets characterised by oligopoly or oligopolistic competition, prices tend to be rigid or sticky. Prices do not change frequently. Kinked demand curves are used to explain this phenomenon. Let us suppose that the initial price is OP and the quantity produced by an oligopolist is OQ. At this price level, there is a kink in the demand curve so that the demand curve looks like DD.

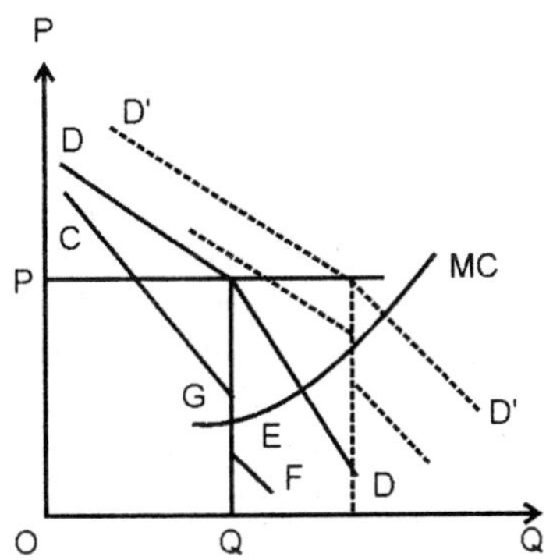

FIG. 25

This is the demand curve that an individual oligopolist faces. The kink means that at price above OP, the demand curve is extremely elastic. And at prices below OP, the demand curve is, extremely inelastic. Why should there be a kink in the demand curve? The answer lies in the expectations the oligopolist has about the behaviour of fellow oligopolists. The oligopolist believes that if he raises his price, competitors will not follow suit. But if he lowers the price, competitors will also match his price cut. Notice what happens when he lowers the price. Since other oligopolists have also lowered their prices, our oligopolist does not gain in market share. However, since the price has fallen, there is an increase in overall demand and our oligopolist obtains a little bit of these enhanced sales, perhaps in proportion to his market share. So when there is a price cut, demand increases a little, but not by that much. Thus, for prices below OP_1 the demand curve is relatively inelastic. If our oligopolist raises the price, competitors do not follow suit. Therefore, buyers move away from him, and begin to buy from his competitors. He doesn't lose all his buyers, because there is some element of product differentiation and some consumers continue to buy his products. Had there been no product differentiation whatsoever, for prices above OP_1 the demand curve would have been infinitely elastic. With some product differentiation, for prices above OP, the demand curve is fairly price elastic. Our oligopolist in fact loses in two ways. First, existing consumers move away from him. Second, as a result of the hike in prices, some consumers now prefer not to consume the product. Having drawn the demand curve, we need to draw the marginal revenue curve. This will have two completely different linear segments. There will be a stretch CG and there will be another stretch EF. In between, one has a broken vertical segment GE. Suppose we initially have a situation where the MC curve passes through this vertical segment. This means that the oligopolist is maximizing his profits, since marginal revenue is equal to marginal cost. Also notice the following. Even if cost conditions change, with the marginal cost curve continuing to pass through the vertical segment, the price (and the output) will continue to be the same. Prices accordingly exhibit a certain stability. Prices can in fact continue to be stable even if demand conditions change and the demand curve shifts to D'D'. Even in such cases, it is feasible that the price remains the same at OP, although the output level will obviously go up.

Full Cost Pricing

So far, we have tended to argue that an oligopolist (subject to a few limited exceptions) should maximize profits. He should equate marginal revenue with marginal cost and fix the level of output, qualified by whatever is assumed about interdependence and the reactions of other oligopolists. It is sometimes suggested that oligopolists do not have information or data on marginal revenue or marginal cost. Data are instead available on average variable cost (AVC). To this, one adds average fixed cost (AFC). Since all these costs are accounting costs as opposed to economic costs, a mark up has to be added for normal profits. Thus, this method of fixing prices is referred to as full cost pricing, cost plus pricing or mark up pricing. You should note that if costs are invariant over long stretches of output, full cost pricing will also lead to a stability or stickiness in prices.

Secondly, full cost pricing has no reference to demand conditions. It deviates from the principle that there must be equilibrium in the market, with demand equal to supply. Even if the prevailing price does not result in market equilibrium, prices will not adjust so as to bring the market back to equilibrium. One way to rationalise this is to argue that if the disequillibrium is temporary, adjustments will take place through changes in inventory levels. The idea behind full cost pricing can also be restated in a slightly different way. We know that MR = P (I-1/e) We also know that given profit maximization, we will have MR equal to MC. If the average variable cost (AVC) remains the same over a long stretch, this effectively means that MC = AVC. Stated differently, AVC = P (I-1/e) We can rewrite this as P = AVC (e/(e-1)). Or as, P = AVC + AVC (1/(e-1)). The ratio 1/(e-1), which varies with the elasticity of demand, can be regarded as a mark up. In this sense, full cost pricing does not necessarily contradict the outcome of profit maximization. The inevitable thrust of full cost pricing theories lie in questioning the quality of information that is available with oligopolists, disputing profit maximization as an objective and in focusing on prices being determined in an administered way.

Sales Maximization

Full cost pricing theories question profit maximization as an objective, although as you just discovered, full cost pricing does not necessarily contradict profit maximization. Let us now consider sales maximization as a viable option under oligopoly, the idea being that managers are often interested in maximizing sales rather than in maximizing profits. Maximizing sales is, of course, the same thing as maximizing revenue. This does not necessarily mean that revenues are maximized irrespective of profits. More commonly, there is a minimum level of profits that is desired. Provided that this minimum level of profits is ensured, revenue is maximized. In Figure 26, revenue is measured along the Y-axis and output is measured along the X-axis. The revenue curve (R) has a reverse U-shape. In the same diagram, we have drawn in the cost (C) curve. The slope of the cost curve progressively increases, indicating the increase in marginal costs as output expands. The vertical distance between the two curves is nothing but profits and we have also drawn in the profit (p) curve. The curve also has a reverse U-shape. Profits are maximum when the vertical distance between the revenue and the cost curves is maximum. This happens when the slope of the revenue curve is the same as the slope of the cost curve.

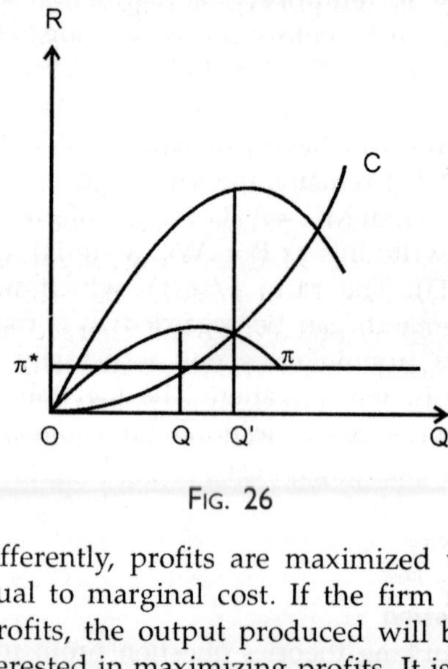

FIG. 26

Stated differently, profits are maximized when marginal revenue is equal to marginal cost. If the firm is interested in maximizing profits, the output produced will be OQ. But the firm is not interested in maximizing profits. It is interested in a minimum level of profits (p) being ensured. Subject to this, it wants revenue to be maximized. Thus, the firm expands output to OQ′. As is but natural, the profit maximizing output is smaller than the revenue maximizing output.

Limit Pricing

In our final section on oligopoly, we will talk about limit pricing, first suggested by an economist known as Bain. The idea behind limit pricing is that oligopolists are not always interested in maximizing short-term profits. They also have the very long run in view. If you remember, the very long run is a time period in which entry by new firms (and exit) is permitted. Thus, existing oligopolists may be interested in preventing the entry of new firms. In a simple framework, existing oligopolists collude so as to prevent entry. They set a price known as the limit price, which may be lower than the price they would have charged had they been interested in maximizing profits. A profit maximizing price may have attracted new entrants. But since the limit price is lower than the profit maximizing price, potential entrants are discouraged. In Figure 27, AD is the market demand curve that existing oligopolists confront. MR is the corresponding marginal revenue curve. For the purpose of simplicity, let us assume that the long run average cost curve of existing oligopolists is the same. This is displayed as LAC_E. The long run average cost curve of potential entrants is LAC_P. Since the long run average cost curve of existing oligopolists is the same, the long run marginal cost curve is also the same as the long run average cost. Had existing oligopolists (who are colluding) been interested in maximizing profits, they would-have produced an output of OQ and charged a price OP. The problem with doing this is that entrants will come into the industry. However, if existing oligopolists fix a price of OP_e, potential entrants will be discouraged from entering. In the, process, existing oligopolists sell an output of OQ′. Their profits are not as high as would have been the case had they only been

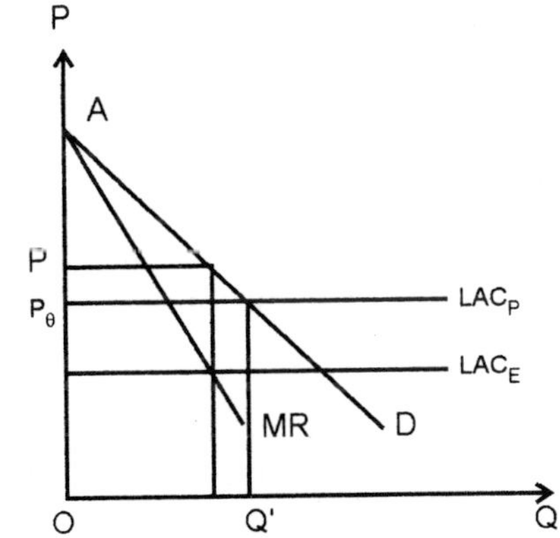

FIG. 27

interested in maximizing temporary profits. But they continue to make positive profits. So far as potential entrants are concerned, at the moment, the market price is equal to their long run average cost. But once they enter, the market supply curve shifts to the right and drives down the price. Consequently, they will incur losses. Limit pricing works because existing oligopolists have an absolute cost advantage over potential entrants and this acts as a barrier to entry.

There can be other examples of barriers to entry as well. Refinements to limit pricing theories are feasible, based on other types of barriers to entry like economies of scale, a minimum needed efficient plant size and large initial capital requirements. But we will gloss over these.

QUESTIONS

1. Describe Price Determination under different market conditions.
2. What are the features of different Market Structures ?
3. Describe about Monopoly Competitive.
4. What do you know about Oligopolistic Competition ?

CHAPTER

8

Pricing Practices

PRICING METHODS IN PRACTICE : STRATEGY AND TACTICS

Marginal Analysis or Traditional approach to price setting : Traditional price theory for the firm establishes relationship beetween price and output in the similar manner as has been discussed in the cost and output relationship under different market situations. The present discussion is extension of the cost output analysis into price-output analysis following the traditional approach for fixation of prices for the products.

Pure competition : In a purely competitive market structure price is determined for a commodity by market forces which include the presence of large number of firms in the industry who are individually unable to influence prices as homogenically identical products, and large number of buyers who demand such products. Each firm has full freedom to enter the market and exit the market and take independent decision about price and output. In such a market situation buyers and sellers interact with each other and such interaction settles the prices, by bringing in force the well-established principle of

Supply and Demand. The price movement is flexible under such a situation. Individual firm is only a price taker and cannot charge price higher than its competitors. If the firm does so it will lose its customers. Therefore, to maximise profit it will have to accept going rate of prices. This is so because of the perfectly elastic demand curve of the purely competitive firm demarcated by horizontal line. In short run the firm operating under purely competitive market situation may make profit by maintaining managerial efficiency or may incur lesses to close down its business for inefficient management because the price which it has to charge for its products is the going rate price. The following diagram may explain the situation of short run price fixation :

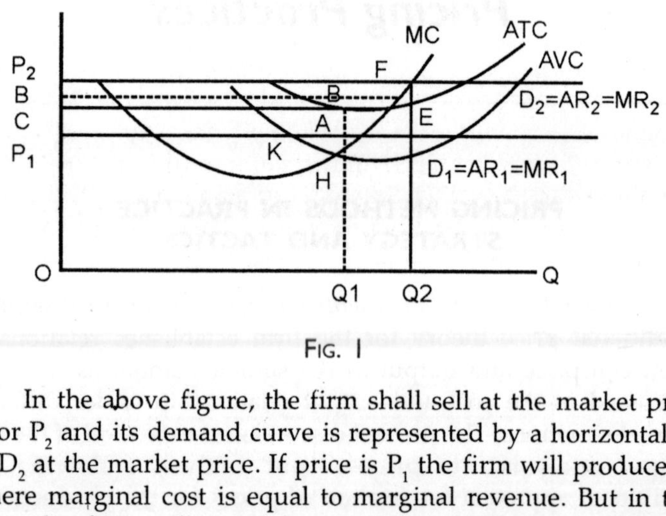

FIG. I

In the above figure, the firm shall sell at the market price P_1 or P_2 and its demand curve is represented by a horizontal D_1 or D_2 at the market price. If price is P_1 the firm will produce Q_1 where marginal cost is equal to marginal revenue. But in this case, the firm will incur loss as it is unable to recover the average total costs. This loss is represented by the distance between B and A or the rectangle CBAP$_1$. But at this level of P_1, losses are minimised because average variable costs are recovered with small contribution as represented by distance between H and A. if the firm does not produce Q_1 quantity then it will have to incur loss equal to BH distance.

So, in short run under purecompetitive market situation only that firm could survive who can produce that much quantity which may offer contribution over the going rate of price to recover average variable cost. Suppose, if the going rate of price is P_2 then the firm will have to produce Q_2 quantity to recover Average Total Cost where MC= MR or price and the profit of the firm will be assessed from the rectangle EFG P_2. The law of supply and demand operating under short-run conditions of purely competitive market can be explained if Marginal Cost curve above the point of its inter-section with the Average Variable Cost curve is taken as firm's supply curve. This is so because the firm shall produce only to the minimum extent when it, atleast, recovers its Average costs Below that point, it will have to close down for heavy losses as losses are minimum at this point. In the above figure K to Z of the MC curve is the firm's supply curve and it inter-section with the given demand curve (which is represented by price line) settles the price at P_1. The market price will move towards equilibrium where quantity demanded equals quantity supplied. Thus, toward the right side of K the firm can increase the quantity if demand rises giving rise to prevailing prices. In the long-run, the supply and demand of the commodity will establish equilibrium point at their inter-section point. The price will be fixed only at this inter-action point. This situation can be explained through the following graph :

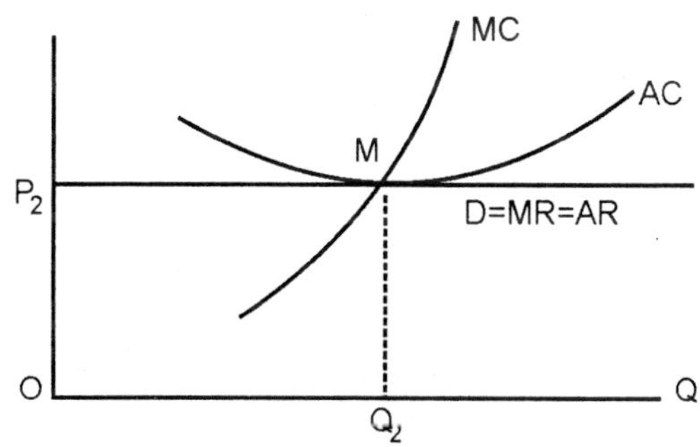

FIG. 2

In the above graph MC intersects demand curve at point M by producing Q_2 quantity which is being sold at P_2 price where MC = MR and the firm has been able to recover its average costs too. In the short-run we had average total costs and average variable costs in our analysis but in long-run all fixed costs become variable so this differentiation has been eliminated by taking into consideration only average costs. In the long-run average cost is just equal to price which means that the firm is not in a position to make any excessive profits.

If the price instead of P_1 becomes P_3 that is any point above AC then firm profitability will increase motivating other firms to enter into the market to take benefit of the price-cost differences but entry of more firms will increase supply of commodity which will reduce price to the level of existing equilibrium where demand and supply inter-sect each other at a equilibrium point. However, shift in demand curve for reasons of change in consumers' taste, income pattern, attitude or price of complementary or substitute goods occurs which will tend to shift the equilibrium point also by suitably adjusting to supply position. In long-run profit and loss of the firm will disappear. The general view of market price determination under pure competition can be had from the following schedule showing price and the quantity of dry-fruits available in the local commodity market:

TABLE

(figures in kg.)

Price (in Rs.)	*Quantity Demanded*	*Qty. Supplied*
10	100	300
8	150	250
6	200	200
4	250	150
3	300	100
2	400	50

From the above schedule it can easily be read that at price 10 very less quantity (100) is demanded where as supplies are huge (300). With the result more firms will shut-down for want of profit avenues in the process supplies will be reduced to the even 200 with the continuous reduction in price. The lowering trend in price gradually motivates more buyers so that the demand is slowly raised to the level of 200 when price falls to Rs. 6. Further fall in the price reduces supplies as many more firms are unable to recover their costs but demand for the dry fruits-increases. Excess demand with very little supplies will further move price up and bring more firms in business for reaping opportunities for profit earnings and in this way again the market force will bring the price to be settled at equilibrium point where supply exactly match with the demand for the quantity. This market mechanism can be depicted by the Figure 3 :

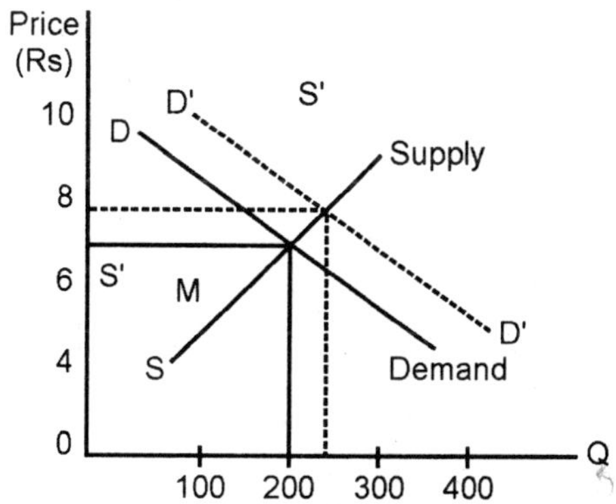

FIG. 3

The above diagram displays an equilibrium position arrived at through the interaction of demand and supply. However, with the given supply, if income of the consumer suddenly increases then their demand curve will shift to right hand side as D^1D^1 for increase in their purchasing power. This will shift the equilibrium price to higher level. For decrease in the disposable income of the demanders the demand curve may also shift to lower side creating a lower equilibrium point. Similarly there may be downward or upward shifts in the supply curve also affecting the equilibrium point : The above situation implies a flexible market wherein price will be determined by the market forces. On the other hand, there may occur situation when the Government may fix price at less than equilibrium point for the commodity so that the price is rendered stable to be within the reach of poorer sections of the society. Government intervention with market situation will create disequillibrium for the time being as lesser firm will supply only at less than equilibrium price. The demand will be more as this policy has been adopted by Government of India in the case of steel, coal, cement, etc. Due to excess demand, the suppliers will be willing to charge higher prices in black market and an equilibrium in disguise will be established for black market pricings of such controlled price commodities. Incidence of reduction or increase in Taxation imposed by Government may also affect the equilibrium position of supply and demand of any commodity under pure competitive conditions. Suppose Government of India has enhanced excise duty on a particular commodity, then how much of this increase will be borne by the suppliers and how much of such increase will be passed on the consumers in the shape of price increase can be reflected from the diagram given below :

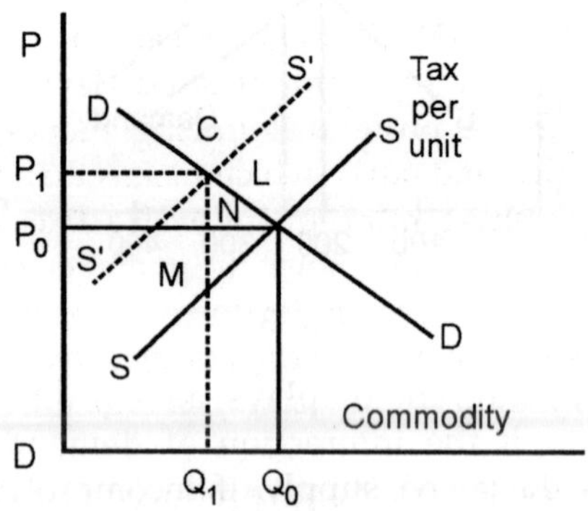

FIG. 4

In the above diagram, suppose pre-tax equilibrium was at a point L with price P_0, and quantity supplied Q_0. Increase in tax compelled the producer-suppliers to raise price to P_1 by raising the cost curve to S'S' (by assumption supply curve is the average cost curve of the firm in long-run). Tax per unit is represented by length of CM but the resulting price increase will be only CN as part of the tax incidence (NM) will be borne by the suppliers and (CN) will be passed on to the consumers. But on such increased prices buyers may not purchase the quantity Q and the fresh equilibrium point will be established at C demanding Q_1 quantity only. To conclude, under pure competition, the firm can not have any price policy. It shall have to accept the going rate market price over, which it has no control as this rate is settled through market forces of supply and demand in which each and every firm participate as supplier collectively. Stock exchange and grain market are the best existing examples of such a market situation.

Pure Monopoly : Pricing of commodity under pure monopoly is the sole job of sole producer who is a firm as well as an industry because the firm has no close substitute. Monopolist exist for many reasons viz. (a) efficient cost function having advantage of economies of scale which smaller firm may not be having under pure competition; (b) huge capital investment which other firms might not afford to incur in plant size, operating process etc.; (c) advantageous financial position and capacity to borrow; (d) efficient management services through highly salaried technical experts, (e) huge administrative structure with better means of communication and co-ordination, through computerised devices and use of modern technology. A profit maximizing monopolist faces a negative sloping demand curve which means that at lower price consumer will purchase more quantity. He fixes up prices at such a point which is much higher the average cost to enhance his margin of profit. He is able to do so by restricting output. Figure 5 illustrates pricing process adopted by monopolist in contravention to a situation obtaining under pure competitive conditions. In Fig. 5 MR is intersected by MC at point A. If monopolist charges P_1 price and produces Q_1 quantity he is benefitted by CB times the quantity because he is able to recover

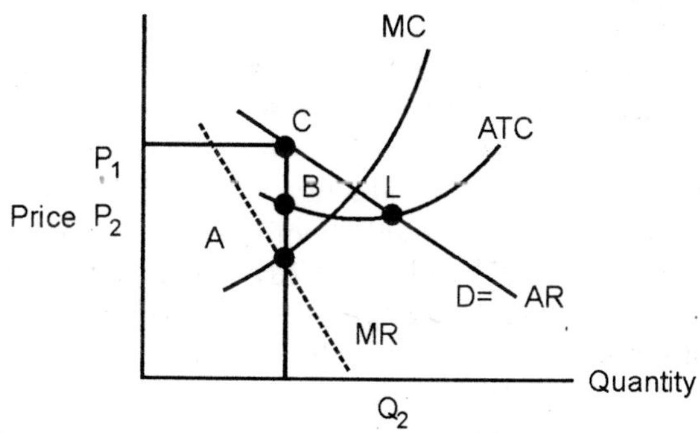

FIG. 5

average total costs at point B. ATC is the supply curve of the firm, its intersection at point L displays the pure competitive equilibrium point with price at P, and quantity at Q_2.

The greatest evil associated with the monopoly is misallocation of resources, which reduces aggregate welfare and distributes national income in favour of the monopolist. The welfare loss through monopolist pricing can be displayed by way of a graph :

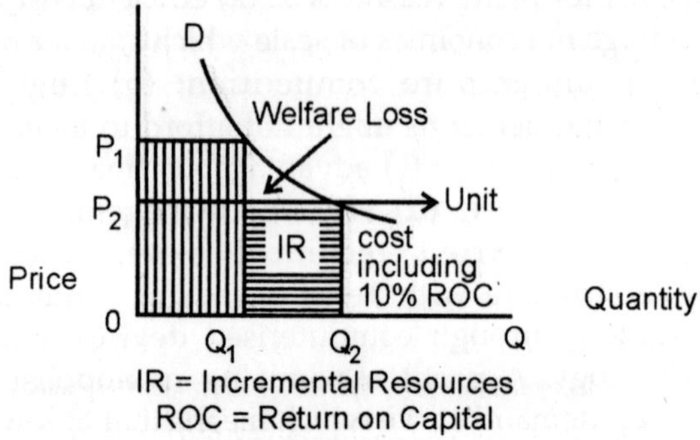

FIG. 6

The above diagram would display a hypothetical case where demand for industry's product is unity. The average revenue for the firm's product cover 10% return on invested capital; but the firm is having 20% return by restricting output at Q_1 and selling it at P_1. This is resulting into misallocation of resources. The firm could have produced Q_2 and sold at P_1 to save the society from welfare, loss as indicated in the figures 6. The firm has employed different resources like capital or labour but has not been making full use of all of them to run to full capacity. These resources if could be saved from this firm could have been used for other productive purposes. Such transfer could increase society's welfare by equalising the profits of the monopolist with other productive firms who could use the resources saved from wastage of excess capacity of the monopolist's production.

Discriminating Monopoly : A monopolist possibly discriminate in pricing the homogenous product so as to charge different price from different customers. Such discrimination in pricing is impossible under perfect competitive market situation but a monopolist can exercise it because of his monopolistic position as sole producer and seller for a particular commodity.

There are three main reasons for such price discriminations viz. (a) Firstly, the monopolist is aware of consumers' ignorance for the cost of a product because of lack of knowledge and communication of proper information. (b) Secondly, in rendering professional services or personal services, discriminating price can be charged by a monopolist from different customers. A doctor specialist having monopoly in his professional specialisation. can charge more fee from rich and lesser fee from poorer clients.

Such discrimination is feasible when the service rendered or commodity sold can't be resold.

Thirdly, price discrimination may be practised under the circumstances when cost difference might exist because of distance between one market or another lower price in poorer markets and higher prices in sophisticated market could be charged. Mostly, such price discrimination occurs when firms' different markets are separated by distance or by national frontiers cheaper commodity in one market may not be resold at dearer markets because of excessive cost of transportation. Price discrimination may, thus, cover transportation cost which are substantial in many cases for example, steel or coal transportation cost are substantial in many cases. Profit maximization is the basic objective before a discriminating monopolist. For this purpose he would like to avail of every opport unity what is available to any ordinary monopolist.

The basic rule, according to W.J. Boumol, which he has to follow, is that marginal revenue in all the markets where he is practising discrimination should be similar. Monopolist can allocate his products in different markets on the basis of available MR from the best combination. Suppose, if monopolist is able to sell more and earn more MR in market A than B then he will transfer his product from B to A so that it could fatch more revenue in A. Monopolist will have to take into consideration the differences in the elasticity of demand from one market segment to another at the same price. James R. McGuigon and R. Charles Moyer have explained the price discrimination by a monopolist into three stages. In the first stage they define it first degree price discrimination where monopolist only knowns market demand curve and the capacity and ability of each customer to pay for the quantities. He then charges each of his customers the highest price they are willing to pay for each unit purchased. Thus, he captures the entire consumer's surplus of the customers. Such type of price discrimination rarely exists in practice. In the second degree price discrimination the price is charged less for consuming more quantity of product and more for lesser. In public utilities this may happen electricity charges. If you consume lesser units than a prescribed minimum you are charged with fixed minimum charges. If you consume more than the prescribed minimum units you are charged with the running rate per unit. Railways also charge flat rate freight for carrying goods etc. This is known as block rate price setting also. In this case, only part of the consumer's surplus is captured. Such discrimination is feasible where services and products are sold through metered units like water, electricity or gas.

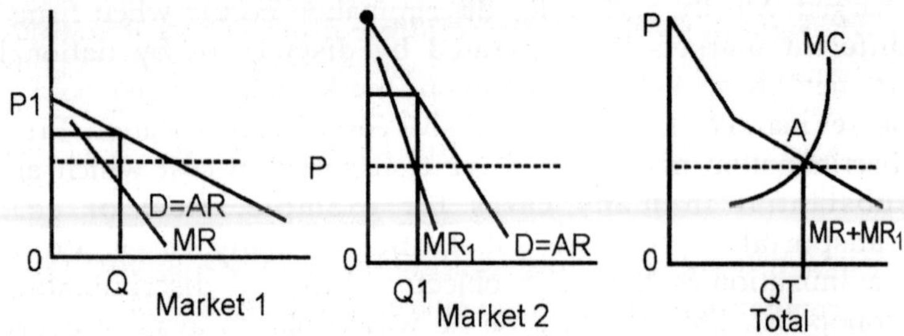

FIG. 7

Thirdly, Third-decree price decrimination is more common. Firms segregate their customers into different small groups like household, individual users, commercial users etc., and follow a different price rate schedule for each of these categories. Allocation of product in these different markets is done in such a way that MR in all markets is the same, that is the profit maximizing equilibrium position of a monopolist. The total output to be allocated to different markets is determined by setting the combined MR of all markets equal to MC. Figure 7 exemplify this situation :

In the Figure 7, if MR curves of market I and 2 are added together horizontally will yield total MR are displayed in the diagram No. 3 in above figure 7 for the aggregate market. The total output is set at a point A where MR intersects MC curve. This quantity is divided into both the markets as OQ and OQ_1 at which the MR are equal in both markets as needed for profit maximization which will be sold at prices P and P_1 in the two different markets with different elasticity of demand.

Monopolistic Competition : (Product differentiation) : Presence of Monopolistic competition in the market is reflected by the following characteristics of the market as assumed by Chamberlim while designing the model of monopolistic competition :

(1) The existence of relatively large number of firms producing and selling differentiated goods which are not homogenous products; (2) In this way each firm is an industry for the quality and quantity of the product it manufactures and sells out; (3) each product is an indirect substitute for the product of other firms. Differentiation in product may be caused by trade mark, packaging, quality design or conditions attached to sales like guarantee or warranty, credit terms and free servicing for longer periods etc, Under the above circumstances, firms have free entry into the trade with their own trade marks and patents. Each firm operates under the conditions of pure competition. The demand curve for the product of the firm has a negative slope. A small reduction in the price of the product may not attract much more customers as they have different degree of loyalty attached to products from different firms. But large reduction of price will break this attachment of the customers with their choiced brand. The firm obtains an equilibrium position where marginal cost equals the marginal revenue. In the short-run the firm may or may not earn profits. But in the long-run more competitors enters in the trade having been attracted by profits. So, excess profits are wipe out. The firm is at an equilibrium where demand line is tangent to its average cost curve as may be seen from the following Fig. 8. At P_1 price and Q_1 output MC is equal to MR. Any price lower

or higher than P_1 will result in a loss to the firm since AC will exceed price.

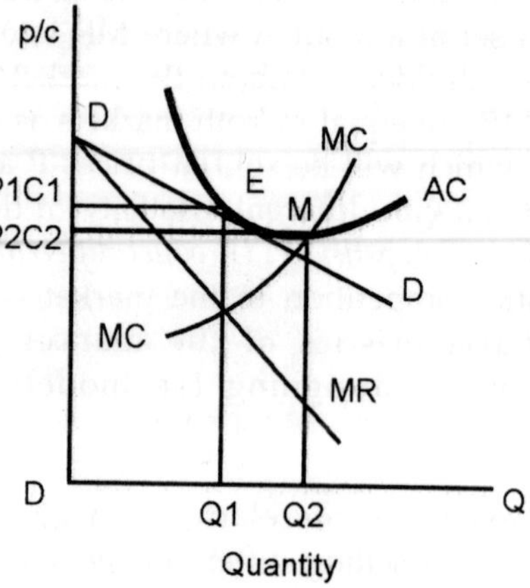

FIG. 8

In the above figure monopolistic competitor's equilibrium is at point E, where cost of output is recovered through price C_1 and MR is equal to MC. Any other level of output than Q_1 will be loss incurring situation to the firm as it may not be able to recover costs. This position is reflected through 'U' shape average cost (AC) curve. Further C_2 position with Q_2 production would reflect pure competition equilibrium at M where average cost will be equal to marginal cost and marginal revenue i.e., price. This situation will not exist in monopolistic competition as monopolist producer will produce lesser quantity and sell at higher price. He will find his profitable position beyond E to left. W.J. Boumol has discussed the possibility of few firms joining their resources together and availing of reduction in cost of production than that at point E. Same level of production can be produced now by lesser firms. If so each firm will expand having lower average cost giving advantage to the society for over all savings in cost of production using up excess capacity which evidence waste of resources. W. W. Haynes has put forth arguments reflecting the tendency of the firm not to join hands because each firm has special advantage of patents and trade marks resulting into discontinuities in the chain of substitutes.

This position can't be wiped out by competition. Due to such circumstances the position will be different and demand curve may not be completely pushed back to be tangent with cost curve. This situation is reflected in the following diagram;

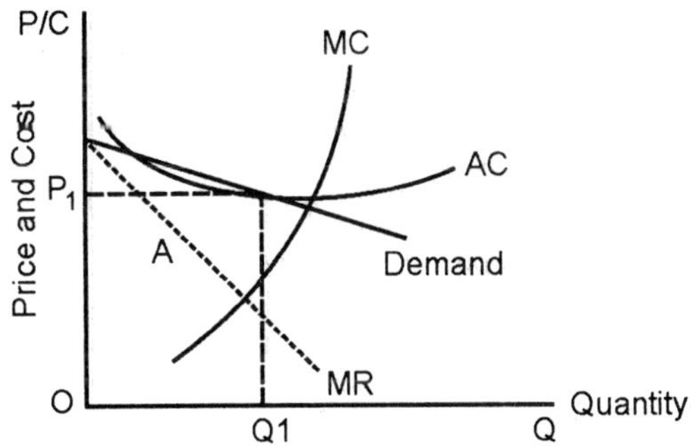

FIG. 9

The above diagram would display the position where the MR is equal to marginal cost but AC is not tangent to demand curve. The firm is making maximum Profit in the monopolistic situation amid competitors. Kalmen Cohen and Richard Cyert, in their book "Theory of the firm" have criticised the model of monopolistic competition. They hold the view that the situation of a monopolistic competition may not exist in the market because of three main reasons, viz. Firstly, if firms are existent in large number then they sell standardized or near standardized goods. Even if, in some degree, product differentiation exists it will keep the demand curve in horizontal shape reflecting pure competition; secondly, if the customers have brand preference for the products of different firms then such situation will be reflected as oligopoly where number of sellers are few; thirdly, if the firm selling in the market has no available substitute for its product then this situation will be reflected as a case of pure monopoly. According to the said authors, in no case, there exist a situation which may reflect the presence of monopolistic competition. Most of the modern writers like McGuigon and Moyer are in agreement with Cohen and Cyert, There are very few real-world market situations which may be most appropriate to Chamberlain's model of monopolistic competition.

Oligopoly : Oligopoly is a situation featured by presence of small number of firms producing any homogenous commodity. Pricing under oligopoly is based on recognition of three situations by the sellers viz.

(i) Existence of inter-dependence amongst the sellers of homogeneous goods i.e. any change in price output, product style or quality, introduction of new model or term of sale carry serious impact upon other sellers which enthuse them into reaction to adopt a change;

(ii) Foreseeing competitor's counter moves i.e. perceiving by the seller the reactions on the basis of past experience which are likely to be set on among other sellers on making any changes in the price structure of the competitive products.

(iii) Perceiving rivals best feasible strategies and preparing to move with them or counter-act against their strategies.

Existence of oligopoly situation in the market is reflected through price-wars, price cuts to drive out competitors, dominate price leadership by firm, collusion in pricing in the form of cartels or pools or in segmentation of markets, non-pricing competition evidenced by advertising competition or sales strategies or exhibitions of brand names etc. On many occasions oligopoly also generates secret price concessions for selected customers to avoid retaliation from other sellers and maintain the share in the market. These situations are observed by us in our daily walk of life more especially in retail as well as wholesale market of goods and services. Pricing under oligopolistic situation can be done by following three basic set model; viz. (1) Regid prices under kinked demand curve model, (2) price leadership and (3) Boumol's revenue maximization model.

Rigid Prices under kinked demand curve model : In 1939 Paul M. Sweezys had noted the rigid price-output behaviour in USA's oligopolistic industries. In subsequent studies made by other American authors oligopolistic tendencies were observed which kept the prices remarkably stable. In Indian industries this tendency is very much observed. Take for example,

Television industry. Prices of all brand are just equal and stable with advertising competition amongst different producers. Same is true with refrigerators manufacturers under different brand names like Godrej Volta's Opal, Kelvinator or Gem etc. In oligopolistic market situation, rigid price is maintained because of the assumption that a cut in price by one seller would motivate other competitive sellers to take a matching step under the common apprehension that they might loose their customers resulting into decline in their sale.

Similarly, a raise in price by one seller would make competitive sellers to be "sticky" so that they might attract new customers on old lower prices. In such a situation the demand curve will be highly elastic for price increases than for price decreases. Because, any increase in price by oligopolist which remains unmatched by other sellers would depress the sales by driving away the existing customers. In this way, total revenue of the firm would decline. Similar is true with decrease in price which is matched by other competitors would not be fully offset by increase in sales and as such its total revenue would be less after price reduction what would have been without making any such reduction. The following graph would depict the pricing change of an oligopolist :

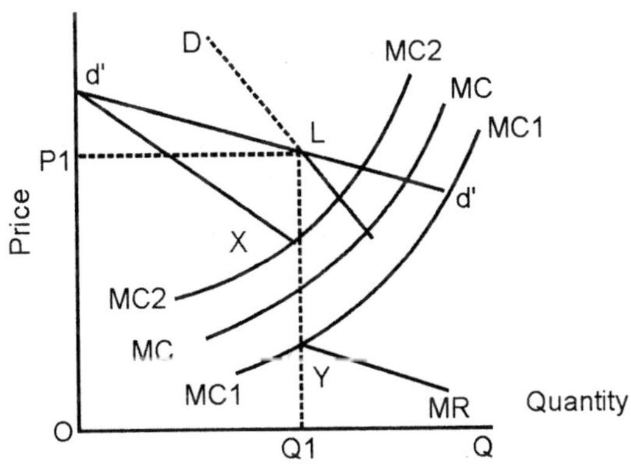

FIG. 10

From a close look on the above Fig. 10 the following points can be of use to explain price mechanism set in by oligopolistic movements.

(i) Curve DD is relatively inelastic showing that any reduction in the price which is matched by other oligopolists would not increase sales. Initially for a short while it might get a few customers but with rival's reactions anticipated jump in sales will not be attained.

(ii) Curve dd is relatively elastic showing that any reduction in price if remains unmatched then sales would increase tremendously.

(iii) Point C is the assumed point of prevailing price-quantity combination. Price reductions by the firm would not allow to increase sales on dd curve and with such reduction of price, the new demand curve of the firm will be inelastic portion of LD. Price increase will not motivate the other sellers to increase their prices; with increased price the new demand curve becomes d^1L. The new demand curve of oligopolist with rigid prices will be d^1LD having a kink at L which represents the current price at Q_1 with Q_1 quantity as price-output combination. The marginal revenue curve in this case will be a discontinuous line as represented by dXY MR. P, is the profit maximising situation for the firm. If marginal cost curve (MC) passes through the gap XY in the MR curve, the most profitable alternative is to maintain current price-output. Change in costs would not disturb the price-level as may be seen by MC_1 or MC_2. Similarly, any shift in demand curve either to right (an increase in demand) or to left (as decrease in demand) may not change the price deviation of the firm.

Maintaining price rigidity under monopolistic situation as explained under kink demand model has been put to emperical testing by a number of economists and their findings can be viewed as under : (i) Stigler' did not find any evidence of kinky demand in his study of seven oligopolistic industries, (ii) Cohen and Cyert, have observed that in short-run the kinky demand curve has little existence when competitors have no knowledge of reactions of others' price changes. This may happen in new industries in early stages. As firms have access to knowledge because of increased means of communications, the kinky demand curve does not exist as all firms increase or decrease their prices following the oligopolist.

Price leadership : It is another explanation to the oligopolistic situation. According to Joel Deen the oligopoly competitors achieve the delicate adjustment to changing cost and demand conditions without precipitating a price war through price leadership. One firm takes lead in fixing initial prices and other competitor firms follow the suit in fixing the prices for their product matching the leader's prices. Such price leadership is observed existing in stable industry with highly standardized product like steel, cement, building materials, etc. According to McGuigon and Moyers' there are two main forms of price leadership which have been observed existent in industries. from time to time viz. (i) Barometric price leadership, and (ii) Dominant price leadership. In Barometric leadership pattern, one firm announces price changes keeping in view the change in demand and cost pattern. This price change can be introduced by any firm, whosoever does so assuming the role of leadership. Other firms initially do not agree to such price changes. Many firms, as a result, announce higher price and many announce lower prices until a general agreement on new price policy arrived at through such moves amongst all firms. In the case of dominant leadership one firm may establish itself as a leader by virtue of its size, economic power, having lower cost structure etc. Such leader acts as monopolist and others simply follow his actions to exist in the market.

The smaller firms who can produce that much quantity which equate their marginal cost with the price fixed by leader exists in the market and those who are unable to reach to this position close down. Other firms who are so small in size follow the leader to avoid cut throat price competition and retaliation a price leader should possess basic qualifications noted by Joel Dean as—(i) A substantial share of market should be captured by price leader, so as to create followers. As a major partner in consumer market the price leader should be equipped with up-to-date information about demand and supply position, the number of competing firms and the customers, the cost of production factors affecting the cost and the income conditions of prospective customers. (ii) A price leader should possess a sound reputation in the industry amongst the follower firms. (iii) A price leader should take initiative in fixing prices, making changes in existing prices and motivating the followers to accept the price changes introduced by the leader. To make price leadership stable, the leader firm should understand the interest of its followers and act to safeguard such interest especially in changing economic situation affected by cyclical fluctuations. It should undertake business forecasting for the industry as a whole for the demand of its product, cost of inputs etc., to maintain its reputation amongst the followers. He should be particular about quality of the products being maintained by his followers.

Many times, firms follow price leadership but give secrete concessions to customers to attract more business. Such underground price competition fades away the impact of price leader and when inferior goods are supplied by certain miscreant firms then the reputation of such price leader is put at stake. Such a situation is obtainable in those industries where demand is in excess and supply position always lags behind. For instance, in India, in drugs industry and tyre industry such mal-practices are in vogue despite the price leadership established by Dunlop India or Fire Stone in the tyre industry.

Boumol's Revenue Maximization Model : W. J. Baumol in his article, "On The Theory of Oligopoly" characterised that "oligopolists typically seek to maximise their sales subject to minimum profit constraints....the firm will aim for that stream of profits which allows for the financing of maximum long run sales... to take advantage of all reasonably safe opportunities for growth and to provide a fair return to stockholders." The process of setting-up prices and output by an oligopolist with a view to maximise sales under the profit constraint has been discussed by Boumol under price-output-determination model under partial analysis. Sales maximization here implies maximization of of total revenue. If at a revenue maximising output the firm earns enough profits to meet the competitive requirements then it will want to produce the sales maximising quantity.

But, if at this output, profits are too low, the firm's output must be changed to a level which meets the profit requirements though it may not maximise sales. In such a situation two types of equilibria appear to be feasible i e. one in which the profit constraints provided no effective barrier to sales maximization and another is which so does. This is displayed in the following diagram with firms total revenue, cost and profit curves :

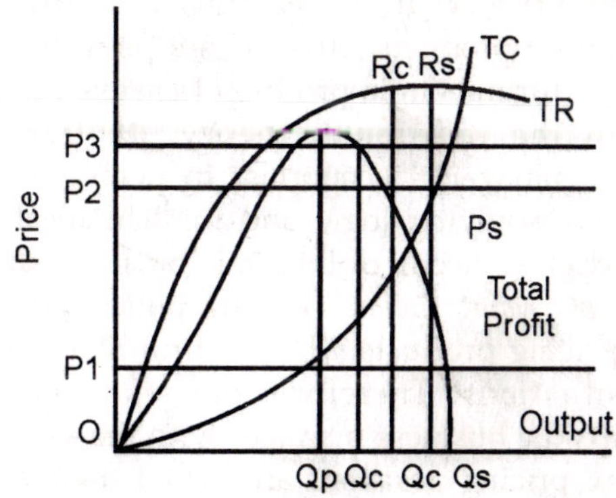

FIG. 11

Profit and sales maximising outputs are OQp and OQs. If OP_1 is the minimum needed profit level of the firm then sales maximising output will be OQs setting selling price at Qs Rs OQ. If profit level is OP_2 then output will be reduced to OQc. QP is profit maximising output which is smaller to sales maximising output OQs or OQc that is, sales maximising output yields lower profits. If needed minimum profit rises from OP_2 to OP_3 so that at the initial output OQc in profit level is no longer acceptable, this level of profit can only be attained by a cut in production and physical sales to OQc by rising price to P_3.

PRICING STRATEGY AND PRACTICES PRICING POLICY

Traditional theory, as discussed above, relating to taking pricing decisions does not respond to the problematic pricing situations in the complexity of economic environment because of inherent weaknesses in its logical frame-work viz. firstly, the traditional theory rests on the assumption of profit maximization as the basic goal of the firm which is not correct assumption. Profit is the end result of successful working of a firm while survival and growth is its sole aim. Secondly, it analyses static situation, a fixed period study and fails to consider short-run and long-run effects of price change. In a way it does not answer to the situation involving future risk because of uncertainty of price change It also ignores discounted effect of todays price on future revenues. Thirdly, traditional theory ignores multiproducts situation and is restricted only to the firm manufacturing single product. However, despite these weaknesses in the raditional. theory, it offers a logical framework for managerial economist to evolve a pattern for pricing decisions applying logic and mathematical properties suiting to the diverse needs of dynamic business situations.

Objectives of pricing Policy : Pricing policy are generalised decisions for pricing products which a firm makes in different competitive situations. Therefore, the study of traditional approach equips the business manager with the analytical tools. The objective of pricing decisions are varied than simple profit maximization assumed under traditional approach. The pricing decisions may be aimed at minimising risk under conditions of uncertainty. Social accountability of business has provided a different set of objectives to the business manager for pricing decisions which are needed to be devoid of monopolistic or discriminatory practices. Revenue maximization objectives may be viewed from social angle for making the product available at cheaper price to all consumers rather than following a restrictive trade practice of charging high prices. Besides these objectives, the firm has to evolve a pricing policy which should respond to strengthen its own structure by assuring a needed rate of return on investors' funds, combat competitive situation for ensuring long term welfare and growth in changing economic situations etc.

Factors Affecting Price Poucy : A firm under pricing decisions should consider the interests, role and accountability of all the parties affected by the pricing. Traditional economic theory name only two parties viz., buyers and sellers but Alfred R. Oxen-feld has named seven main parties to the pricing process, viz., (1) those responsible for sales promotion; (2) the ultimate customers for product; (3) rival sellers; (4) potential rivals; (5) middlemen; (6) suppliers; and (7) the government. The author of this book would like to add three more parties viz. (8) the investor-shareholder; (9) the employee and (10) the society in general. All these parties are elements of pricing decisions. Their interests be protected through pricing decisions. They individually and combinedly affect the pricing decisions. These parties are responsible for introducing changes in existing price policies and practices.

Internal Structure of Firm's For Pricing Decision : Besides the above factors, firm's own internal structure affects pricing decisions. Top management's accountability is limited to framing out a pricing policy. It is only the delegated power and accountability from sales-manager to sales-man that needs taking price decisions with in the the framework of pricing policy laid down by top management. The internal Organisation of the firm should be responsive to different situations requiring different pricing decisions. The internal Organisation should have a quick information system reporting about the market conditions and other needed matters which may enable the staff for taking decisions at a frequency speed level.

Common steps in Pricing decisions : Having set the above pre-requisites for pricing decisions the following steps are discussed by Oxenfeldt in the process of pricing decisions : viz. (1) selection of market target fixing market segments insulating competition and developing market for complementary products (2) creating brand image in public mind for justifying high, prices (3) deciding composition of marketing mix viz. role of advertising in influencing the customs and the prices of products; (4) selection of price strategy with reference to longtime objectives of the firm; (5) evolving a price policy. For instance, setting markup, follow leader's price, adopt price line suggested by wholesalers or distributors or follow discriminatory price or uniform price etc. (6) having taken above steps, then prices should be set for each commodity with flexibility and adaptability to a change.

CLASSIFICATION OF PRODUCTS FOR PRICING DECISIONS UNDER COMPETITIVE MARKET SITUATION

Joel Dean has divided the product for pricing decisions under three main groups viz. (1) product with lasting distinctiveness, (2) perishable distinctiveness of product; and (3) little distinctiveness with few competitors.

Durable products have lasting distinctiveness : For such products no substitutes come up over long-period. Such a situation may exist for products with patents and trade marks or licences from research bodies. This situation symbolises monopoly with differentiated goods. For taking price decisions for such products Joel Dean suggests following main steps : (A) Estimate demand pattern and cost behaviour for such product so that target rate of return could be planned on such product; (B) make econometric estimate and project maximum profit price for the product; forecast data for shortrun behaviour of cost and demand schedule can be used in profit planning over the sale price of product; (C) having obtained price in above manner, then adjust the present price to influence future sales or to prohibit entry of potential competitors and to affect the price of substitutes.

(2) Perishable distinctiveness of a product presents a different situation averse to the above monopolistic one. The product loses its distinctiveness as it grows older allowing more firms to enter into trade to produce it and influence its price through substitute productsThe seller can't take independent decisions without considering such changing situation for pricing his product. Therefore, the pricing decision should be made taking into consideration the whole product life cycle of a product touching in details all the three stages viz., (a) technical maturity stage when product get standardized with spread of knowbow of process to others,; (b) market maturity when new brand enters market and customers compare the price, quality and strength of new brand with existing ones; and, (c) competitive maturity of the product to be stable in market with existing and newly forthcoming substitutes. Pricing of products with perishable distinctiveness can take two forms viz., (i) pricing at pioneering stage of a new product, and (ii) pricing at maturity stage of the existing product. Pricing decisions at the first stage should be made by considering the nature of the new product as protected from competitors through patent rights, secrets of production process, control of scarce resources etc.

Steps for pricing such products should comprise of the following viz. (a) estimate demand; (b) Decide markets share target; (c) decide promotional strategy; (d) elect channel of distribution from alternative choice. For a new product, the most difficult task amongst all these steps is the estimation of demand as product is new to buyers, and their preferences can not be determined easily. In such a situation educability of buyer be considered to create demand. Their income pattern be taken into consideration to judge their willingness to purchase the commodity. For such a situation the survey of market should be adopted by sample introduction and interviewing the prospective buyers. Price of market substitute be taken into consideration while pricing for new products, Possibility of retaliation by displaced sellers of substitutes by pricecutting be also taken into account. The above information so collected will provide insight whether it will be advantageous to the firms to follow a policy of skimming price or penetration price. Skimming price is known as charging high price in initial stages.

This can be followed by a firm by charging skimming price for a new product in pioneering stage when demand is either unknown or more inelastic at this stage, market is divided into segments on the basis of different degree of elasticity of demand of different consumers. This is a short period device for pricing. It is safe policy for pricing where elasticity is not known and product is not accepted by market forces. Penetration price is known as charging lowest price for the new product. This is aimed to quicken sales, capture market share, utilise full capacity and economies of scale in productive process and keep the competitors away from the market. Penetration price policy can be adopted in the following circumstances viz. (i) price elasticity of demand is very high; (ii) lower cost of production is feasible by. reaping savings in enhanced production process; (iii) product by nature suits to the mass consumers' baskets; (iv) Imminent threat from Potential competitors exist to capture market quickly. Penetration price is a long term pricing strategy and should be adopted with great caution. Pricing at maturity stage requires altogether a different treatment than the pricing at pioneering stage.

At maturity stage the product develops certain features which distinguish it from pioneering stage. These features includes : (i) with standardistation of product, consumers' preferences diminish for leading brand and they become indifferent to the brand distinctions; (ii) production process is known and stabilised which forces more competition in the market; The market stands exhausted by competitors and replacement demand for goods become dominant then the original demand. Pricing of product in maturity stage is an easy process.

Firm should adopt a going rate of price. If it fixes higher price it might find itself unable to market its products and if it lowers the prices more than going rate price it might not recover its average total cost. So, by compulsion of market forces the going rate of price has got to be embraced by the firm. Less distinctive product with few competitors implies oligopolic situation. In last section, pricing under such a situation has been dealt with in detail and readers should refer to the same.

Practice of Pricing Method

Cost-Plus-Pricing or Full Cost Pricing or Target Return Pricing. (Single Product Analysis) : It is a short-cut method in pricing a product. This method suggests that price of a product should cover its full cost and generate the returns on investments at a fixed markup percentage. This method ensures a profitable business operation by stressing on the cost should be recovered through pricing. Costs carry main influence on price and it is a long term price determinant. For cost-plus pricing two steps are essential : firstly, determine percentage markup over cost, and secondly, apply this markup to particular products in particular category of products. In determining appropriate markup the firm should carefully evaluate cost, demand elasticity and degree of competition faced by the product. The firm should also consider the brand image and long-run strategy in fixing markup. Once markup is fixed it should be added to the cost of a product to determine its market price. Cost-plus-pricing can be divided in two categories on the basis of "markup." viz. (a) Rigid cost-plus and (b) flexible cost-plus.

Rigid Cost-Plus Price : In rigid cost-plus pricing, it is customary to add a fixed percentage to the cost to get price. Only direct cost i.e. variable-cost are taken and a fixed markup percentage is added to it. This markup is large enough to cover overhead and untraceable costs as well as profit. For instance, if a pen costs Rs. 8 and a 25% markup on its cost is desired then the price for pen will be Rs. 8 plus Rs. 2 (being 25% of Rs. 8) that is Rs. 10. This could be expressed in the form of margin on sales which is in this case 20%. This method is simple to calculate and is consistent with profit motive.

But it fails to consider demand elasticities, degree of competition and aimed market share of the firm. It is a rough method which is used by small traders and retailers Hall and Hitch's had established in their famous study of 38 British firms in 1939 revealing that 12 firms had used this method in almost all cases of their products whereas 15 firms used it in "normal" situations.

Flexible Cost-Plus Pricing : In flexible cost-plus-pricing markup is not rigidly fixed on cost but it is allocated on different heads of variable and fixed costs. This has two significant results i.e., firstly, competition and demand may affect cost of different inputs in cost structure and should be accounted for in pricing the product; secondly, cost is comprised of different elements and markup on each element of cost provided a more scientific and reliable approach. A mature product will bear a lesser markup than new product. For a more competitive product flexible markup would provide firm basis for profit margin. In view of heteriogeniety of costs flexible markup considers all aspects of costs viz. labour, material, machine hours and all over-heads.

The following example will distinguish the rigid and flexible markup cost-plus pricing.

	Product X	*Product Y*
Labour	Rs. 50-00	10
Material	10.00	40
Machine time	10.00	20
Overheads	3000	30
	Rs. 100.00	Rs. 100

If the firm follows 20% marking over cost then both the products will be sold out at 100+20 i.e., Rs. 120 each. This is fixed markup on assumption that all the elements of cost were the same which is not correct.

In the case of flexible markup the firm shall distinguish between different elements of cost by allowing different markup for example, markup for labour cost would be fixed having assessed the labour productivity. It may be less or more in different firms in the same industry. The material to be used as input in production process may have no difference in producing it and so the markup may be similar in all firms. Machine and other costs may be different and give different markup depending on the ratio of mechanical specialization, involved in the production process and the firm's commitment to different overheads. We may allow equal markup for both the above products X and Y for different elements of cost. Suppose labour is given markup at 40% material at 10% machine time at 10% and overhead costs at 20%. Then we have the following cost-plus price for each product :

TABLI

	Elements of cost		*Markup*	*Total Unit cost*	
	Product X	*Product* Y	%	X	Y
Labour	50	10	40%	20.00	4.00
Material	10	40	10%	1.00	4.00
Machine time	10	20	10%	1.00	4.00
Overheads	30	30	20%	6.00	6.00
	100	100	28-00	16-00	

Application of flexible markup has revealed in the above Table difference in prices. Price for X would be fixed at Rs. 28 as against price of Y for Rs. 16.00. Thus, by using flexible markup the firm can take into consideration different market conditions affecting the price of different inputs used in the production of the commodities. For fixing markup, the firm is supposed to undertake demand analysis, assess degree of competition and attribute needed allowance for specialisation and managerial efficiency. Flexible cost-plus Pricing is quite in vogue in all the major firms which recognise that cost should be a flexible and adjustable phenomenon. However, this method violates marginal pricing rules of traditional theory. Further, this method is based on accounting data and neglects opportunity cost analysis.

Mark-up and Turnover : Markup may have direct link with turnover. High turnover items may carry low mark-up for two reasons : firstly, customers are aware of the prices of such items anti would shift to other sources of supply if price is higher with high mark up; secondly, for high turnover goods, storing space is a big problem and opportunity cost of space utilisation and inventory build-up should be taken into account. With lower markup turnover can be enhanced and opportunity cost of space utilisation be minimised.

Mark-up and Rate of Return : Mark-up may provide Rate of Return pricing with a view to obtain desired rate of return on investment. For fixing rate of return mark up on cost two things are essential; firstly, calculate capital turn-over rate. This is calculated as ratio of invested capital to years normal production cost; Secondly, the capital turnover rate be multiplied by goal rate of return. The resulting figure will give markup figure on standard cost for example, if capital turnover is 0.10 and goal rate of return is 45% on invested capital than markup would be 0.10 · 45% i.e. 4.5%.

Mark-up and Target Return on Investment : A study" in pricing techniques adopted in U.S.A. was conducted: by A.D.H. Kaplan, J.B. Dirlans and R.F. Lanzidlotti who bad observed that large U.S. Industrial firms have adopted mark-up pricing to achieve target return on investment. The firm sets an acceptable profit.

Pricing under this method can be expressed by following formula :

$$P = Lc + Mc + MKc +$$

where P = Price per unit.

L_c = Unit labour cost.

M_c = Unit material cost.

MK_c = Marketing cost per unit.

F = Total Fixed cost.

X = No. of unit to be produced.
K = Total gross operating assets.
a = Desired profit rate or investment.

The target return pricing method is based on cost standard and fosters price stability. It is useful to firm in planning its profit in situations where skimming pricing or penetration pricing for products is aimed at.

Going Rate Pricing : This is another short-cut method used for pricing by adopting the going rate market prices. This method is used where it is difficult to assess costs, but it is desirable to adopt market price. For doing so, the price structure of the industry should be examined by the firms' business economist and then fix the firm's own price accordingly. In oligopoliy leadership a firm has no alternative but to accept the going rate pricing which is fixed for a particular product under competitive market conditions. Such going rate pricing may adopt different forms. The most significant form is "inverted price" approach or product tailoring approach which sets into motion the backward analysis of price and cost where price determines cost. The steps to be followed in such analysis are comprised in four forms viz. (i) first chose the price of the product which presents a going rate; (ii) deduct retailers' discount; (iii) then, deduct whole-sellers' discount; (iv) Then the remainder would afford the margin over cost which should be more than cost. For instance, if the going rate of price is Rs. 100 per item then the following analysis would be undertaken by the firm :

	Rs.
Retail Price	100.00
Less retailers, gross margin 40%	40.00
	60.00
Less wholesellers' markup 15% on retail list price	15.00
	45.00

Rs. 45 per item is the return. This return should cover cost and offer a handsome margin of profit to the producer i.e. cost should be below Rs. 45. If, suppose, cost is Rs. 30 only then producers' margin of profit will be Rs. 151 per item i.e. 15% on sale price. The above pricing is adapted when product design is fluid and target price is sharply defeated by economic situation in respect of substitutes. It looks on pricing problem from point of view of buyer in term of what he wants and what he will pay.

Such pricing is adopted to satisfy specific consumers' wants. For instance, in India, the price for Ambassador car was fixed by Govt. of India and the company, M/s. Hindustan Motors Ltd. had to adjust the cost within cost structure. However, such pricing, many times, results into two major dis-advantages viz. Firstly, the quality of product deteriorates in such circumstances. Secondly, cheap and inferior goods are also marketed in the same price and consumers are cheated. For instance, Drug industry in India presents a burning citation where imitations under brand names are sold at prevailing prices.

METHODS OF PRICING AND PRACTICES (MULTI-PRODUCTS AND JOINT PRODUCT ANALYSIS)

Setting Policy for Pricing Multi-products : Firms usually produce more than one product. Such products may be joint products or the multi-products. Joint products are those where inputs are common in productive process. Multi-products are creations of the productline activity with independent inputs but common overhead expenses. Pricing of multi-product or joint product require little extra caution and care than has been stressed under the single product price analysis. For evolving price policy for multiproduct firm certain basic considerations involved in decision making are : (1) price and cost relationship in product line, (2) demand relationship in product line, and (3) competitive differences. These considerations influence pricing decisions as under : Price and cost relationship is the basic consideration for evolving a price policy for any product.

Cost conditions determine price. Therefore, cost estimates should be correctly made for each product for depicting profit margin on the available price structure. Cost estimates instil foresight whether a price equal to cost estimates be accepted or not. A price that offers maximum contribution over costs is generally acceptable but in multi-product cases, incremental cost becomes more inevitable to make such decisions. A set of alternative price policies should be considered and the one which suits best be adopted. These alternative price policies have been dealt with by Joel Dean as being five in number, as discussed below :

(i) Prices of multiproducts may be proportional to full cost. This price may produce equal percentage of profit margin for all products. If full cost for all products are assumed equal then the pricing will be equal. Readers may refer to example given on back pages while explaining cost-plus pricing method. With full cost of Rs. 100 for each product X and Y a fixed markup of 20% should fetch price at the rate of Rs. 120 each.

(ii) Pricing for multi products may be proportional to incremental cost. Prime costs of labour and material for X or Y are Rs. 60 and Rs. 50 respectively. If markup at the rate of 100% is added up to each, the proportional incremental costs would be Rs. 120 and 100 respectively.

(iii) Prices of multiproducts may be assessed with reference to their contribution margin as proportional to conversion cost. if we take the cost of labour and over-heads together (which converts raw material into useful product by adding value to it) for each product and add up at the rate of 100% then we may fix price for each multiple product of product line. In our example, labour cost, machine time and overhead cost for X and Y are given as Rs. 90 and Rs. 60 which will give price under this formula as Rs. 180 and 120 for each product.

(iv) Prices of multiproduct may be fixed differently keeping into consideration market segments. Market, for sophisticated product meant for sophisticated class is less elastic and high price can be charged from such buyers than those with elastic demand.

(v) Prices for multi-products may be fixed as per the product life cycle of each product. Such pricing may be different at pioneering and maturity stages for each product depending upon the degree of degeneration of a product into undifferentiated commodity. Such pricing is quite different to cost-plus-pricing policies.

Each of the above pricing alternatives has its advantages and disadvantages. Business manager should select the price strategy keeping in view the demand pattern for products and competitive differences. The demand pattern for products as related to pricing decisions of multi-products is discussed below. Inter-relation of demand for multi-product is significant phenomenon for pricing decisions of the product line. Each product being produced by the firm may have inter-related demand either is the shape of substitutes or in complementary forms. Sale of one product may effect the sale of another product.

Different demand elasticity of different consumers may allow the firm to follow policies of price discrimination in different market segments. Two products of the same price may be substitutes to each other with crosselasticity of demand because of high degree of competitiveness. In such circumstances, pricing of the multiproducts will have to be done in such a way that maximum return could be obtained from each market segments by selling maximum products. Another significant point needed to be considered for making pricing decisions for a product line is the assessment of degree of competitiveness which the product faces with outsider competitors. Such an examination will set up market share for each product. A product having large market share can stand a high markup and can contribute to bear the losses which another product with intensive degree of competitiveness is sold at very low price so as to exist in the market even under cut-throat competitive conditions. The firm should also analyse the product commanding large market share whether the competitors have free entry to the market or are barred by the presence of any type of barriers of financial or technological nature or patents and trade mark rights.

Marginal Technique for Pricing Multi-products : Marginal technique of pricing multi-products is based on the logic that when firm has spare capacity, unutilised technical resources, managerial and organisational abilities and capabilities, the firm enters into production of different other products with most profitable uses of alternatives. These products are technically independent in the production process. For selecting these alternatives firm considers marginal costs of each such alternative and adopts those which offer higher margin on cost through sales. Productive resources of the firm may be transferred from one product to another on the basis of differences in price and marginal cost. The firm may face different market conditions ranging from pure competition to pure monopoly for its different products. Whatever may be circumstance, a firm shall produce the multiproduct to the level where Marginal Revenue from sales of all these products equals the marginal cost. If marginal costs are more than MR then firm shall stop producing and selling one of the products which offer less marginal revenue than marginal cost. The above explanation can be illustrated through Figure 12.

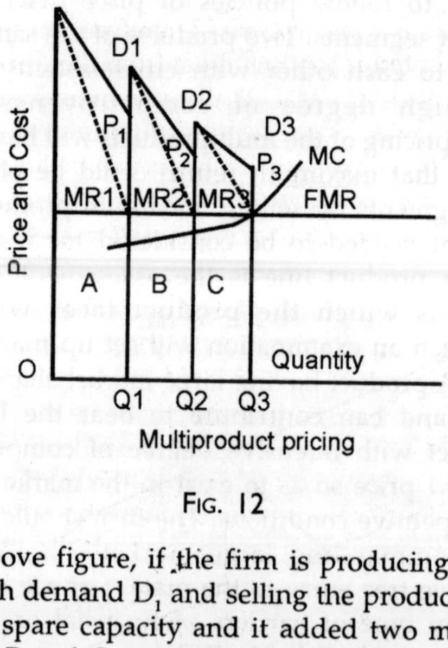

Multiproduct pricing

FIG. 12

In the above figure, if the firm is producing only 81 % of product A with demand D_1 and selling the product at price P_1 it was left with spare capacity and it added two more products, consecutively, B and C to exhaust its capacity with the existing market for each product at price P_2 and P_3 selling quantities Q_2 and Q_3. By adding product C, the firm has exhausted its production capacity although it can produce more of C and sell it in the market but by doing so it has to incur heavy marginal cost which remain unrecovered as EMR is intersected by MC at Q_1 of product C. Although the firm has been charging lower prices for B and C yet it is able to recover marginal costs.

Pricing of Joint Products : Joint products are those products which a firm produces with common production process. These products are interdependent to each other in such cases production cost of one affects the production cost of another. Take for example, coconut oil producing company may have coconut biscuit manufacturing process. Increase in cost of coconut will cause increase in cost of biscuits too which uses coconut husk for biscuit manufacturing. Pricing of Joint product can be explained under two different circumstances viz. (1) when there is fixed proportion of products and (2) when there is variable proportions of products. In joint product case with fixed proportion of quantity, there is no possibility of increasing one at the expense of another.

In this situation the costs are joint and cannot be allocated to each product on any sound basis. Therefore, the production of both is to be accepted if total revenue from them in short-run is more than incremental costs. If the revenue is expected to cover all long-run costs including opportunity cost of capital, then the joint products are worth producing in long-run. The revenue of both the products. will be taken into account together. Pricing of joint product is illustrated in the figure given below :

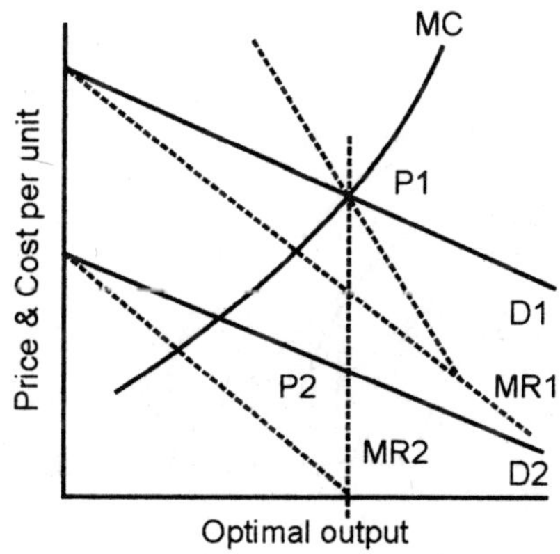

FIG. 13

In the above figure P_1 and P_2 represents most profitable price for the joint products. The total marginal revenue curve (MR1+2) cuts the marginal cost curve nearest to the optimum level of production of the joint products. The above graph carrys the assumption that each product is produced in fixed proportion because the output point for both is one and the same where as their demand and marginal revenue curve are separate for different market existing for them. Pricing of joint product which can be produced with variable proportions present interesting analysis of price, cost and output relationship. Figure 14 illustrates the pricing method of joint product pricing with variable proportions wherein three main thing are to be observed viz., firstly, the production possibility curve is concave to origin indicating imperfect adaptability of productive resources in producing A and B. In other words, it indicates the quantity of A and B which can be produced for the same total cost If total cost is equal to Rs. 8 then any combination of A&B can be produced within this total cost, For instance, the firm may produce either QA and QB quantities or QA^1 and QB^1 quantities of the two products. If output of A is to be increased then output of B will be decreased and *vice versa*.

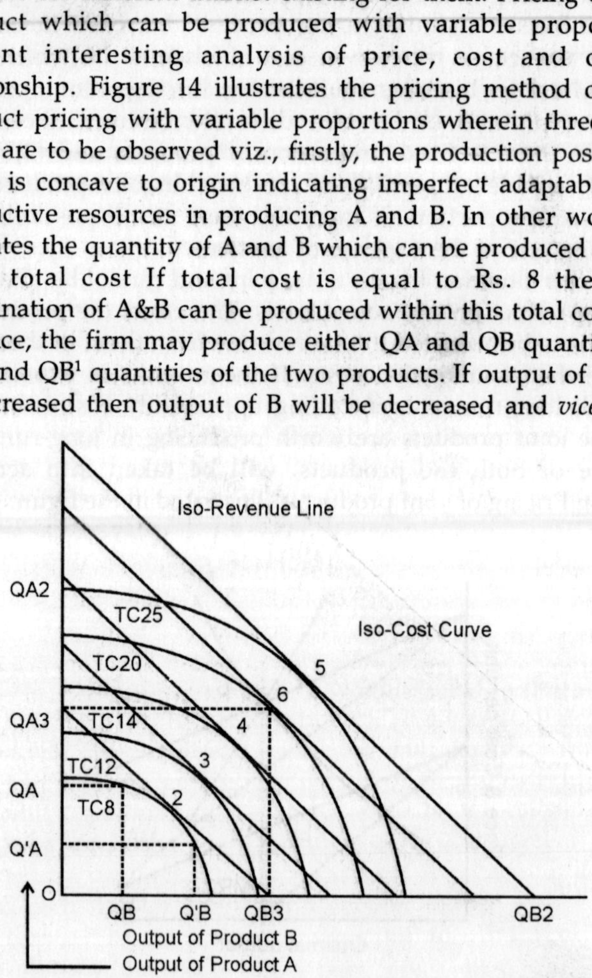

FIG. 14

For increasing the quantities of both A and B the new total cost constraints will have to be adopted by adding to more resources. Cost curves display increased resources with TC = 12, TC = 14, TC = 20 and TC = 25 respectively. Secondly, the Iso-revenue lines defines the prices which firm receives for the two products irrespective of any combination of their out. This would mean to say that it is immaterial whether the firm produces QA^1 and QB^1 or QA and QB TC − 18 but the total revenue in all positions will remain limited to Rs. 10 only. At different levels of TC the different quantity of Iso-revenues are generated. Thirdly, the best combinations are the points of tangency of Iso-cost curves and Iso-revenue lines for optimum production and maximization of sales revenues. At this point, MC equals the MR which each product generates. Addition or deletion of any product shall be considered only on the basis of the capacity of the product to generate sufficient marginal revenue to cover marginal cost combinedly.

The Figure 14 studies only two joint products. The analysis can be extended to cover large number of products with the help of linear programming and mathematical programming.

PRICING DECISIONS : PROBLEMS IN IT

Problem of Multi Products or Joint Products : The problem of transfer pricing in production of multi-product or joint product arise because of decentralised production activity. A product may be manufactured in two, processes in separate production divisions. The decision making process of one division shall be dependent upon the other division. Further, the two divisions may be cost dependent through either technological interdependence or the cost of in puts used in production activity. One division may use the output of another division as its major input. In all such situations of interpendence of one division upon the other is valued in terms of money it involves transfer of more resources from one product to another. In such two stage process of manufacturing a product is transferred to another process at an internal transfer price before the product is ultimately transferred to the marketing division which give finishing touch after packing the product and sells in the market. In above explanation two situations arise for taking pricing decisions viz. (1) when product is in manufacturing process and is transferred from One division to another for completing process and final touch-up and sale. At this stage the product in its half-finished form is to be priced for internal transfer from one department to another. Such product is known as intermediate product and it is assumed that it has no immediate market outside internal division of the firm. Determination of Transfer price when no external market exist for the intermediate product can be explained by way of following graph:

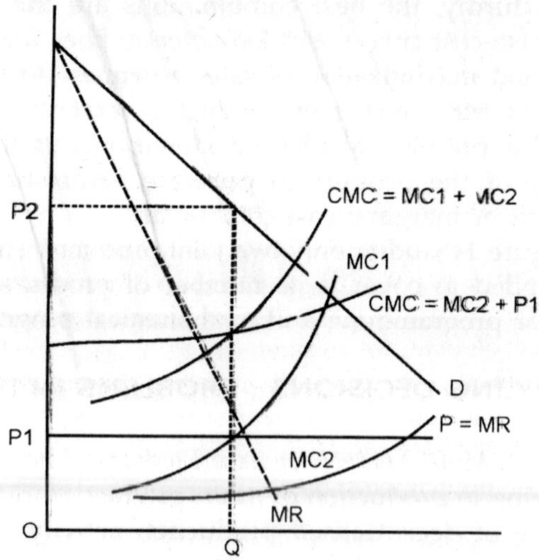

FIG. 15

In the Figure 15, Division 1 and 2 have different marginal costs curves in the production process denoted as MC_1 and MC_2 and the combined marginal cost of the two is given as CMC. Demand and Revenue curve for the external market are also given. At P_2 price the quantity Q can be sold in external market once the product is finished supposing Division 2 is the sale department of the firm. At Q level of product transfer price for internal movement of product is needed to be fixed which is optimum level for division I at P_1. Division 1 will maximise its own profit on this level. So is the case with division 2 at this level with P_2 once P_1 is settled the demand curve for intermediate product in the internal market of the firm will become horizontal and will represent marginal revenue as P= MR D. The profit for division I will be maximised at this point as MC_1 intersects P, With the assessment of price for intermediate product, the combined cost for division 2 becomes MC $2+P_1$. At this point intersection of MR by CMC (= $MR_2 + P_1$) the Q will be optimum production which suggests that product be sold at or above the intersection level. The above situation will be different if the assumption of treating market for intermediate product confined only to internal market is relaxed so as to enable the firm to sell the product in the external market. This will be Possible when the firm produces more of intermediate product than it can use for final product internally. In such a situation if competitive market exists externally for the intermediate product then the demand for the product will be horizontal line and the point of intersection of this horizontal demand line by the division's marginal cost curve will give market's existing price with profit maximising quantity of production. Marginal cost curve for division 2 will be above the demand curve of external markets because MC of Division 2 will be total sum of price available in the market for the product plus the cost of its own processing department. The point of intersection of MR for the firm's product will set the total requirement of internal product. This can be depicted in the Figure 16.

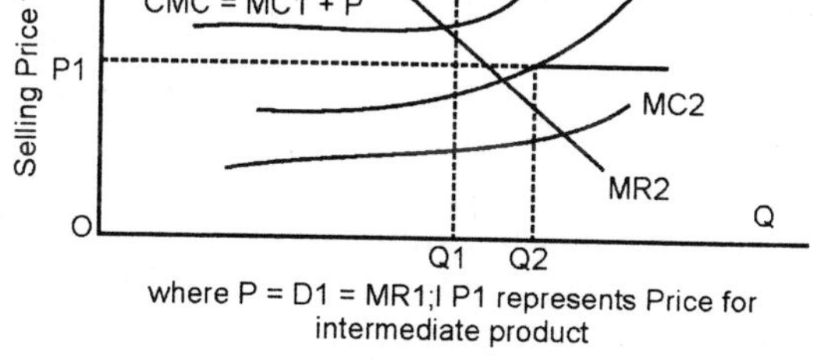

where P = D1 = MR1;I P1 represents Price for intermediate product

FIG. 16

In the above figure, MC_1 is marginal cost curve for division I producing intermediate product. The demand curve for the intermediate product in external competitive market is given as P = D = MR which is marginal revenue curve for division I also. Intersection of MC_1 with MR_1 sets the quantity limit which the firm should produce at level Q_2. On the other hand, combined marginal cost CMC, of Division 2 is arrived at as total sum of MC, plus price. The point of intersection of CMC with MR_2 sets the quantity needed by Divisions 2 to finish the product and sell at price P_2. So, the firm will sell $Q_2 - Q_1$ quantity in external market at price P, is the transfer price for the intermediate product for both internal as well as external markets. This analysis can be extended to these situations where external market is not competitive as assumed above. Thus, transfer pricing reasoning instil adequate insight in the business manager of setting inter and intra firm prices for intermediate products or unfinished products.

Pricing Strategy under Business Cycles : Business cycles affect prices and compell business managers to introduce changes in price structures. Impact of business cycles on prices can be studied by analysing the demand pattern, the degree of competition, the cost structure of the industry and the profit margin available. Cyclical conditions may cause boom as well as depression in business activity and influence above parameters of price function. In boom demand may increase for goods offering better margin of profit over cost in initial stages and create more intensive degree of competition. In depression, demand may slacken, even lower prices may not boost the demand and thus disallow the firm to cover production cost. Thus, uncertainty and risk always envelopes the business activity. To pursue price policy under cyclical conditions, Joel Dean has given a vivid description of alternatives to make adjustment to cyclical changes. These alternatives may be adopted keeping in view the degree, timing and pattern of cyclical influences on the prices. Accordingly, the firm may adopt a change in list price, or it may introduce changes in product-mix and product-line differentials or it may overhaul its incentive structure of discounts to merchants etc. The firm may adopt one or more of the above alternatives depending upon the intensity of cyclical influence on its price, structure. Cyclical pricing policy may assume varied forms ranging from price rigidity to flexible prices conforming to the nature of' fluctuations affecting the price structure of different commodities.

Alternative price strategy could be suggested under these circumstances viz. firstly, price rigidity is one strategy which may be followed over the period of business cycle if changes in demand have been caused by those factors which are beyond the control of the firm like decrease or increase in real income of consumers and growing optimism or pessimism of their expectations of future incomes. The firm can't change these conditions. Even slight increase or decrease in price will not bring any material changes.

Secondly, if cost structure of the firm's productive activity has been influenced through cyclical changes then the firm will have to follow a policy of price adjustments, so as to attain just prices to conform to cost changes. However, these adjustments will differ as per the technique of costs followed. This strategy suits where "cost plus" concept is followed. But it ignores demand considerations and competition It is mechanistic approach which seeks price reduction during depression stage of business cycle; such price reduction is limited to firms' savings in unit cost. In boom period increase in price is restricted to sellers' increase in costs. If flexible markup is used in cost elements then this price strategy answers to the questions which are posed in continuing inflationary conditions.

However, such a price policy is most suited in oligopolistic conditions because under competitive conditions prices of substitutes will have to be taken into consideration and it may not be feasible for many firms to compete for their survival successfully for their inability to have cost saving advantages. This suggests a third price strategy in which firm should adopt a price for its product conforming to the prices of substitutes which have been influenced by the cyclical fluctuations. Many time firms become cautious to preserve the market share which its product commanded. This happens when the firm faces a recessionary phase of business cycles with receding demand and declining prices with the same cost pattern of the productive process. To affect economies in productive process, the firm might have to follow policy of drastic cuts in expenditure to maintain lower prices to attract its customers with the same level of their demand. To conclude the above discussion, it may be pointed out that there can not be any cut and dry method which could be followed by all firms under business cycles to regulate their pricing policy as such policy for cyclical conditions will differ from industry to industry according to the degree of influence excercised upon the parameters of price function under different stages of business cycle.

Peak load Pricing : Business cycles may create a temporary excessive demand situation for service rendering firms like electricity supplying firm of transportation industry etc. who developed a limited capacity to cater the existing demand for the consumers. The service rendering industries have to face excessive demand in peak season when they find themselves unable to meet the demand. They take advantages of charging different prices for peak period which are higher than the off-season prices. In off season because of lack of demand, the existing capacity is not utilised to the full extent and prices are lowered to attract the customers. Marginal cost analysis is applied to assess optimal prices for peak periods. However, marginal analysis do not respond to social problems involved in peak-load pricing resulting into exploitive behaviour towards consumers."

Pricing under Inflation : A general rising trend in prices is termed as inflation. Purchasing power of money declines during inflation. In the production process of a firm fixed and overhead costs remain constant during short-run period but other costs including material costs and labour wages rise, this increase in input costs pushes the price up for the individual firm. However, for the health of economy, in general,. inflation is considered a healthy sign for growth as it generates new wants of the people influences production of new goods to cater new wants and create employment bringing all round prosperity. In traditional economic theory Quantity Theory of Money analyses the impact of money supply on prices and emphasizes the role of money in maintaining price stability by checking inflationary pressures.

The theory holds that price level move in direct proportion to money supply i.e., P = KM where P is price K is positive proportionality constant and M is money supply. But, in practice, this hypothesis has not been proved. Paul A. Samuelson has stated that in 1972 money supply in America was seven times more than it was in 1939. According to the quantity theory of money, price rise should also have been seven times but it remained only three times." However, this is macro approach to price analysis bearing impact of money supply. This theory does not give any guidance to a firm for formulating pricing policy, during infationary condition. For evolving a sound price policy the firm is needed to take into consideration the demand and cost conditions and competitive forces to analyse their impact on its price policy. Demand conditions may instil insight in the business manager that excessive demand in the economy has been the main cause for price increase as the production capacity of an industry is limited and the firm's working in the industry can not meet this excessive demand during the short period.

However, the increased prices during the short period get stabilized over the long-run with the increased capacity of the industry to satisfy this increased demand. Under such circumstances, the firm should reap the advantages caused by demand push inflation by adjusting the price to a new higher level. Demand push inflation is caused by excessive money supply and extra purchasing power in the hands of the buyers. Monetary and fiscal measures taken by government put check to inflationary tendencies but at the same time it suppresses the march of the economy towards prosperity. Firms expands their productive capacity under the demand push inflationary conditions and face stiff competition in the market at the entry of new firms, attracted by expectations of heavy profits, compete with the existing firms causing the price to be settled at the level when MR – MC. As regard cost-push inflation, it becomes suicidal for certain firms who are compelled to close down for higher prices of inputs raising cost more than the revenue generated from the sale price under competitive conditions. Cost push inflation is known as sellers' inflation. The firm has to face price increase for raw materials, wage rise for labour and so on which inflate cost and are needed to be reflected in the prices. Thus, the best policy for the firm is to follow a costplus pricing policy under such inflationary conditions so as to recover cost with a markup for desired level of profit. There has been lot of controversy over pricing during the inflationary conditions today when firms follow safe price-policy. This policy is known as "price ruling at date of delivery". This pricing approach is based on the logic that cash flows generated by the price today should not be less than at the current prevailing market price.

Discounts Role in Price Policy : The objectives of price policy for a firm will set norms for adopting a price differential strategy rest on the types of discounts the firm offers to buyers at particular time and location and for prompt payments. Price differentials for different classes of purchasers may cause differences in average net realised price per unit for the firm. Therefore, the objectives planned to be attained by following a price differential policy will have to be specified. These objectives may vary in different circumstances and conditions. For instance, these objectives may include implementation of firm's marketing strategy which may adopt different forms like profit oriented strategy of market segmentation or customer oriented strategy of market expansion or competitive adaptation of prices. To accomplish the planned objectives through medium of product pricing, the strategy of price differential to be followed by a firm include different forms of discounts viz. trade channel discount, quantity discount, cash discount or geographical discounts. Trade channel discount is allowed by a manufacturer to the whole sale traders or distributors. It is a deduction from the list price of a certain percentage which is enough to cover the cost of distributors for marketing the product to retailer with his scheduled or planned margin of profit.

Many times distributors profit include a successively applied discount which he gives to retailers on list price like 30% + 15%. on the listed price. If suppose the retail price is fixed at Rs. 10 per item then it will be passed on to whole-sellers or retailers at a price of Rs. 5.50 only (i.e. Rs. 10 minus Rs. 4.50 which is successive discount per item being Rs. 3 + Rs. 1.50 = 4/50). Distributors dictate their terms of discount by taking into account their operating cost of selling to different channels which may include segmented market also. Quantity discount reduces net price available to producer firm at the proportionate rate of selling goods in bulk quantity. Quantity discounts are significant pricing tools for many business firm. The firm may give discount on the basis of rupee value of goods sold or on the basis of physical units.

The product quantity sold should be the sole criterion for allowing the quantity discount to one dealer which may comprise his different orders. The size of discount should be decided keeping in view the market strategy, objectives of the firms, the operating cost of the purchaser-retailer and the prevailing market price. Many times the retailers are given quantity discount by manufacturers purchasing bulk quantity without pack aging. Such discount size is supposed to be large enough to cover packaging cost of retailers in beautiful covers. Pricing of the product shall be dependent upon the fact that how much cash discount the firm will allow on cash payments on the value of the goods sold. Retailers usually give such discount to their consumer buyers. But a firm while fixing price for a product should take into consideration the feasibilities of cash discount to distributors also. Lastly, discount may differ on account of locations when determination of pricing takes place through negotiations between the traders and the buyers. Thus, price differentials may arise on account of geographical locations in three specific ways viz. firstly, seller may deliver the goods at different location at uniform prices so that retail price remains the same every where. Just like postage stamps. Bata shoes are available at the same price every where through out in India. Further, a seller may discriminate on the basis of areas for delivered prices too. He may charge different price on the basis of different market zones because of heavy transportation costs. Delivered prices will be uniform within the zone but differ from zone to zone to the extent of tansportation cost differences; Secondly, price differentials may arise on the basis of sellers dispatching locations. He may charge uniform price for dispatching goods from his different plants located at different places or he may base the price differently from different locations or he may deliver the goods equalising the freight from all points of dispatching locations.

All these three types of price differentials are respectively known as single base pricing, multi-base pricing and freight equalisation pricing. Thirdly, price differentials may arise on account of differences in treatment of f.o.b. pricing. For instance, seller may not agree for freight absorption and may keep exfactory prices uniform regardless of buyersilocation; on he may agree to postal freight absorption in the form of subsidy on a regulated basis, or alternatively be may follow a discriminatory freight absorption policy by agreeing for some customers and declining for others on f.o.b. price. In such cases freight absorption will differ from individual to individual buyer. In all the above circumstances the pricing policy will be guided by market conditions viz. the elasticity of demand, the degree of competitiveness, the stage of product life cycle, the impact of transportation cost on pricing, etc.

PRICE DISTRIBUTION

Distributors purchases products directly from manufactures. They perform some significant functions like offering the product to the retailers on credit with a view to clear the product from the godowns. They maintain an organisation with men and equipments in order to deliver goods and offering free services whenever needed. For instance, the distributors of refrigerators, TVs, and other durable household equipments maintain technicians to provide free servicing, which is one of the conditions of sale. This free servicing for a specific period forms a kind of discount. Trade discounts cover the operating costs and the normal profits of the distributorsThese distributors undertake sales promotion and get higher discounts. Discounts rate depend upon the type of services offered by the distributor. The discount must be such that, it should cover the entire Operating costs, and also bring a certain amount of profits to the firm. Most of the manufacturers, either by custom or practice have been following a fixed discount structure. In the case of high priced luxury goods which are slow moving, the rate of discount is high. But those companies which face stiff competition offer discounts twice as high as those given by Market leaders. Besides a discount, the dealers also get price advantage.

Trade channel discounts are used to achieve profitable market segmentation. In order to make effective sales of particular products, the market has been divided into sub-markets. If there is a main distributor in a region he provides for sub-markets. If there is a main distributor in a region, he provides for sub-dealership in different places of his region. These sub-dealers in turn may appoint local dealers who supply the product to the retailers. Since demand elasticities in these sub-markets are different, the prices are also different. The discount structure is arranged in such a way, that it becomes feasible to have different prices suitable for each sub-markets. For instance, in the case of components, prices would not influence demand. The demand for a car tyre does not depend upon the price, but it depends upon the requirement. If the need persists, the owner has to buy the product even at a high price. But the dealers have to maintain adequate stock at the local level for which an attractive discount is needed to be given. The bulk buyers of the components are the manufacturers and the producers are needed to offer higher discounts.

The quantum of discounts given to distributors and dealers depend upon the price elasticity of demand for goods. In the case of replacement goods like tyres for cars and other automobiles, the manufacturers have to provide huge discounts to dealers. Here, the consumers prefer to buy a product for which they have preference and price has no effect on them. In order to shift the demand from one preferred product to an alternative product, the dealers also have to offer discounts. The dealers in such cases discriminate prices between the old customers and new customers. They charge somewhat higher prices to the old customers and lower prices to the new customers. The discount facility has given rise to various kinds of problems in the pricing of products. The main problem is whether to fix a high price and produce products of high quality or to fix a low price and produce goods of low quality.

Whenever the discounts are offered, they become the item of cost and as such the price will be naturally high. Discounts are indispensable until the product becomes popular. When the product becomes popular, its demand increases sufficiently, making it feasible for the company to reach an optimum capacity. The manufacturers generally depend upon the goodwill of the distributors. If the distributors do not display any interest in the brand product, the manufacturers are put into difficulties. The distributors have, by experience, the capacity to judge whether the quality of the product and its price are favourable or not. Therefore, the manufacturers have to satisfy the distributor and dealers more than the consumers, as consumers are guided by the dealersIf the dealers say that the product is better than product 'B', then the consumers prefer product. It is therefore, very significant for the manufacturers to secure the goodwill of the distributors. This can be done by riot only supplying the products of good quality with reasonable price, but also offering handsome discounts. If the product is a highly advertised one, then the dealer's influence on the consumers is limited. In such cases, the dealers have to be content with a small percentage of discount.

Cash Discounts : Cash discounts are price concessions offered when the payment is made promptly. For instance, if the dealers make the full payment within the specified period, a discount of two percent is allowed. Firms offer cash discounts with a view to improve the liquidity position and to minimise bank borrowing. Cash discount is a very good device. It eliminates the accumulation of credit, If the buyers make payment on receipt of the consignment, the manufacturers are also willing to offer higher discounts. If the buyers decide to Purchase the product on credit, they have to forego the discounts also. It is essential to compare the benefit of cash discount with that of the cost of cash discount. The rate of cash discount must be lower than the benefits which the firm gets by offering these discounts.

Quantity Discounts : These are price concessions offered to the distributors on the ground of the quantity of the product purchased. Quantity discounts are concerned to the size of a single purchase. The size of the lot purchased may be measured either in terms of physical quantity or the value of the product. In case of similar type of products like refrigerators, scooters or cars etc., it is the physical quantity considered. In the case of heterogeneous products, which are difficult to add, like furniture and scientific instruments, the money value of these products is preferred.

Therefore, the quantity discounts are related to either physical units of the products or the money value of the products. High discount is offered if the dealer purchases a bigger lot size. The chief purpose of quantity discounts is to encourage the dealers to buy the product in large amounts, thereby, the manufacturers can reduce their cost of selling, packaging, delivery, etc. It is said that quantity discounts was examined by Monopolies and Restrictive Trade Practices Commission. Initially, the MRTPC Commission agreed with the grant of high discounts to big orders in several cases referred to it. But later on, the Commission came to the conclusion that this practice distinguishes between larger buyers and small buyers finally coming to the conclusion that this practice is unsound.

Price Differentials : A significant aspect of price differential is price discrimination. In open price discrimination, the producer divides the market into several sub markets and charges different prices in each market, depending upon the elasticity of demand for the product. If the demand for the product is inelastic, he charges a higher price.

Time Differentials : There are various ways of discrimination of prices. One such discrimination is that of time differentials. The producers take the advantage of change in demand elasticities over a period of time. The demand for a product may be high in a particular season, for instance, the demand for woollen goods is high in winter, while the demand for cotton cloth is high during summer. Let us take up another example: Demand for telephones is higher during day time than during the night. There are two cases of time differentials. (i) Clock time price differential and (ii) Calendar time price differential.

Clock Time Price Differential : Let if the demand elasticities change during a day, sellers can charge different prices at different points of time during the 24 hour period. Such a price differential is called clock time price differential. It's object is to charge a higher price when the demand for the product is inelastic and a lower price when the demand for the product is elastic. The common examples are telephone services and the differences between morning displays and afternoon displays in cinema, houses. In the case of telephone services, day time charges are higher than night time charges. It is because of its inelastic demand during day time, that the charges are high and at night time, the demand is elastic and hence the rates are low.

The following conditions are to be fulfilled if the clock time differentials are to become profitable:

(i) The seller must be in a position to offer his product at a lower price in the slack period.

(ii) Buyers must have a definite preference for purchasing a product at a particular time.

(iii) The product offered for sale is not a storable item either wholly or in parts. If the product is a storable one, the buyers buy it when its price is low and use it whenever it is needed.

Calendar Price Differentials : In the calendar price differentials, the period of sale of a product or a service is more than 24 hours like days, weeks, months, etc. For instance, swimming pool charges and charges for hotel accommodation on hill stations differ on the basis of seasons.

During winter, the charges are low and in spring, they are higher. The seller of these services charge higher prices in spring in view of its inelastic demand. Taking this opportunity, the sellers of the services exploit the consumers. The economics of pricing points out that the pricing of product or services must be related to cost. The prices are differentiated during a whole period of a year or so in such a manner that higher cost of maintenance must be overcome by charging a higher price during seasons.

Price Discrimination : Price discrimination is made by the public utility organisations such as railways, electricity organisation, etc. on the basis of use of the services. Railways are used to transport various commodities and they can be used not only for long distance travel but also short distance travel. Charges for these uses are different. The sellers of these services divide the market into different segments and charge prices according to the demand. In order to make use of price differential effective, the demand elasticities for the product or services must be different.

Geographical Price Differential : Price discrimination is practised by sellers on the ground of buyer's location. Such discrimination is known as geographical price differential. For instance, at the place of production of a commodity, the price of the product is low, while at different centres of the nation, the price is high. The price of the product at the point of production is called as FOB Price (i.e. free on board), while the latter is a delivered price. The delivered price comprises the cost of shipping the goods.

Practising FOB Pricing : It connotes that the buyers have to pay the transport and handling charges and they are responsible for any loss of goods during the transport. Sellers charge uniform price to all categories of buyers at the point of production. The sellers do not make any discrimination between a buyer of large quantity and small quantity. But they have to bear the entire transport cost. It is the accountability of the buyers to arrange for their own mode of transportation. If the sellers take up the accountability of transportation, then they include the transport charges in the price of the commodity. In order to practice FOB Pricing, the sellers have to fulfil the following conditions:

(i) If the transport cost is small when compared to the production cost of the commodity, the sellers will sell outside the place of production or local market,

(ii) The fixed cost must not be very high to force the sellers to go out searching for customers in distant markets.

(iii) If the firm sets up plants at different demand centres, it can cater to the regional market needs easily without bothering about excess production.

Homogeneous Delivered Pricing or Postage Stamp Pricing : It means that the seller charging similar price for his product without looking into destination of the product, is known as 'Postage Stamp Pricing', In the case of postage stamp pricing, the seller sells the product at a uniform price at all centres of a country. The quoted price comprises the transport cost also. Postage price is quoted in two ways : (i) the seller sells the product at a single price all over the country, and (ii) secondly, a uniform FOB Price is quoted and the buyers are permitted to deduct a certain percentage from the price towards the freight charges. In these two cases, there is a certain amount of discrimination. Postage pricing is commonly practised by sellers in selling popular brand products and having wide national markets. For instance, most of the soap manufacturing firms sell their brand soaps at a uniform price all over the country. They advertise the prices of their products in newspapers. For instance, the Lakhani Shoe Company sells its different brand shoes at a uniform price across the country. Most durable goods are sold like this. Postage stamp prices are very suitable when the transport cost is insignificant to their actual cost of production. Goods like clothes, cosmetics, soft drinks, electrical and electronic equipments, radios, typewriters are few examples for postage pricing. This pricing gives the producer easy access to all markets regardless of the location.

Zonal pricing : Several times, the producers, instead of charging a uniform price in all regions of the country, differentiate between zones. They divide the country into several zones and the price in each zone is different from the other zone. This is called zone pricing, This is done with a view to cover transport charges. Zonal pricing is preferred when the transport cost on goods is too high. If the transport cost is high, the producers fix different prices for different zones.

Point Pricing : A great production centre for a particular product is chosen for pricing, which consists of a factory price and transportation price. This is known as base point pricing. A delivered price is quoted on the ground of base point. In other words, a base point price includes mill price or ex-factory price and transportation costs.

The transportation cost, which is taken into consideration, is not the actual freight charge, but transportation charge from a designated centre. A seller of the product may use single base point pricing or multiple base point pricing. Under the single base point, all sellers quote a uniform price irrespective of their locations. In the case of multiple base point pricing, two or more producing centres are chosen as base points. The seller then quotes a delivered, price which comprises mill price and transportation charge from the base point to the buyer's nearest point. Base point pricing is used extensively by heavy machinery manufacturers.

Pricing of Products : Pricing of a product is a difficult task, for several aspects have to be looked into. In recent years, the producers have to take into consideration several aspects like competition, advertisement and the quality of the product to fix a reasonable price for their products. In modern times, the firms are producing various products which may be related to the main product or unrelated to the main product. The multiplicity of the product by a firm creates three types of relationships :

Demand Relationship : When a firm produces different products, either substitutes or complements, it has to see how a change in the price of one product affects the demand for others.

Costs Relationship : When a firm is producing multiple products within the same plant and machineries, some costs are directly chargeable to each product, while other Costs are common to all.

Capacity Relationship : If the firm has idle capacity, it can produce one or more extra products. When a new product is produced, the fixed costs are shared among several products which alter the optimal output and price structure of all products.

A multi-product line can be divided into: (a) Joint product firm, (b) firms producing unrelated products, and (c) firms producing relating products.

(i) There are firms producing unrelated products. For instance, a company manufacturing steel almirahs and refrigerators is also manufacturing locks and soaps. These products are made using various kinds of raw-materials. The firm producing multiple products which are unrelated to each other, take advantage of the goodwill of the company and the marketing network. If a firm adds one more product, the marketing of it may be done by the existing network.

(ii) A joint product firm is one where amain product and a by product are produced. For instance, in a sugar factory, sugar is the main product and alcohol is a byproduct. Let us take another instance. In soap factories, soap is the main product and glycerine the by-product.

(iii) A firm is producing several related products, for instance, a textile firm is producing yarn, cloth and apparel. These different products are produced from the same plant. They are very inter-dependent.

PRODUCT LINE PRICING

For most of the industrial enterprises it is an significant practical problem. The problem of product-line pricing comprises of determining the proper relationship among the prices of the members of a product group. Many alternative methods of product-line pricing may be given. Prices which are Proportional to full Costs, i.e., they produce the same percentage of net profit margin for all products. Under this system, each product assumes its fun allocated share of common and overhead expenses as well. Particularly, these allocations are arbitrary which impairs the soundness of this method. Moreover, this method gives no consideration to demand conditions. Prices which are Proportional to Incremental Costs, i.e., they produce the same percentage contribution margin over incremental costs for all products. This method also suffers, although not to that extent, from the arbitrary allocation of common costs. Besides, it also fails to take into account the conditions of demand and competition. Coversion costs are the costs of converting the raw materials into finished products, i.e., labour costs and overheads. Pricing on the ground of conversion costs has been supported by some economists mainly by W.L. Churchill on the ground that they represent the value added or the real contribution of the firm. However, this view has not found much support. The following illustration provides a comparative view of the prices which would result by utilising the above three cost bases, viz., full costs, incremental costs and conversion costs. A copy manufacturer makes two different types of copies. The second copy needs more labour cost but less material cost per cake than the first copy. Also the second copy takes more overhead than the first.

Price which Produces Contribution Margin Depending upon the Elasticity of the Demand of Different Market Sectors/Segments. Buyers with high incomes are generally less sensitive to price than those which constitute the mass market. Obviously, it is profitable for the firm to charge higher profit margins on products consumed by the wealthy class than those meant for the common man. In 1985, American car manufacturers increased prices for large, luxurious cars but held steady or reduced the prices for small cars.

Price Related to the Stage in the Life Cycle of the Product. A product may start as a novelty, later become a speciality, and finally degenerate into a common product. According to these stages, prices and profit margins may be varied. A product as a novelty can be priced very high and will still command consumer acceptance. When it becomes a speciality, its price and the profit margin on it may have to be reduced to some extent because by this time, various rivals may come in the picture. Finally, when the product becomes a common commodity, it may have to be priced competitively to stay in the market in the face of severe competition.

PRODUCT-LINE PRICING : SPECIFIC PROBLEM

Pricing Products which Differ in Size : Two approaches to this problem are feasible:

Charging a Price Irrespective of Size Differences. This practice is common where buyers' benefits do not vary with size and the costs also do not differ materially due to the difference in size. The very common instance of this practice is the shoe industry where all shoes of the same quality for adults are priced uniformly.

Different Prices for Different Sizes. This approach is based on the proposition that size is a measure of value to the buyer.

By a variety of dimensions size can be measured, and it is significant to find the most appropriate one. For some products, the choice is not difficult to make, i.e., weights for different sizes of sugar bags. For other products which represent intricate and sophisticated equipment, it becomes difficult to find out an objective measure of size which measures the value of the goods to the buyer. In selecting the pattern of relationship of price to size, much depends upon whether the buyer has freedom to substitute one size of the product for another so that the two sizes are in competition.

In such cases, the firm may find it beneficial to quote lower prices per unit for the larger size than for the smaller one so that the buyer may be persuaded to go in for the larger size. The firm will find it more appropriate where it can avail itself of economics of large-scale production by producing goods in large sizes (or packages).

The very common instance is that of oil in tins. Oil in bigger tins is cheaper per kilogram than in smaller tins. So also, advertisement rates per square centimetre are lower in the case of full-page advertisements than in the case of fractional page advertisements. In order to have a price-size relationship, it is useful to prepare in advance a systematic pattern of price in relation to each size. Having a pattern has several advantages. Price determination is made easier when new sizes are added to the line. Besides, the appearance of equity is given to buyers. Management also saves time in deciding about price fixation in the case of a new size.

Special Order Pricing : In pricing special designs, it is a general practice to estimate normal full cost and then add to cost a fixed percentage to represent a fair or desirable profit.

The problem of special order pricing resolves itself into answering three questions:

(a) What is the highest price that can be quoted without the risk of losing the order?

(b) What is lowest price which the seller can afford to accept considering his alternatives? If the alternative is idleness, then the incremental cost concept becomes relevant. The incremental revenue from a special order must exceed the incremental cost of accepting the order. If there is any other alternative for employing the resources, the opportunity cost concept becomes relevant. Here, the minimum price to be quoted would be the revenue forgone by discarding the best alternative.

(c) What adjustments in the short-run prices are essentially or desirable in view of the long-run future benefits (or drawbacks)? For example, sometimes a firm may consider It essential to quote a very high price amounting to refusal price. The objective of this refusal price may be to discourage special orders and thereby persuade the customers to go in for the standard brands of the manufacturers.

Pricing Repair Parts/Spare Parts : All manufacturers ot durable goods face the problem of pricing spare parts. It is a significant problem. For some firms, the sale proceeds from spare parts exceed those from new equipment. The pricing of spare parts comprises the following considerations:

Where a purchaser of original equipment is committed to the purchase of spare parts from the original supplier/ manufacturer, the latter has a sort of monopoly depending upon alternative sources of spares, and can charge monopoly prices. However, there are some limitations on the part of the manufacturer of the original equipment in doing so:

(i) If the prices of spare parts are kept too high, the buyer may decide not to purchase the equipment from that manufacturer.

(ii) The buyer may find that it would be economical to manufacture the spare parts himself. The buyer's cost of making the part himself along with opportunity profits thus set an upper limit to the price of the spare parts.

Generally, some ancillary industries specialise in the production of spare parts and they offer keen competition to the manufacturer. The manufacturer of the original product or equipment may charge prices reasonably higher than the prices charged by these manufacturers of spare parts but not beyond a certain limit.

Some of the rule-of-thumb methods that may be adopted by the manufacturer axe:

(a) The sum of the prices of all spare parts should not be more than double the price of the complete product or equipment.

(b) The price should be consistent with the prices of other spare parts keeping in view the complexity and the size of the spare parts.

(c) Spare parts may be priced on the ground of weight adjusted roughly for complexity.

(d) Cost plus a reasonable margin of profit may be the base for pricing.

Practically speaking, low prices should be quoted for spare parts (1) which are easily available from specialised parts manufacturers, and/or (2) which can be easily made by the buyer himself in his own shop. But in the case of repair parts where there is no competition, present or potential prices can be fixed at high levels taking advantage of the profit opportunities. To conclude, the pricing of repair parts would be governed mainly by the alternatives available to the buyers.

During the detemination of the rent on equipment given on lease, the approach may be one of perfect price discrimination. That is, each user of the equipment may be charged different prices similar to the benefits received by each one of them. As there are great differences in the benefits accruing to users from a piece of equipment, there is scope for charging high rents from those getting great benefits and low rents from those getting small benefits. The production, selling and servicing costs of the equipment will set the minimum limit. The manufacturer can fix a minimum rent which would set a kind of price barrier for those whose uses of the equipment will be less advantageous.

During the determination of the royalty charges for the use of patents, or grant of licences, the price policy may be determined on the basis of the following considerations:

(a) The cost of developing the patented process is entirely irrelevant being a sunk cost.

(b) The incremental costs of administering the patent or operating expenses in case of licensing arrangements, where the licensee is entitled to the use of patents as well as technical know-how, are relevant and in fact determine the minimum limit of the royalty.

(c) The principal consideration in pricing should be the worth of the process to the licensee. This sets the maximum limit for fixing the royalty.

(d) In between the maximum and the minimum limits, the lessor will have to look to the feasibility of the development of potential competition, infringement of the patents and the intervention of government in case too high royalties are fixed.

(e) Where the objective is to stimulate wide use of the patent, royalty rates may be fixed at a comparatively lower rate.

Instances. In case of films, the cost of production of the film is irrelevant being a sunk cost. The minimum limit for the royalty is fixed by the incremental costs of distributing it. And the maximum limit is fixed by the anticipated response of the public to the film. So, also, for the patentee of the 'Sanforizing Process', the maximum limit is fixed by the expectation of higher prices and/or greater sales volume for the shrinkproof fabrics.

Pricing of Complementary Goods : The eventual objective in pricing complementary goods is to determine a price structure which produces the largest contribution margin according to the separate demand elasticities of the market segments. In case of complementary goods, a decrease in the price of one commodity may lead to an increase in the demand of the other. Hence, the seller may find it profitable to sell the product at a lower price, and even at a loss, if he feels that he can sell another complementary product at an above-average margin. The objective of the seller is to take advantage of the cross-elasticity of the demand for his products. There are two significant forms of complementary pricing:

Loss Leader. The practice comprises selling a product at a price below the customary price, or even at a loss, with a view to stimulate the sales of some other product, and publicising this fact through wide advertisement. For a product to be an effective loss leader, the cross-elasticity coefficient between the loss item and other products must be large (ideally infinite), the price elasticity of demand should be low (ideally zero), and the supply elasticity should be high, so that the direct losses do not only outweigh the indirect gains from other complementary products.

High elasticity of supply will mean a reduction in the supply with a reduction in the price. The stage is then set for the seller to ration the sale of loss leaders and encourage the sales of other complementary products. Further, the commodity should be well known. purchased widely and frequently, unsuitable for storage by consumers and standardised so that its customary price is widely known and low price or bargain price set for loss leaders is easily recognised. In fact, it is a misnomer to call such a commodity as a loss leader. It should be better known as profit leader because a change in the price of a loss leader produces larger sales of all products so that the increment in revenues exceeds the increment in costs.

In case of tied sales, buyers are asked to combine the purchases of main (profit giving) products with the subsidiary products which do not sell well. For instance, a dealer purchasing tyres from 'Goodyear' has to purchase locks, solution tubes, etc. along with his purchases of tyres. And these other items very often sell at a loss while in the case of tyres, the dealers can make a good profit. Tied sales are feasible only when the company's main products are difficult to substitute or are in short supply. Seldom, the dealer is forced to purchase the entire product-line of the manufacturer as a precondition for the purchase of the chief product. For instance, for purchasing Eveready cells in times of scarcity (rainy season), the dealer has to purchase different varieties of torches as well. A foreign-owned chemical company resorted to tied sales of its products by forcing consumers to lift slow-moving items like butanol and butyl acetate along with their requirements of polyethelene powder. Tied sales are also called clubbed sales. A variation of tied sales is packaged sales where an offer "buy one product and get the other free" is made to the buyer. For instance, with a large packet of 'Surf a free 'Signal' toothpaste was offered without cost by Hindustan Lever. The practice of "tying up" sales constitutes a restrictive trade practice under Section 2(9) of the MRTP Act. A redistribution stockist of Hindustan Lever Ltd. was asked to discontinue the practice of 'tying up' two brands to force the sale of one of them. Earlier, cooking gas distributors were restrained from forcing people to buy hot plates from them.

QUESTIONS

1. Describe about Pricing Methods in Practice.
2. What do you know about Price Distribution ?
3. What is Product Line Pricing ?
4. What is Pricing Strategy and Tactic ?

CHAPTER

9

Profit Management

NATURE AND SCOPE

Essentially profit is a residual sum. Under contracts, land, labour and capital are frequently used whereby they receive a predetermined return. Net profit is a sum over and above the ordinary costs of business including such contractual outlays. Nobody contracts to pay the entrepreneur the residual sum which constitutes net profit. Business profits are, therefore, especially contingent upon successful management of risk. Business is faced with a number of uncertainties: (a) technical uncertainties-those relating to the physical process of production, (b) cost uncertainties either because of change in the prices of raw materials, wages, rent, etc. or because of technology changes, (c) demand uncertainties either because of changes in consumer preferences or because of innovation of new products and obsolescence of the existing products, and (d) market uncertairities—those relating to the future price of the product and the volume of sales. The entrepreneur receives a reward for combining the factors of production to meet the economic needs of a world faced with uncertainties. He takes a risk which others are unwilling to bear, and if he successfully manages the risk, he receives profits. This means that a businessman, in order to earn profits, has to do two things: (i) select the risks which he wishes to bear, and (ii) manage them successfully.

The selection of risk is made at almost every step of a businessman's career. His great problem is the selection of business in which he wishes to engage himself. In fact, success or profit would depend upon the ability to foresee the future and prepare for it so that when opportunity arises, it can be fully availed of. But even after selection of a business, many risks arise. Some of them he may have to bear even though he would rather not, others he may transfer to people more willing to bear them (or unable to escape them), still others he may shift by insurance. Profits vary from industry to industry and from businessman to businessman. In business or industry the greater the risk and uncertainty, the greater are the opportunities for large profits. Correspondingly, those businessmen who are temperamentally cautious and are not willing to assume large risks get a smaller margin of profit as compared to those who are more confident and adventurous. Since risks and therefore, profits (and losses) appear due to changes and uncertainties in a dynamic society, profits vary from year to year as well. Profits are likely to be high in industries in which methods of production are constantly changing so that there is continuous adoption of new techniques, in nascent industries the prospects of which are rather uncertain, in industries in which there is a large gestation period; and in industries in which resources are irrevocably committed to narrowly specialised tasks. Profits are also affected by the level of business activity. If business is brisk and firms are operating at their maximum capacity, their average costs would be reduced to the minimum while their sales would be the maximum. This would lead to higher profits. Profits would be reduced if the business activity is at low ebb.

IMPORTANCE

For bearing risk and uncertainty, profits are necessary. No sane person would think of investing in a manufacturing industry for a return of 6 per cent if he can get that return on a

Government Security. He would aspire for a much higher rate because of the greater risk of a feasible loss. The greater the risk, the higher must be the expected gain in order to induce an entrepreneur. However, it is not every risk that can account for the emergence of profit. According to Prof. Frank H. Knight, risks inherent in any business are of two types-insurable and non-insurable risks. Those risks which can be calculated statistically and thus insured with an insurance firm are of two kinds: (a) risks of loss of property because of earthquakes, fire, flood and other natural calamities; and (b) risks of dishonesty such as loss because of theft, robbery, burglary, etc. These insurable risks are not the responsibility and worry of the organiser, because by paying insurance premium he is relieved of this worry.

Thus, insurance premium becomes a definite part of the entrepreneur's cost of production and, hence, enters into price. However, there are certain non-insurable risks of modern business which are not capable of being reduced to statistical measurement and are not borne by insurance companies. These risks must necessarily be borne by the entrepreneur himself, if he has to carry on production. These non-insurable risks are:

(i) Technical risks which arise from the possibility of a newly installed machinery becoming obsolete because of discovery of a new and economical process of production.
(ii) Risks of competition which arise when more rivals enter the industry or because of development of some new and competitive products.
(iii) Risks arising from government actions like price control, tax policy, import and export restrictions, etc. which may result in profits or losses.
(iv) Business cycle risks which arise due to the occurrence of business depressions when prices fall much more than costs.

The above mentioned risks are not insurable with any insurance company because there is no way of calculating the probability of particular events occurring and hence, are undertaken by the entrepreneurs themselves. These non-insurable risks are known as "uncertainties" by Prof. Frank Knight. In his view, the term 'risks' should be applied only for those risks which are known and foreseen and, in principle, insurable. Profit is an award for undertaking and managing uncertainties of business. Knight has advanced the well-known theory that pure economic profit (whether positive or negative) is concerned with uncertainty. The investor who outguesses the market makes a profit with certainty.

Another investor might make a loss because his guess turns out to be worse than that of the market. It might be useful here to pinpoint the distinction between risk and uncertainty. The probability of occurrence of risks can be calculated fairly accurately on the basis of past experience. Uncertainties are not capable of being reduced to statistical measurements. Risk can be insured against but uncertainty is not insurable. Premium paid for insurance of risks enters into the cost of production whereas uncertainty has an impact on profits.

Market Imperfections and Monopoly

Where a firm possesses monopoly power, it can restrict output and obtain a higher profit than' what it could under competitive conditions. Profit is the outcome of contrived scarcity. It can exist only in an imperfect market where output is, for various reasons, restricted and the consumers are deprived of the opportunity of alternative sources of supply. Sources of such power are generally found in legal restrictions, sole ownership of raw materials or sole access to particular markets. Even some degree of uniqueness in a firm's product confers some power. Contrived scarcity must be distinguished from natural scarcity. Natural scarcity exists in the supply of central urban building sites or high grade farm lands, These earn rents rather than monopoly profits, since particularly nothing can be done to alter supply.

For Successful Innovation

Innovation refers broadly to any purposeful change in production methods or consumer tastes that increases national output more than it increases costs. The increase in net output is the profit that comes from innovation. It comprises not only new products such as synthetic fibres but also new organisations, new markets, new promotions and new raw-materials. It may also include a new way of doing old things or a different combination of existing methods to accomplish new things. To a significant degree, innovation has been built into the competitive system complete with research and advertising staff. There is an important distinction to be made between invention and innovation. Invention is the creation of something new whereas innovation is the application of an invention to business use.

Many inventions never become innovations. The innovation theory of profit is related to Schumpeter. The innovator is one who turns a new idea or invention into a commercial proposition. Many try to do this, but only a few succeed. Those who do earn high profits by bringing their new revolutionary product into the market, do so because the public is attracted by the new and apparently superior product and is willing to pay the innovator a high price for it. Thus, the innovator reaps the profits of innovation. Following a successful innovation comes a period of adjustment when new competitors come in and sooner or later innovational profits die out. Meanwhile, in a dynamic economy other innovations are hitting the market.

All the above mentioned theories of profit are in some sense complementary, since uncertainty, innovation and monopoly power are factors which affect every business as regards its profit-earning capacity and hence its policy decisions. To a businessman, knowledge of profit theories is quite useful because they throw light on the three important factors giving rise to profits and thus enable the phenomenon and quantum of profits in a firm to be examined in a proper perspective. Practically, business firms may often be required to justify the profits being earned by them. Uncertainty bearing profits and innovational profits have a justification because they constitute a reward for performing two important productive functions, and can be so defended. Monopoly profits, however, are usually frowned upon and are often a target of attack. Being a symbol of exploitation, they can hardly be defended in the context of social obligations of business. Generally, government has to take measures to regulate monopoly profits by putting legal restrictions such as profit ceilings. In fact, large business profits often lead to a suggestion of something being wrong from the public point of view.

FUNCTIONS OF PROFIT

The basic function of profit lies to provide businessman with an incentive to produce what consumers want, when and where they want it at the lowest feasible cost. This comprises innovation of new products and new methods. In fact, the profit motive is the kingpin of private enterprise, nay, of every business activity. Besides, as pointed out by Peter Drucker, profit serves three main purposes:

Performance Measurement

It measures the net effectiveness and soundness of a business effort. A higher profit is an indicator that the business is being run successfully and effectively. It is true that profit is far from being a perfect measure of business efficiency but it is probably the best indicator of the general efficiency of a firm. It is essentially the only one which allows quick and easy comparison of performance of various firms.

To Cover the Costs of Staying in Business

Profit is the premium that covers the costs of staying in business-replacement, obsolescence, market and technical risk and uncertainty. Seen from this point of view, it may be argued that there is no such thing as profit, these are only the costs of being and staying in business. The management of a business has to provide adequately for these costs by generating sufficient profit.

Making Sure the Supply of Future Capital

Profit makes the supply of future capital for innovation and expansion, either directly, by providing the means of self-financing out of retained profits, or indirectly, through providing great inducement for new external capital which will optimise the company's capital structure and minimise its cost of capital.

The chief point of a business firm is to ensure its own survival. From this stand point, the firm must make a profit because profits are indispensable to remaining viable and to remain alive. Again, the firm must have growth because that is the only way it can perpetuate itself as an institution. And profits are a natural concomitant of the growth and development of business over time. In fact, "profits are essential as a means to an end, they are not an end in themselves, although essential for the continuity and growth of the firm".

MEASUREMENT POLICIES

The issues of measurement are: (i) Profit and Depreciation, (ii) Capital gains and losses, (iii) Profit maximisation vs Profit Optimization, (iv) Reasons for limiting profits, (v) Standards of reasonable profits, and (vi) Profits for Control.

Profit and Depreciation : Depreciation is considered as one of the essential aspects of determining the divisible profit. Divisible profit here refers to the net surplus available for distribution to the owners of the company. Net surplus is equal to gross earnings minus of depreciation and tax. In accounting terms it is "Profit after depreciation and tax".

Therefore, in order to arrive at true profit, depreciation is considered as a vital deduction, out of gross earnings. To determine the periodic net income, the cost of using the long-term assets should be properly calculated and charged to the P&L A/C of each year during which the assets are to run in the books of accounts. The use costs are called by various names such as depreciation, depletion, amortisation, etc. In the case of tangible assets, Land has unlimited life and hence there is no necessity for creating use cost against it. Assets like plant, equipment, building, furniture, tools, fixtures and vehicles are having 'use costs' and hence have depreciation. Natural resources like oil, timber, coal, mineral deposits are also exploited and their 'use cost' is termed as depletion which refers to the systematic and rational allocation of acquisation cost to the future periods in which the revenue is derived from that asset. Intangible assets like copyrights, trademarks, patent, and goodwill will have the use cost known as amortisation. In these cases also, there will be rational allocation of costs to future periods in which benefits contribute to the revenue. Whether it is depreciation, depletion or amortisation, the charge is definite against profit. If the use costs are not charged, profit will be inflated and real profit will not be arrived at. The Institute of Chartered Accountants of India defines depreciation as "a measure of wearing out, consumption or other loss of value of a depressible asset arising from use, effluxion of time or obsolescence through technology and market changes. Depreciation is allocated so as to charge a fair proportion of the depressible amount in each accounting period during the expected useful life of the asset. Depreciation includes amortisation of assets whose useful life is pre-determined," Therefore, various factors such as obsolescence, effluxion of time, wear and tear, change in technology, cause depreciation and the use cost of assets have to be rationally allocated to future periods on the ground of utilisation of assets each year. "The chief emphasis in depreciation accounting is on the computation of periodic charges to be allocated as an expense and to be matched with revenues reported in each period." The relevance of depreciation in profit analysis is that it has to be set aside before arriving at divisible profit. "Depreciation accounting is a system of accounting which aims to distribute the cost of tangible capital assets, less salvage (if any) over the estimated useful life of the unit in a systematic and rational manner It is a process of allocation, not of valuation. " (AICPA (USA). From this definition, we understand that depreciation is related to the expected benefits derived from the assets and it is feasible to measure the benefit. Depreciation makes efforts to measure the value of benefit, the asset has provided during a given accounting period and not an attempt to measure the value of an asset at any given time. The benefit is valued as portion of the cost of assets. This means, "The balance sheet value of depressible asset is that portion of the original cost which has not been allocated as a periodic expense in the process of income measurement." Depreciation charged to the P&L A/C will not itself provide funds for replacement of a depreciable asset. But the charging of depreciation to income ensures the maintenance of the original money capital of the enterprise". Depreciation is not identified with cash or any other specific asset. A rational allocation of use cost is made and charged against revenue before arriving at disposable profit. Depreciation is not a valuation process. Valuation considers depreciation as the fall in value of an asset over a period of time. However, the depreciation does not arise because of fall in value, but rather from the process of ensuring a return on capital invested. Even in periods of appreciation in value of an asset at a point of time, there will be depreciation. The increased value is not brought into books of accounts. The increase in value may be a temporary phenomenon.

Interim fluctuation have to be ignored as the assets are bound to reduce to below scrap value. Hence the rational and scientific allocation of the cost of assets against the revenue over the period is known as for.

Profit Maximisation and Optimisation

The terms 'Maximisation' and 'Optimisation' are confusing ones. Here an attempt is made to distinguish between these terms. The concept of 'maximisation' will be a myth. There is no limit for earning profit. Unless a standard is fixed, the concept cannot be properly understood. Profit maximisation can be measured, if a comparable parameter is provided.

Otherwise it will be simply a usage without any specific position. The following example will throw light to understand the concept. Supposing a T.V. Manufacturing firm is willing to maximise the profit. The firm is producing to the full capacity and is having stiff competition in the market. However, the product is sold in the market with certain distribution strategies. How to maximise profit in this context? The only way to assess the maximum of profit is to know the industry profits and compare the profit of the firm with that profit to know the level of maximisation. Supposing the T.V. industry in making 15% per annum. This firm can take this as a parameter to know the concept of maximisation. If the firm is earning only 10% p.a., it has not maximised its profit. Any earning beyond 15% (industry profit) will be the maximisation. Thus, only with certain standards, the concept of maximisation can be understood. The term 'optimization' of profit refers to reaching the normal earning level. If the firm, on an average, is earning a percentage of profit every year, the firm's profit is said to be epitomised.

The profit earned is 'best of most favourable', and may be known as 'optimum' profit. The concept of favourable profit depends upon the environment in which the firm works. In the present business environment, if the firm makes a reasonable profit, the profit is said to be optimised. The concepts 'maximisation' and 'optimisation' in a real sense have no meaning, unless they are quantified and standards are set to measure these levels. However, it may be only an academic exercise to distinguish between these two terms.

Causes for Limiting Profit

Earning of excess profit is not prevented. But it is not feasible to earn super profits. Every business firm works with the aim of earning huge profits. But there are several uncontrollable factors which restrict the firm to earn maximum profit or super profit. When we analyse the profit curve of an enterprise for a long period of five to ten years, we observe that the firm will be earning only normal or optimum profit or even below the optimum level. Regular earning of super profit even by monopoly firms will not be feasible as uncontrollable factors influence such profits to come down. In real situations, profit earned will be a normal profit. The reasons for earning normal profit are as follows:

(i) Resource crunch.
(ii) Threat of entry of rival to the market.
(iii) Government policies on tax matters, quote policies, monetary policies etc.
(iv) Consumer behaviour and to retain customer goodwill.
(v) To keep labour cool.
(vi) Disturbance in distribution channels.
(vii) Market behaviour.
(viii) Weak promotion policy of the firm.
(ix) Rapid change in production technology.

These are the major factors which cause the reduction in profit. One or some of the above factors come in the way of making extra profit or even to earn optimum profit. Firms also don't wish to earn super profits for long. They want to limit the profit as they have to stay long in the business. They have social responsibility and ethics. This obstructs them to aim only at profit maximisation, Society will not pardon the business houses, if they squeeze the consumers. After certain fluctuations in earnings in the initial years, firms get stabilised in their business operations and make only normal profit. But there will be steady growth of profit. Abnormal situations rarely arise. Since each firm is interested in the longevity of the enterprise, they restrict profits to a certain limit. This limit may marginally change each year, because of the growth in business volume or because of price fluctuations. Super profit is a temporary phenomenon, even in monopoly firms. Thus, limiting the profit is both a natural and forced phenomenon.

WHAT ARE REASONABLE PROFITS?

Reasonable profit here implies the profit which gives a fair return on capital employed. The term fair may refer to a certain quantity in the existing circumstances. Industry profit is the average profit earned by a group of firms producing identical products. If an individual firm's profit reaches the level of industry profit, then it can be said that the firm is earning a reasonable profit. To determine and earn the reasonable profit, we have to set certain standards. Profit standard can be in the following forms:

(i) Standard in the form of 'Return on Investment' (ROI).
(ii) Standard in the form of percentage of sales.
(iii) Standard in the form of aggregate rupee terms.

If the firm depends upon its uses and if the firm has to avoid competitors, the ROI is the relevant standard that the firm can adopt. If it has to satisfy the customers, keeping certain margins over unit cost is the standard to be adopted. The ratio of profit to sales as a standard is not a viable one. This ratio varies widely in many firms with various production plans, and the varied turnover, various composition of capital etc., will be inappropriate having the same ratio of return on invested capital. As every investor looks at net profit, ROI is the most important standard that can be adopted.

Setting a Standard

Setting a standard for earning reasonable profit is not to influence the standard setting. They are as follows:

Attracting Outside Capital: The profit earning of a firm should be such that it attracts outside capital. Investors invest in firms which are making good profits, declaring reasonable dividend every year and maintaining sufficient reserves to plough back in times of necessity. While setting the standard, this aspect has to be considered. The focal point in this issue of attracting outside capital is that profit earning should be steady and normal. This, certainly is influenced by factors like capital structure of the enterprise, cost of capital, rate of retained earning, the financial decisions of the management etc., and outside capital should be capable of making good profit.

Internal Resources and its Importance: Internal resources here refer to retained earnings. How far the firm can depend upon the retained earning to finance a desired rate of growth without seeking external funds is important. Maintaining high reserves to plough back to improve the business operation is not that desirable. High plough-back does not have public acceptance. The feelings is that all earnings should be distributed to shareholders. This means there should be of high dividend pay-out. If all the earnings are retained or heavy retention of earnings reduces the dividend payout, it affects the shareholder's interest. Maybe their holdings may sell at premium in the stock market. But their intention is not selling the equity for premium. Equity holders expect a good dividend for which a good portion of earnings have to be earmarked. Retained earnings can be used for business expansion or maintenance which may result in additional revenues to the firm. This may enhance the rate of dividend to equity holders.

Retained funds will be under the exclusive control of the management. But the management may not properly use it. If all or major portion of earnings are distributed to the shareholders, they will have the choice to increase their portfolio. They can use their dividend earnings in acquiring equities of other firms of their choice. Maintaining retained earnings at a higher scale remains a debatable point. However, it is one of the factors which influences the standard setting for earning reasonable profits.

Maintenance of Normal Profit: Another standard that can be considered for earning a reasonable profit is 'maintaining normal profit over the normal years'. If the firm's average profit for previous years is taken as an indicator, if the earning capacity of the firm and if investors confidently invest in the firm as per the indicator, then 'normal profit' can be taken as one of the standards for earning reasonable profit. But how to fix the normal period and normal profit? In a developing economy like ours, the economy will be oscillating and there will be no price stability. It will have its impact on the firms.

Therefore which is a normal period and which is an abnormal period cannot be strictly assessed. However, average profits of previous years can be considered as a standard to indicate the reasonable earning capacity of the firm. These standards can be considered for earning reasonable profits. Eventually, the factors that decide the profit earning capacity of the firm are situational analysis and quick and sound business decisions. Which standard has to be chosen depends upon the factors like avoiding competition maintaining liquidity for business operations, keeping the human force at work happy, preparing sound long-term growth plans etc., Standards are heterogeneous and the choice of a standard depends upon its purpose and its persuasive values.

The Concept of Profit for Control

'Profit for control' is a concept which recognizes profit centres the organisation and each centre is made to work actively to contribute to the overall profitability of the firm. Identifying profit centres and fixing responsibilities to centre heads to contribute so much profit to the total profit of the firm is profit for control. It is a thinking that workers who work at various levels of organisation do not think of profit concept of the firm. They always work in their ambit without considering the cost of their operations.

The waste or idle working hours or slackness on the part of workers will contribute to the increase in cost of production and it will have a bearing on the profit earnings of the firms. To check attitudes of workers like : (i) spending heavily on perfection of production over work without recognising cost and usefulness of such operations, (ii) lack of incentives for bottom line workers for their creativity and innovations, and making them feel that they are insecure will hamper the profit earning capacity of the firm. The firms have now recognised these problems and are restructuring managerial operations to see that every worker identifies with his work and eventually with the organisation. In the process, the functional organisation system has emerged and profit centres are created in the organisation.

Each functional manager (marketing, finance, production, human resources etc.,) will be given the responsibility of his functional department and is delegated with certain authority to make his department viable. These functional bosses have to prepare periodical reports about their revenue, expenditure and operations and submit to the top for appraisal. How to fix the profit standard for each department is a point to be examined. There are two ways of setting standards for the functional departments (i) Setting profit goals with regard to net profits for the firm and (ii) Confirming profit goals for the contribution to the total profits determined by costs and revenues of that centre or department. Fixing profit standards to the first method is not feasible as it is very difficult to measure the entire revenue cost of the firm by individual departments. The reasonable approach is to take into account only the cost and revenue of that functional department and fix the standard. Each functional executive should be given the widest discretion in pricing and promoting to reach his profit goals. While determining the profit goals, some of the general overheads can be proportionately charged to functional departments as the operational aspects of the firm is an integrated activity and each department is interlinked. So many activities take place in the general interest of the firm and expenses on these activities may be proportionately charged to each department while setting "controllable profits". Thus, 'Profit for Control' comprises identifying work magnitude of each department and costs incurred thereon, fixing profit standards for each department, considering the cost and revenue of each department, receiving periodical reports to measure the work in terms of profit and adopting corrective measures to achieve optimum profit/targets set for each department. This is a control technique adopted to achieve operational efficiency in each department.

PLANNING FOR PROFIT AND FORECASTING

The sign of healthy business is to make regular profit in the midst of various risks and uncertainties. These uncertainties arise on account of the diverse nature of competition, uncontrollable cost elements and the continuous technological developments and so on.

Modern businesses have to withstand various shocks which they face in society. If the prices of products are high, the businessmen have to face consumers' resistance. If the prices fall, then they may not earn good profits. In these days of technological developments, several products become obsolete. If the scope of market segmentation and product differentiation is great, the risk of product obsolescence also increases. If such a scope is less, the risk of price competition increases. At the same time, the risks involved in product competition are greater than price competition. Therefore, business in such an economic environment is very risky. These risks will have to be covered by means of accurate business planning and strategic operations. Profit planning is an integral part of business policy and planning. Profit policy is programmed through profit planning, which gives a concrete shape to the profit policy of the firm. It is a sign of good business which can make profit consistent with myriad of risks and uncertainties in business. These risks and uncertainties are faced boldly with profit planning.

Break-Even Analysis or Cost Volume Profit Analysis (CVP)

The break-even analysis (BEA) is defined as an important technique in the study of relationship between costs revenue and profit at various levels of sales of a firm. Joel Dean says that Cost Volume Profit Analysis (CVP) presents a flexible projection of the impact of volume of output upon costs revenue and profits, As such, it provides an important bridge between business behaviour and economic theory of the firm. When a firm breaks even, it means that it has not made profit nor incurred loss in its operations. In order words, (CVP) is defined as the point at which the level of output and the level of revenue is equal to the cost of production and marketing. This is also known as no profit and no loss point. The object of cost volume analysis is not just to determine break even point but to understand the financial relationship between cost, revenue and the rate of output. The revenue and expenses situations at various levels of output or sales of a firm are drawn in a map and this is known as break-even chart.

Cost Volume Chart

Cost Volume charts are being used in recent years by the managerial economists, company executives and government agencies in order to find out the cost volume point. In the breakeven charts, concepts like total fixed cost, total variable cost and the total cost and total revenue are shown separately. The following diagram illustrates the typical cost volume chart.

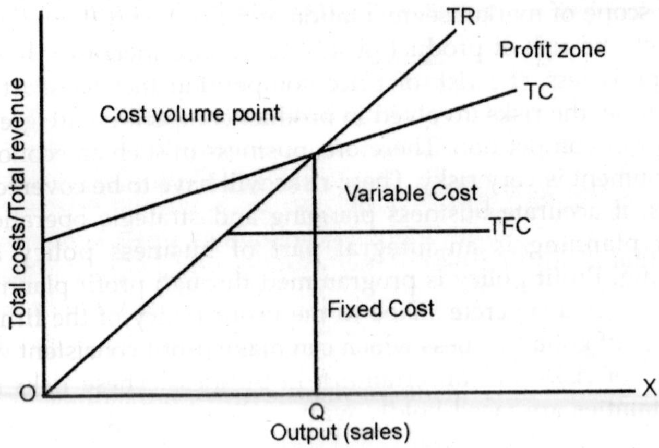

FIG. I

In the above diagram, the volume of output or sales is measured along the OX axis and the costs and revenues are measured along the OY axis. For the sake of simplicity, assuming constant factors, linear revenue function is drawn. Similarly, a linear total cost function is drawn. It is composed of total fixed cost which is represented by (TFC) on the chart. The variable cost function is assumed to change linearly in a constant proportion to the change in output. The cost volume point is the point at which total revenue equals total cost at the level of output 'Q'. So, the net profit is zero at the level of output

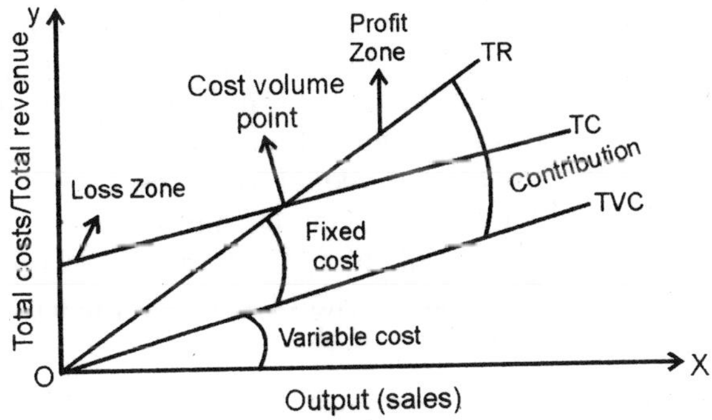

FIG. 2

OQ. The area between TR and TC depicts the profit function. It means that the firm incurs loss when it produces output below OQ. OQ is the level of output where the firm makes neither profit nor loss When it expands output, it makes profit. The cost volume chart can also be represented in an alternative form where the contribution to fixed cost (contribution margin) and profits is clearly depicted in Figure 2. Prof. F. V. Gardner in his book 'Profit Management and Control, considers that the cost volume chart is an excellent instrument panel for the guidance of businessmen in determining the profitable output and controlling his business. Break even point can be determined either in terms of physical units or in terms of sales value of the output.

BEP in Terms of Physical Units

Break even point may be determined either in terms of physical units or in money terms (sale value of the output). The cost volume point in physical terms is determined by a formula as follows :

$$BEP = \frac{TFC}{P - AVC} = \frac{\text{Total fixed cost}}{\text{Price per unit - Average variable cost}}$$

P – AVC means the contribution margin per unit.

Taking into consideration the contribution of per unit cost and revenue, BEP is located at the level of output at which the price per unit or average revenue is equal to average cost. That is the selling price should cover average variable cost in full and a part of fixed cost. The price of the unit in excess of the average variable cost is regarded as contribution margin per unit which contributes towards the fixed cost. Thus, the BEP is reached at a point where sufficient number of units are sold so that its total contribution margin becomes equal to the total fixed costs.

Let us consider the following examples:

Suppose the fixed costs of a factory are Rs. 20,000 and the variable costs are Rs. 4 per unit and the selling price is Rs. 8. per unit. The breakeven point would be:

$$\text{BEP} = \frac{\text{Rs. } 20{,}000}{(8-4)} = 5000 \text{ units}$$

If the company sells 5000 units, it would not make any loss or profit. Let us work it out it as follows:

Sales = Rs. 40,000

Cost of goods sold:

Variable cost 20,000
Fixed cost 20,000 40,000
Net profit Nil
It may also be arrived at by applying the above formula

$$\text{BEP} = \frac{\text{Total fixed cost (TFC)}}{\text{Price per unit} - \text{Average variable cost}}$$

$$\text{BEP} = \frac{\text{Rs. } 20{,}000}{(8-4)} = 5{,}000 \text{ units}$$

Break even point is reached when the firm sells 5000 units. When 5000 units are produced, the total revenue will be Rs. 40,000. The total cost

FC + VC
= Rs. 20,000 + Rs. 20,000 = Rs. 40,000

Thus, at BEP, TR = TC, so there is no profit and no loss. Net profit is zero, which is the break-even point.

Break Even Point in Terms of Sale Value

The above method holds good when a firm is producing only one product. But, in many cases, a firm is producing more than two products. It may be known as multiproduct firm, where BEP is calculated in relation to the total sales expressed in terms of money. In this case, we decide the fixed cost by the difference between sale value and the variable costs. That is BEP is a point where the contribution margin (Sale value - variable costs) would be equal to fixed cost. For example, if the sales are Rs. 400 and the variable costs of these sales are Rs. 280 and the contribution margin ratio (400 - 280)/400 i.e. 0.3

The formula for calculation BEP is fixed cost/sales value - variable cost.

For example : Sales Rs. 12,000
Variable cost = 800
Fixed cost = 4000
Let us take up a problem

AB firm produces four products. Sales value is Rs. 40,000. Variable costs are Rs. 12,000.

Fixed cost is Rs. 28,000. Calculate the BEP.

$$BEP = \frac{\text{Total Fixed Costs}}{\text{Contribution ratio}}$$

Contribution ratio is measured as :

$$CR = \frac{TR - TVC}{TR} = \frac{40,000 - 12000}{40,000} = \frac{28,000}{40,000} = \frac{7}{10}$$

$$BEP \doteq \frac{TFC}{CR} = \frac{28,000}{7/10} = \frac{28,000 \times 10}{7} = 40,000$$

The cost volume point is reached when the firm's sales value is Rs. 40,000. At Rs. 40,000 sales value, there is no profit and no loss.

Problem No. 2 : The fixed costs of a factory is Rs. 15,000 per year. The variable costs per unit of the product is Rs. 3 per unit. The selling price is Rs. 5 per unit, Find out the cost volume point.

$$BEP = \frac{\text{Fixed Costs}}{\text{Contribution ratio}}$$ (selling price – variable cost per unit.)

Let us find out the units of the products produced

$$\frac{15,000}{5-3} = 7500 \text{ units.}$$

That means, the company would not make any profit or loss at a sales volume of 7500 units.

Sales = 7500 units × Rs. 5 = 37, 500
Costs of goods sold at Rs. 3

	Rs. 22,500
Fixed costs	Rs. 15,000
	Rs. 37,500
Net profit is	Nil

BEP of company manufacturing multi-products:

Product	*Selling price*	*Variable cost per unit*	*% share of each product to total sale*
A	Rs. 5	3	20
B	Rs. 8	5	25
C	Rs. 10	6	30
D	Rs. 12	7	25

The capacity of a firm in terms of Rs. is one lakh. The fixed costs are Rs. 15,000. Calculate BUR

Solution : $\text{BEP} = \dfrac{\text{Fixed Costs}}{\text{Contribution ratio}}$

In this case, the fixed costs are Rs. 15,000,

The contribution ratios have to be calculated.

Contribution ratio of each product is the difference between selling price per unit and its variable cost.

Contribution ratios of each product:

A = Price – VC	Rs. 5 – 3 = 2
B = Price – VC	Rs. 8 – 5 = 3
C = Price – VC	Rs. 10 – 6 = 4
D = Price – VC	Rs. 12 – 7 = 5

The contribution ratios will have to be expressed as percentage of prices.

$$A = \frac{2}{5} \times 100 = 40 \qquad B = \frac{3}{8} \times 100 = 37.5$$

$$C - \frac{4}{10} \times 100 = 40 \qquad D = \frac{5}{12} \times 100 = 41.66$$

To obtain contribution ratios for each product, the contribution percentage has to be multiplied by the percentage share of each product.

A. 20% × 40% = 8%
B. 25% × 37.5% = 8%
C. 30% × 49% = 12%
D. 25% × 41.66% = 8%
Total = 36%

Thus, 36 per cent is the contribution of all products.

$$\text{Now, BEP} = \frac{\text{Fixed Costs}}{\text{CR}} = \frac{15{,}000}{36\%} = \text{Rs. } 42{,}000$$

If the firm makes a sales revenue of Rs. 42,000 per year, it will make no profit and no loss.

Managerial Uses of Break-even Analysis

The BEA provides a microscopic view of the profits of the firm. Based on the analysis, the management can chalk out the plans, programmes and policies pertaining to the development of the firm. Suppose a firm wants to know the volume of sales required to achieve a certain amount of profit, BEA may be utilised. Then the following formula will have to be used:

$$\text{Volume of sales necessary} = \frac{\text{Fixed costs + Profit (Target)}}{\text{Marginal contribution per unit}}$$

Let us take up the following example :
Fixed costs Rs. 15,000. The profit target is Rs. 5,000.
Selling price is Rs. 5 per unit. Variable cost: Rs. 3 per unit.

$$\text{Then, } \frac{15{,}000 + 5000}{\text{CR} = 2} = \frac{20{,}000}{2} = 10{,}000 \text{ units.}$$

If the firm sells 10,000 units, it can make a profit of Rs. 5,000.

(2) The cost volume profit helps the management to know at a glance the profits generated at various levels of sales. The BEP can be used in determining 'the safety margin' regarding the extent to which the firm can permit a decline in sales without causing losses. The formula to determine 'safety margin' is :

$$\text{Safety margin} = \frac{\text{Sales} - \text{BEP}}{\text{Sales}} \times 100$$

Taking the above examples,

$$\frac{50,000 - 37,500}{50,000} \times 100 = 25\%$$

That is, the firm can afford to lose sales up to 25% of the present level before incurring a loss. 25% is the safety margin.

3. The cost volume analysis is very much helpful in decision making pertaining to price policy, sales projection and capital budgeting.

4. In modern business situations, many times firms may be faced with the problem of reducing the prices of their products. Whenever the firm reduces the price, there will be a reduction in the contribution margin (towards fixed cost). This means that, to remain at the same level of profit, the firm has to increase its output. The firm cannot assume that a fall in price will result in a rise in sales. Assuming there is no change in sales, the firm has to calculate the increase in volume of output in order to remain at the same level of profits, following a reduction in the price. The following formula can be used:

New volume of sales necessary

$$= \frac{\text{Total Fixed cost} + \text{Total Profit}}{\text{New Selling Price} - \text{Average Variable cost}}$$

Let us take the following example :

If FC of a firm is Rs. 10,000, profit target is Rs. 22,000, selling price is Rs. 10 per unit and variable cost is Rs. 5 per unit, then the total volume of sales necessary, using the earlier formula is 6,400 units; given the target profit of Rs. 22,000. Suppose the firm decides to reduce the selling price from Rs. 10

to Rs. 9 per unit, then the new volume of sales necessary using the above formula would be

$$\text{New volume of sales necessary} = \frac{10{,}000 + 22{,}000}{9 - 5} = \frac{32{,}000}{4}$$

$$= 8000 \text{ units.}$$

Thus, after reducing the price from Rs. 10 to Rs. 9 per unit, if the firm wants to maintain the target profit of Rs. 22,000, it has to increase sales from 6,400 units to 8,000 units. In other words, a reduction in price by Re. 1 should be followed by an increase in sales volume by 1600 units, if the firm has to maintain the same profit level.

Limitations of BEA

(a) In the BEA, everything is assumed to be constant. This implies a static condition. But costs and revenues may change over a period of time, making the projection based on the past data wrong. As such, BEA is useful in situations of stable and slow moving entities.

(b) Since BEA is based on many assumptions which do not hold good in practice, we assume cost and revenue functions are linear. We assume again selling price as constant, etc. In fact, the linearity of cost and revenue functions are real only for a limited range of output.

(c) The cost volume analysis is based upon the accounting data, as such, it neglects imputed costs, takes arbitrary depreciation estimates and considers inappropriate allocation of overhead costs. In order to make the best use of BEA, a good accounting system is to be followed.

(d) The BEA regards profit as a function of output only. It fails to consider the impact of technological change, division of labour, improved productivity, etc.

(e) It assumes horizontal demand curve which means, any quantity is sold at one price which can be true only under the conditions of perfect competition. Hence, to be realistic, calculations have to be made at several price levels. Thus, several total revenue curves are required instead of one. It is so because in the real world, imperfect competition is prevailing. Otherwise, the demand schedule will not get its due weightage.

In spite of these limitations, the BEA is very simple and easy to understand and hence, it is frequently used by the management.

PROFIT FORECASTING

Profit forecasting is indispensable for profit planning, Profit forecasting means projecting the future profits, assuming the factors like growth of the size of the business, the pricing policies of the firm, the cost control policies, depreciation policy and so on. It is also necessary from the point of view of economic health and stability of the firm to project for certain years the growth of sales, increase in costs and consequently the profits also.

Joel Dean points out three approaches to profit forecasting.

Spot Projection means projecting the entire profit and loss for a specified period, say five years, seven years or ten years. The projection of profits and loss statements for this period depends on the projection of sales, costs and prices of the same period. Since profits are surpluses resulting from the forces that shape the demand for the company's products and govern the behaviour of costs, their prediction is subject to wide margins of error, from the culmination of errors in forecasting revenues and costs and from the inter relation of the various components of the income statement.

Break-even analysis identifies functional relations of both revenue and costs to output rate with profits related to output as a residual or surplus.

Environmental analysis relates company's profits to key variables in the economic environment, such as the general business activity and general price level. It is based on the movement of business cycles.

The profit forecast is intimately related with variables like the growth rate of output, changes in prices, wages, material costs and productivity or factors of production. All these are related to the aggregate business activity of the nation.

In practice, these approaches are used in combination to project future profits.

QUESTIONS

1. Describe the nature and scope of Profit Management.
2. What do you know about Measurement Policies?
3. What is Cost Volume-Profit Analysis?

CHAPTER

10

Inflation

Inflation means rise in price level or fall in the value of money. According to Kemmerer, "Inflation is too much money and deposit currency-that is too much currency in relation to the physical volume of business being done". This is what Coulburn also means when he defines inflation as "Too much money chasing too few goods". That volume of money is responsible for the fall in the value of money or rise in prices is expressed by several writers as"abnormal increase in the quantity of money" (T.E. Gregory), "the issue of too much money" (Hawtrey), etc. The implication of these definitions is that prices rise because of an increase in the volume of money as compared to the supply of goods. This is the quantity approach to the rise in the price level. But it should not be forgotten that the prices may rise because of other factors also such as rise in wages and profits. Besides, there can be an inflationary pressure on prices without the prices actually rising.

While discussing the concept of inflation, Keynes mentions the following four related terms:

(1) Reflation (2) Inflation (3) Disinflation and (4) Deflation.

Using a trade cycle model, we may clarify these terms as under:

What is Reflation? It implies a situation of rising prices, deliberately undertaken to relieve depression. With rising prices, employment, output and income also increase till the economy reaches the full employment ceiling.

What is Inflation ? It occurs when prices rise after the stage of full employment in the economy, with no similar rise in employment and output.

The following are the chief characteristics of inflation:

(i) Inflation is a long-term dynamic process.

(ii) Inflation is a process of persistently rising price level.

(iii) Inflation is fostered by the interaction of a multitude of economic factors.

(iv) Inflation, in a real sense, is a post-full-employment phenomenon.

(v) A cyclical movement is not inflation. Inflation is rising trend in the price level.

(vi) Inflation price rise is persistent and is irreversible within a short time, thus, it should be distinguished from a price rise which may occur temporarily because of short-term scarcity or during a cyclical upswing.

(vii) Inflation is indigenous to the economic system.

(viii) By and large, inflation is also a monetary phenomenon. It is generally characterised by an overflow of money and credit. In fact, the root cause of inflation is the expansion of money supply beyond the normal absorbing capacity of the economy.

Disinflation: When prices are falling because of anti-inflationary measures adopted by the authorities, with no corresponding decline in the existing level of employment, output and income, the result is "disinflation'.

When acute inflation afflicts the community, disinflation is adopted as a curve. Disinflation is said to take place when deliberate attempts are made to curtail expenditure of all sorts to lower prices and money incomes for the benefit of the community.

Deflation: It implies a condition of falling prices accompanied by a decreasing level of employment, output and income. Deflation is just the opposite to inflation. Deflation takes when the total expenditure of the community is not equal to the existing prices. Consequently, the value of money goes up and prices fall. However, each and every fall in price cannot be called deflation. For example, when the inflationary spiral is controlled by an effective monetary and fiscal policy, along with increase in output and employment and prices begin to fall, it is not called deflation. The process of reversing inflation without either creating unemployment or reducing output is known as "disinflation" and "deflation".

Deflation is an under-employment phenomenon.

INFLATION : MAIN CHARACTERISTICS

(a) It is a continuous rise in prices.
(b) Inflation is a long term operating dynamic process.
(c) Inflation is purely a monetary phenomena.
(d) It is not a high price but a rising price.
(e) Inflation is endogeneous to economic system.
(f) A cyclical movement not inflation but continuity in price rise must be there.
(g) In real sense, true inflation occurs after full employment.

KINDS OF INFLATION

On different grounds, economists have divided inflation into several types. Some of the important categories are discussed here.

Creeping, Walking, Running and Hyper Inflation

According to the rapidity with which prices increase, we have:

Creeping Inflation: It is the mildest type of inflation. Keynesian economists do not consider this kind of inflation dangerous at all for the economy. When prices rise within a range of ten per cent over a decade or approximately one per cent per annum, there occurs creeping inflation in the economy.

Kent, for instance, opines that when prices rise by not more than three per cent a year, there is creeping inflation which does not disrupt the economic balance.

Walking Inflation: When the rise in prices becomes more pronounced as compared to a creeping inflation, there exists walking inflation in the economy. Roughly, when prices rise by more than ten per cent and within a range of 30 per cent to 40 per cent over a decade or by 3 to 4 per cent a year, walking inflation is the outcome. Walking inflation presents a warning signal for the occurrence of running and galloping inflation.

*Running or Galloping Inflation:*When the movement of price accelerates rapidly, running inflation emerges. Running inflation may record between 80 and 100 per cent rise in prices over a decade. In case of hyperinflation, prices rise every moment, and there is no limit to the height to which prices might rise. Therefore, it is not easy to measure its magnitude, as prices rise by fits and starts. If, within a year, the prices rise by 100 per cent, it is a case of hyperinflation or galloping inflation.

Hyper Inflation: It refers to a situation when prices rise at an unexpected rate. There is an escalation of price rise, thereby sometimes called Hydra-headed monster of inflation. It was witnessed in Germany after 1932, which made people lose all their confidence in the German currency.

War, Post-war and Peace-time Inflation

Under the criterion of time, we have:

Peace-time Inflation: It implies the rise in prices during the normal period of peace. Peace-time inflation is often a result of increased government outlays on capital projects having a long gestation period, so a gap between money income and real wage goods develops. In a planning era, thus, when government's expenditure increases, prices may rise.

War-time Inflation: It is the result of certain exigencies of war on account of increased government expenditure, which is of an unproductive nature. By such public expenditure, the government apportions a substantial production of goods and services out of total availability which causes a downward shift in the supply, as a result, an inflationary gap may develop.

Post-war Inflation: This type of inflation is experienced in immediate post-war period. It is the gift of war. This may happen when the disposable income of the community increases when war-time taxation is withdrawn or public debt is repaid in the post-war period.

EXCESSIVE, COST DEFICIT AND FLIGHT INFLATION

On the basis of process of rise in prices and the factors which influence money supply and demand for goods and services, we have :

Wage Induced Inflation: When inflation occurs due to rise in factor cost, it is known as cost inflation. It occurs when money incomes (wage rate, particularly) expand more than real productivity. Powerful labour organizations have strong bargaining power vis-à-vis the employers. They succeed in getting their wages increased, thereby resulting in higher cost of production and increased prices. This process of spiraling may reach higher and higher levels. In this case, however, cyclical anti-inflation remedies of monetary controls are not relatively effective.

Excessive money supply inflation: This inflation is classical types of inflation, where there is an excess of money supply in comparison to the availability of real goods and services. This type of inflation is usually conceived with reference to the cyclical fluctuations in the economy and measures of monetary controls to check inflationary or deflationary trends.

Deficit Inflation: When the government budgets contain heavy deficit financing, though creating new money, the purchasing power in the community increases and prices rise. This may be referred to as deficit-induced inflation. During a planning era, when government launches upon investment, it usually resorts to deficit financing, when adequate resources are not found. An inflationary spiral develops because of deficit financing, the production of consumption goods fails to keep pace with the increased money expenditure.

Flight Inflation: This kind of inflation implies the relationship between money supply and goods, where there is a flight from the currency, reflecting increased velocity of spending. This is the result of peoples' psychological reactions when they find an intolerable decline in the value of money. It has been said that this stage is always reached by recurring budget deficits and then the creation of new money under deficit financing.

Stagflation: It characterizes a situation in which on the one hand prices rise but on the other hand, there is no increase in production and employment. According to Samuelson, "Stagflation involves inflationary rise in prices and wages at the same time that people are unable to find jobs and firms are unable to find customers for what their plants can produce". That is Stagflation occurs when inflation rises while output is either falling or atleast not rising.

SPORADIC AND COMPREHENSIVE INFLATION

From the coverage or scope point of view, we have:

Sporadic Inflation: This is a kind of sectional inflation. It consists of cases in which the averages of a group of prices rise because of increases in individual prices which might be due to abnormal shortage of specific goods. When the supply of some goods becomes inelastic, at least temporarily, because of the physical or structural constraints, the sporadic inflation has its way. For instance, during drought conditions where there is failure of crops, foodgrain prices shoot up.

Sporadic inflation is a situation in which direct price control, if skillfully used, is most likely to be beneficial to the community at large.

Comprehensive Inflation: When prices of every commodity throughout the economy rise, it is known as economy-wide or comprehensive inflation. It is a normal inflationary phenomenon and implies rising prices of the general price level.

REPRESSED AND OPEN INFLATION

An inflation is open or repressed according to government's reaction to the prevalence of inflationary forces in the economy.

Repressed or Suppressed Inflation: When the price rise is interrupted by the government, there is repressed or suppressed inflation. Thus, suppressed inflation implies those conditions in which price increases are prevented at the present time through adoption of certain measures like price controls and rationing by the government, but they rise in future on the removal of such controls and rationing. The inevitable characteristic of repressed inflation, in contrast to open inflation, is that it seeks to prevent distribution through price rise under free market mechanism and substitutes instead a distribution system based on controls. Thus, the administration of controls is a significant feature of suppressed inflation.

Open Inflation: When the government does not make efforts to prevent a price rise, inflation is said to be open. Thus, inflation is open when prices rise without any interruption. In open inflation, free market mechanism is allowed to fulfil its historic function of rationing the short supply of goods and distributes them according to consumer's ability to pay. Therefore, the inevitable characteristics of an open inflation lies in the operation of the price mechanism as the only distributing agent. The postwar hyper-inflation during the nineteen twenties in Germany is a living example of open inflation. However, many economists like Milton Friedman and G.N. Halm opine that if there has to be any inflation, it is better open than suppressed. Suppressed inflation is condemned as it breeds a number of evils such as the phenomenon of black market, hierarchy of price controllers and rationing officers and uneconomic diversion of productive resources from inevitable industries to the non-inevitables or less inevitable goods industries since there is a free price movement in the latter and hence becomes more profitable to investors. We may add to the above list, the following different types of inflation, based on different other causes.

PROFIT INFLATION

Professor Brahmananda in his recent book, 'Growthless Inflation by Means of Stockless Money', mentions profit inflation as a unique category of inflation. The concept of profit inflation was developed by Keynes in his Treatise on Money. According to Keynes, the price level of consumption goods is a function of the investment exceeding savings. He considered the investment boom as a reflection of profit boom. Inflation is unjust in its distribution effect. It redistributes income in support of profiteers and against the wage-earning class. During inflation, thus, the entrepreneur class may tend to expect an upward shifting of the marginal efficiency of capital (MEC), hence entrepreneurs are induced to invest more even by borrowing at higher interest rates. Ultimately, investment exceeds savings and economy tends to reach a higher level of money income equilibrium. In an economy operating at full employment level or if there are bottlenecks of market imperfections, real output will not rise proportionately, so the imbalance between money income and real income is corrected through rising prices.

FOREIGN-TRADE INDUCED INFLATION

Prof Brahmananda for an international economy, has categorised the following three kinds of inflation as being caused by factors pertaining to the balance of payments:

(1) Key-currency Inflation,
(2) Export-Boom Inflation and
(3) Import Price-like Inflation.

When a country having a sizable export component in its foreign trade, experiences a sudden rise in the demand for its exportables against the inelastic supply of exportables in the domestic market, it naturally means an excessive pressure of demand which is revealed in terms of persistent inflation at home. Again, trade gains and sudden influx of exchange remittances may lead to an increase in monetary liabilities which is further reflected in the rising pressure of demand for domestic output causing an inflationary spiral to get further momentum. Such a permanent case for an export-boom inflation is, however, ruled out in the Indian economy, because neither export trade is a great portion of Domestic National Product nor is there a continuous boom of export demand, causing terms of trade to move up favourably all the time.

Inflation: Its Causes

The general price theory says that a price rise may take place because of either of the following two situations:

(i) when the aggregate demand increases, and/or
(ii) when the aggregate supply falls.

If there is an increase in aggregate demand, without any similar increase in supply or if there is a fall in supply without any fall in aggregate demand, the prices will go up. Thus, price-rise or inflation is caused by the two sets of causes viz:

(i) Causes which induce an increase in demand and
(ii) Causes which produce a fall in supply because of increase in costs.

Inflation caused by the first set of causes is known as 'demand-pull inflation' while that caused by the second set of causes is called 'cost-push inflation'

Demand-Pull Inflation

This inflation takes place when the aggregate demand increases without any increase in output. It implies that the prices will not go up if output increases along with the demand. If production is not increasing with the increase in demand, it is a state of full employment and therefore, demand inflation occurs only when the production reaches at full employment level. Here, demand is in excess of the available supply at the existing prices. The following are some inflationary factors that induce demand of goods and services:

Raising the Velocity of Money: During boom period, velocity of money pertinently goes up. It happens when people stop preferring liquid money and their consumption function dominates the saving attitude. People prefer spending on consumption which brings an increase in the velocity of money and thus gives a spurt to prices.

Money Supply: Increase in money supply is the chief factor that induces demand for goods and services. Increase in money supply increases, on the one hand, money income of the people that can be spent in purchasing the goods on the other hand, increases bank deposits which are the basis of the expansion of credit. The policies of central and commercial banks are also responsible for expansion of credit money. For instance, a slash in the bank rate makes the credit cheaper. Expansion of actual money and credit money increases the demand for loans for production purposes. Increased supply of money and bank credit adds something to the demand of goods and services on one hand and to the cost because of interest element on the other hand. These factors push up the prices.

Disposable Income: This refers to the income payments to different production factors after personal taxes have been paid. An increase in the disposable income results in an increase in the absolute amount of consumption expenditure in the economy,that boosts up prices.

Deficit Financing: Deficit financing is a technique through which the government covers the budgetary gap. When the government spends more than what it expects to collect as revenue, the deficit is met by issuing more currency in the market or by borrowing the funds from foreign governments or international agencies. It will result in more money in the market and will increase the price level, because the disposable income of countrymen increases.

Increased Foreign Demand: Increased foreign demand will obviously push the prices of the domestic goods and services because it increases the overall demand. This factor is especially significant if country's balance of trade is favourable or exports are higher than imports.

Rise in Business Outlays: Increase in business outlays or capital expansion takes on a speculative character during an inflationary boom. Majority of the new equipment and plants are financed by speculative borrowing, not to mention an increase in their replacement demand. Most of the expenditure of the business find way into income stream via dividend wages, interest and other income payments. These income payment are also inflationary in character.

Rise in Population: If the population of a country increases speedily, it will pressurise the demand of goods and services. If money supply does not increase, the velocity of money will consequently increase the prices, provided the increase in output is less than proportionate to increase in demand because of increased population. Prof Coulborn in this regard says, "If population increases rapidly, while the aggregate of money remains stable, the consequent rise in the velocity of circulation is likely to outweigh the countervailing decrease in the volume of money per head. Further a rapid increase of population may increase output less than proportionately, another factor tending to raise prices." The cumulative effect of all these factors is that the aggregate demand function in an economy shifts upward, resulting in an inflationary rise in prices.

Cost-Push Inflation

The second chief cause of inflation is the increase in the cost of production. When cost of production increases, the supply curve will go downward, provided there is no increase in demand at the prevailing prices Thus, increase in cost of production, decreases the supply resulting in upward trend in price level. The following factors are responsible for the increase in cost and consequently higher prices:

Higher Profit Marginals: Another factor causing cost push inflation is higher profit margins fixed by the producers. It is especially feasible in monopolistic or near-monopolistic market situations where the producers (or heading producers) fix up higher profit margins arbitrarily without any increase in other elements of cost. If some powerful producers succeed in revising their profit margins upward, the other followers-producers also increase their profit margins and this phenomenon would push up the prices because profit becomes the part of selling price. Thus, higher profit margins inflate the price level.

Higher Wage Rates: Generally strong trade unions demand for higher wages for their members and successfully manage to get it because the enterpreneurs have no other choice. This increase in wages is not linked with the increased productivity and hence the cost of production goes up. The producers shift this increased burden on the consumers by charging higher prices for their commodities. This is a never ending wage price spiral. Higher prices of goods amount to higher cost of living and a fall in real wages. To neutralise the fall in real wages, again higher wages are demanded and granted which again are passed on to the consumers and thus inflationary trend continues.

Decline in the Supply of Basic Inputs: Whenever fundamental and strategic raw materials and other inputs like cement, cotton, iron and steel etc. go in short supply, their prices will tend to move upward. The cost of production of finished goods in which such raw materials are used increases thereby and consequently their selling prices would be a source of cost push inflation.

Higher Taxes: Another source of cost-push inflation is higher tax particularly indirect tax like sales tax, excise duties etc. imposed by the government. Such taxes increase the selling prices of the commodities because producers generally shift the burden of such taxes to consumers. Thus, higher indirect taxes push the commodity prices in the market.

Inputs Administered Higher Prices: Sometimes, the prices of so many significant inputs are administered by the government or by supplying agency or organisation. Such administrators of prices keep on revising the prices of controlled inputs at regular or irregular intervals. The revised prices are generally fixed upward. Higher prices of inputs raise not only the prices of outputs in which they are used but they raise the general price level as basic inputs are used as basic raw materials in a number of industries. For instance, prices of crude oil are administered by the Organisation of Petroleum Exporting Countries (OPEC) which keeps on revising the prices of crude oil upward from time to time. As oil is a basic input for several industries, it raises the general price level and therefore establishes powerful cost push inflationary forces in the economy.

Natural Factors: Fall in agricultural production due to insufficient or excessive rainfall, and other natural calamities such as earthquakes, floods, drought conditions, famine and other destructive mishappenings moves the prices of agricultural consumer goods upward. In addition to that, industrial production is also affected as the supply of inputs falls short. Both these factors exert inflationary pressures.

Low Industrial Production: Different causes tend to affect the industrial production negatively resulting in the short supply of consumer goods. Such factors are strikes and lock outs, nonavailability of factors of production, break down of power supply, operation of law of diminishing returns, etc. Fall in supply will naturally increase the prices.

Government Policies: Different types of the policies made by the government also help raising the general price level in the country. For instance wage policy fixing the wages of workers working in specified industries; industrial policy, not allowing certain industries to be in operation without license or providing excessive protection to industries; export policy, making export of certain commodities obligatory, thus leaving the domestic demand unsatisfied etc., affect the supply position of industrial production unfavourably and price trend displays an upward move. The cumulative effect of all the above factors sets in cost-push inflation in the economy. Demand pull and cost push inflation in an economy go together and no demarcation line can be drawn between the two. Both affect each other. In both the cases, demand exceeds supply and prices of factor inputs rise.

INFLATION : EFFECTS OR CONSEQUENCES

Inflation has its effects on various sections of the society and on the economic activities as well. Some effects are good and some others are quite undesirable for the economic development of the country and to various sections of the society. Modern economists are of the view that a mild degree of inflation is not only desirable but also a essential condition for growth specially in developing countries where manpower and natural resources are underutilised. A slow rise in prices may induce the investors to undertake innovations and expand the level and scale of production. But, it is desirable only as long as it is kept within control table limits and is not allowed to gallop further. Galloping inflation, certainly, has same serious consequences. The consequences of inflation can be discussed under two subheads:

Effects of Mild Degree Inflation on Production and Economic Activities: As it has been explained in the above lines that a mild inflation serves as a tonic for the economy of the country and therefore, is an essential condition for the growth of the economy. A mild degree of inflation has some good effects:

With an increase in the price level, the profit margins of producers tend to widen. Rise in price level also increases the costs of inputs but the prices of inputs move slowly, as compared to the prices of the final products. The producers thus, have a wider profit margins. It encourages more investments in industries because investments in industries shall be more attractive because of greater profit margins. It will lead to industrial progress of the country as new and new industrial units will be promoted by the industrialists to earn more profits. The industrial expansion boosts up the employment level. Expansion of industrial base requires the employment of more and more labour and thus unemployed manpower and resources are used. But this favourable trend continues so long as the prices are rising at a slow speed and the state of full employment is not achieved. But as soon as the full employment point is achieved, it becomes self-generating and creates uncertainty in the economic system. It degenerates into runway inflation or hyper inflation. This situation is not desirable for investment and production activity and has the following adverse effects on the productive activities of the economy:

(i) Reduced capital accumulation shall effect the investment in productive activities adversely that will consequently hamper the industrial production in the country.

(ii) The hyper inflation results in the fall of money value that discourages savings on the part of general public. With the reduced savings, capital accumulation suffers a serious set back, because of the increasing propensity to consume, rather than to save something for future.

(iii) Runaway inflation also affects the pattern of production as the rise in general price level disturbs the price relationship. The prices of some commodities go up rapidly, while of some others move rather slowly and of some remain stationary or may even fall. There is, therefore, a diversion of resources from production of some to others mainly from the inevitable goods industries (which are low profit generation) to luxury goods industries (which are more profit-prone industries). This results in further shortage of inevitable consumer goods to the common man, pushing the prices upward.

(iv) As inflation creates uncertainty in the economic activities, the production will be affected adversely on this account. The enterpreneurs will be discouraged from taking business risks in production.

(v) The worst effect of hyper-inflation is that, in course of time, it results in a flight from domestic currency on account of its constant diminishing value. The people lose confidence in their home currency and rush to buy foreign currencies of stabler value to safeguard their interest.

(vi) Inflation disrupts the smooth functioning of the price mechanism, thereby creating allround confusion in the economy. Artificial demands and supplies take place, disturbing the forces of demand and supply.

(vii) Inflation gives stimulus to speculative activities on account of the uncertainty generated by continually rising price level. In order to earn more profits, businessmen prefer to engage in speculative activities rather than to invest money in productive activities.

Thus, on production side, mild degree of inflation, gives encouragement to produce more till the stage of full employment but later on, production activities are discouraged.

Impact of Inflation on Society or on Distribution: A long period of persistent inflation results in redistribution of income and wealth. Inflation does not effect all sections of society alike. Some gain from inflation while some others lose. These 'gains' and 'losses' results in redistributing the income and wealth within the society. The effects of inflation on different sections of society may be discussed as under:

Impact on Debtors and Creditors: When inflation sets in debtors as an economic group tends to Again. The value of money during inflation, falls sharply but the debtor has to repay the same amount of money he had borrowed few years hence. In ' this way, he returns less purchasing power to the creditor than what he actually borrowed. Creditors, on the other hand, are losers during inflation because they receive lesser purchasing power than what they had actually lent.

Impact of Inflation on Wage and Salary Earners: Wage and salary earners usually lose during inflation. Although their wages and salaries also go up in the wake of rising prices but wages and salaries generally do not rise in the same proportion in which the price level or their cost of living rises. Thus, the real value of their fixed income falls and they are badly hit during inflation. It penalises consumers, labours, creditors, small investors, and fixed income group while it rewards businessmen, debtors and farmers.

Producers or Businessmen: Producers or businessmen gain during inflation as the prices of their stock suddenly go up. It is a tonic for the businessmen and producers. Though, the cost of production also goes up but prices rise at a faster rate than the cost of production and thus, it results in higher profits.

Investors: We can distinguish two kinds of investors:

(i) investors in equities (equity shares), and
(ii) investors in fixed interest-yielding securities like bonds and debentures. Inflation bestows favours on the former and is rather harsh on the latter. In case of former type of investors, equity dividends increase as a result of increasing corporate profit during inflation, On the other hand latter types of investors get fixed dividend (on preference shares) or interest on bonds and debentures. Inflation erodes the value of such dividend and interest with the rising prices. Therefore, their interests are adversely affected.

The small middle class investors generally keep their savings in fixed deposits in commercial banks or in their provident fund accounts maintained by their employers through insurance covers. The value of their savings fall sharply on maturity and therefore, household savings during inflation get discouraged. People prefer to spend more of their income in purchasing consumption goods and therefore, their will and ability to save is affected seriously. It badly hits the process of capital formulation, in the absence of which rapid industrial development cannot be expected.

Impact on Farmers: Farmers gain during inflation. Like other producers, farmers gain because of the time lag involved in the purchase of inputs and sale of output. Moreover, the prices of farm products go up while the costs incurred by them do not go up to the same extent. Again, farmers are generally debtors and as debtor, they are to pay less purchasing power during inflation. To conclude, we say that inflation redistributes income and wealth but it increases disparity of income and wealth in the society.

HOW TO CHECK INFLATION?

Inflation is harmful to the economic development and to the different sections of society and, therefore, should be contained. There are three lines of action that can be adopted to check inflation namely:

Government's Monetary Measures: Monetary measures are those measures of the government which aim at regulating the money supply in an economy. Such boom, as Central Bank is the sole authority measures directly hit the inflationary to control the money supply, this step is, therefore, taken by the Central Bank of the country. Money supply, at any time, consists of currency and bankcredit. Bank credit creates a proportionately larger share of money supply in an economy. Therefore, the bent of monetary authority is to regulat : the flow of bank credit. The following monetary measures are popular curbing inflationary pressures:

Bank-Rate: Bank rate is a rate at which Central Bank of the country accepts and lends money to the commercial banks. This rate affects the bank-credit issued by the commercial banks to businessmen. An increase in bank rate, definitely, makes the bank credit dearer because lending rate of interest is increased accordingly. It will discourage borrowing by businessmen from banks, resulting in a fall in the intensity of inflationary measures in the the economy. Again, increased interest rate, consequent upon the increase in bank rate, will attract savings and induce people to save more rather than to spend money on consumer goods. The measure will, reduce the supply of bank-credit and currency.

Re-discount Rates Enhancement: To check inflation, the Central Bank generally increases the re-discount rates. An increase in the rediscount rates leads to an increase in bank rates, because there is definite relationship between the two. An increase in bank rates tends to discourage borrowing by businessmen from banks, resulting in a fall in the intensity of inflationary pressures in the economy. An increase in interest-rates consequent upon the increase in the bank rate will make savings attractive than before and induce people to spend less on consumer goods. But the increase in rediscount rates as a weapon to check an inflationary boom has its limitations too. Firstly, if the bank rates do not rise with the rise in rediscount rates, there will be no decline in business borrowings, and hence, the inflationary pressures will continue, even though the rediscount rates have been raised. Secondly, the effectiveness of higher rediscount rates as an anti-inflationary weapon shall be considerably undermined if the commercial banks have an easy access to additional reserves.

Resorting to Sale of Government Securities to the Public: Another method to control the inflationary boom is to resort to sale of government securities to the public by the Central Bank. As the buying public purchase and pay for those government securities, the commercial banks, reserves with the Central Batik are correspondingly reduced and they are obliged to adopt a restrictive credit policy in relation to business requirements. But the sale of government securities as an anti-inflationary weapon is also subject to limitations. Firstly, this policy may be rendered ineffective if the commercial banks are able to increase their reserves by selling their stocks of government securities to the Central Bank. Secondly, this policy may also be offset by increased borrowing from or by increased sales of treasury bills to the Central Bank of the commercial banks.

Higher Reserve Requirements: During inflation an increase in reserve requirements of the member banks also serves as an anti-inflationary weapon. It absorbs the excess reserves of the banking system and, thus, prevents them from forming a basis for further credit expansion. But this method is also subject to limitations. Firstly, if the commercial banks happen to have very large excess reserves, even the raising of the reserve requirements may not significantly curtail their power to create credit. Secondly, the ability of commercial banks to increase the reserves through sale of government securities may render higher reserve requirements ineffective to check credit expansion.

Methods of Higher Margin Requirements: It is a kind of method of selective credit control. The Central Bank in its pursuance of an anti-inflationary policy may raise the margin requirements of loans to higher levels. The higher the margin requirements, the lower the amount of loan that the borrower can obtain from the bank. Thus, higher margin requirements have the effect of checking undue monetary expansion.

Consumer Credit Control: During an inflationary boom, facilities for instalment buying are reduced to the minimum to curtail excessive spending on the part of the consumers. This is done (i) by raising the minimum initial payments on specified goods, (ii) by extending the application of consumer credit control to a large number of consumer goods, and (iii) by reducing the length of the payment period, etc.

Anti-inflationary Fiscal Measures: The major anti-inflationary fiscal measures are the following:

Government Expenditure: To counteract increased private spending at a time of inflation, the government should, at such a time, reduce its own expenditure to the minimum extent feasible to help limit the aggregate demand. As against this, it may, however, be said that it is not so easy to reduce government expenditure especially during the war period. Secondly, any drastic cut in government expenditure to cure inflation may actually land the economy in a slump.

Object of Public Borrowing: The purpose of public borrowing is to take away from the public excess purchasing power which, if left free, would surely exert an upward pressure on the price-level in view of the limited supplies of goods and services in the economy. If voluntary borrowing does not yield adequate results, it may become essential to resort to compulsory borrowing from the public.

Management of Public Debt: The present public debt should be managed in such a manner as to reduce the existing money supply and prevent further credit expansion. Anti-inflationary debt management usually requires the repayments of bank held debt out of a budgetary surplus. The idea is that the government securities held by commercial banks should be retired by the government out of the budgetary surplus. This would check the power of commercial banks to encash their securities and add to the reserve for the purpose of credit expansion.

Purchasing Power in the form of Taxes: The problem during inflation is to reduce the size of disposable income in the hands of the general public in view of the limited supply of goods and services in the market. It is, therefore, essential to take away the excess purchasing power from the public in the form of taxes. The rates of existing taxes should be steeply increased, while new taxes should be imposed on commodities so as to leave less money supply with the public to spend.

Substantial Income Policy: During inflation, the government must also adopt a suitable price-income policy. It should strictly control wages, salaries and profits to keep spending at a low level to fight inflation.

Over-valuation: In terms of foreign currencies an over-valuation of domestic currency will also serve as an anti-inflationary measures. Firstly, it will discourage exports and thereby increase the availability of goods in the domestic market. Secondly, by encouraging imports from abroad, it will add to the domestic supply of goods in the economy. But over-valuation as an anti-inflationary weapon suffers from several limitations.

Other Measures: These measures can be brought into use to supplement monetary and fiscal measures undertaken to contain inflationary pressures:

Expansion Output Enhanced: Increased production is the best antidote to inflation because inflation arises partly because of inadequacy of output. But it becomes rather difficult to increase output at a time of inflation because of the full utilization of resources. It is suggested that if it is not feasible to increase output as a whole, steps should be taken to increase the output of those goods which seem to be extremely sensitive to inflationary pressures by shifting productive resources from the less inflation-sensitive goods. In other words, a re-allocation of productive resources is suggested to step up the output of inflation-sensitive goods, such as, food, clothing, housing, etc. Steps may also be taken to increase supply of consumer goods through large-scale imports from other countries to absorb excess money supply.

Objective of Controlling the Prices and Rationing: The object of price control is to lay down the upper limit beyond which the price of a particular commodity would not be allowed to rise. To ensure the successful functioning of price control two conditions will have to be satisfied. Firstly, the government should have under its control adequate stocks of the commodities concerned. Secondly, the demand for the concerned commodities should be controlled through rationing, failing which the richer sections shall be able to buy a major portion of the available stocks.

Inflation and Wage Policy: During an inflationary boom, the wages have to be controlled so as to curb the inflationary pressures in the economy. Wage increases may be allowed to workers only if their productivity increases. If this principle is observed, higher wages shall not lead to higher unit costs and hence, to higher unit prices. Thus, the above steps taken simultaneously, may improve the situation a lot.

THEORIES OF INFLATION

There are two theories relating to the causes of inflation:

(1) Demand Pull Inflation
(2) Cost Push Inflation

CONCEPT OF DEMAND PULL INFLATION

This is the oldest theory of price rise.The chief reason for inflation is the pressure of ever rising demand on a stagnant or less rapidly increasing supply of goods and services. The expansion in aggregate demand may be the result of rapidly increasing private investment and/or expanding government expenditure for war or for economic development. At a time when demand is expanding and is exerting pressure on prices, attempt may also be made to expand production. But this may not be feasible either because unemployed resources are not available or due to shortage of transport, power, capital and equipment, etc., may prevent output from increasing in proportion to expanding demand and inflationary situation in the country. In the words of Peterson, "Demand Pull Inflation Theory holds that inflation is caused by an excess of demand (spending) relative to the available supply of goods and services at existing prices."

Expansion in aggregate demand, after the level of full employment, will push up only in the short period, resources are used for growth and for creating fixed assets and for the production of consumer goods. Necessarily, large expenditure will create large money income and large demand but without a corresponding increase in supply of real output. According to the demand-pull theory, prices rise in response to an excess of aggregate demand over existing supply of goods and services. The demand-pull theorists point out that inflation might be caused, in the first place, by an increase in the quantity of money, when the economy is operating at full employment level. As the quantity of money increases, the rate of inflation will fall and consequently investment will increase. This increased investment expenditure will soon increase the income of the different factors of production. As a consequence, aggregate consumption expenditure will increase, leading to an effective increase in the effective demand. With the economy already operating at the level of full employment, this will immediately raise prices, and inflationary forces may emerge. Thus, when the general monetary demand rises faster than the general supply, it pulls up prices. Demand pull inflation, therefore, manifests itself when there is active cooperation, or passive collusion, or a failure to take counteracting measures by monetary authorities. Demand-pull or just demand inflation may be defined as a situation where the total monetary demand persistently exceeds total supply of real goods and services at current so that prices are pulled upwards by the continuous upward shift of the aggregate demand function. However, demand-pull inflation can also occur without an increase in the money supply.

This can happen when either the marginal efficiency of capital increases or the marginal propensity to consume rises, so that investment expenditures may rise, thereby leading to a rise in the aggregate demand which will exert its influence in raising prices beyond the level of full employment already attained in the economy. According to the demand-pull theorists, during the process of demand inflation, rise in wages accompanied or follows the price rise as a natural consequence.

Under the condition of rising prices, when the rate of profit is increasing, investment and employment, in that they bid against each other for labour, so that labour prices (i.e. wages) may rise. In brief, the inflationary process, described by the demand inflation theory, implies various sequences like-increasing demand increasing prices-increasing costs-increasing income-increasing demand-increasing prices and so on. It should be noted that the concept of demand-pull inflation is associated with a situation of full employment where increase in aggregate demand cannot be catered to by a corresponding expansion in the supply of real output. There can be many reasons for such excess monetary demand:

(i) A diversion of resources from the consumption goods sector either to the capital goods sector or the military sector (for producing war goods) will lead to an inflationary pressure because while the generation of income and expenditure continue, the current flow of real output decreases on account of high gestation period involved in these sectors. Again, the opportunity cost of goods is quite high in terms of the consumption goods meant for the civilian sector. This leads to an excessive monetary demand for the goods and services against the real supply, causing the prices to move up. Keynes, in his article, 'How to pay for the war' (1940) has explained this type of demand pull inflation as Inflationary Gap. It is the difference between the quantity of money to be spent on consumption goods and the actual availability of such goods.

(ii) There may be an increase in the autonomous investment in firms, which is in excess of the current savings in the economy. Hence, the flow of total expenditure tends to rise, causing an excess monetary demand leading to an upward pressure on prices.

(iii) There may be an increase in the public expenditure in excess of public revenue. This might have been made feasible (or rendered essential) through public borrowings from banks or through deficit financing, which implies an increase in the money supply.

(iv) There may be an increase in the marginal propensity to consume (MPC), causing an excess monetary demand. This could be because of the operation of demonstration effect and such other reasons.

(v) In an open economy, an increasing surplus in balance of payments also leads to excess demand. Increasing exports also have an inflationary impact because there a generation of money income in the home economy because of export earnings but simultaneously, there is reduction in the domestic supply of goods because products are exported. If an export surplus is not balanced by increased savings, or through taxation, domestic spending will be in excess of the value of domestic output, marketed at current prices.

Therefore, it is said that the demand-pull inflation can be averted through deflationary measures adopted by the monetary and fiscal authorities. Thus, passive polices are responsible for demand pull inflation.

CONCEPT OF COST PUSH INFLATION

Such kind of inflation is caused by an increase in production costs. It is generally caused by two factors: (i) an increase in wages, and (ii) an increase in the profit-margins of the entrepreneurs. The increase in wages may be caused by a monopolistic labour unions through pressure tactics. This attempt on the part of the trade unions to push up wages invariably causes cost inflation in the economy. Cost inflation is also caused by an organized effort on the part of the industrialists to push up their profit margins. But the profits-push elements are not so significant in causing inflation as the wage-push elements are. Powerful trade unions get the wages pushed up even without an equivalent increase in the productivity of the workers. Under these circumstances, the increase in wages cannot but result in an increase in prices. When cost inflation arises in one industry, it soon spreads to the other sectors of economy as well, the reason being that the different sectors of the economy are closely linked with each other. According to A.S. Compgana, "Cost Push Inflation is the consequence of rise in costs. It is characterized by insufficiency of aggregate demand, unemployed resources and excess capacity."

Cost-push inflation may take place either because of wage-push or profit-push. Cost-push analysis assumes monopoly elements either in the labour market or the product market. When there are monopolistic labour organisations, prices may rise because of wage push. And, when there are monopolies in the product market, the monopolists may be induced to raise the prices in order to fetch high profits. Then, there is profit-push in raising the prices. However, the cost-push hypothesis rarely considers autonomous attempts to increase profits as a significant inflationary element. Firstly, because profits are usually a small fraction of the total price, a rise in profits would have only a slight impact on prices. Secondly, the monopolists generally hesitate to raise prices in the absence of obvious demand-pull elements.

Finally, the motivation for profit push is weak since at least in corporations, those who make the decision to raise prices are not the direct beneficiaries of the price increase. Hence, cost-push is usually conceived as synonymous with wage push. When wages are pushed up, cost of production increases to a considerable extent so that prices may rise. Since wages are pushed up by the demand for high wages by the labour unions, wage-push may be equated with union-push.

QUESTIONS

1. Define Inflation. What are its chief characteristics ?
2. What are the effects of Inflation?
3. Explain in brief the measures to control Inflation.

Index